STYLE

Ten Lessons in Clarity and Grace

STYLE

Ten Lessons in Clarity and Grace

SEVENTH EDITION

Joseph M. Williams
The University of Chicago

Longman

New York   San Francisco   Boston
London   Toronto   Sydney   Tokyo   Singapore   Madrid
Mexico City   Munich   Paris   Cape Town   Hong Kong   Montreal

Senior Vice President and Publisher: Joseph Opiela
Acquisitions Editor: Susan Kunchandy
Executive Marketing Manager: Ann Stypuloski
Supplements Editor: Donna Campion
Production Manager: Donna DeBenedictis
Project Coordination, Text Design, and Electronic Page Makeup: Elm Street
  Publishing Services, Inc.
Cover Design Manager: Wendy Ann Fredericks
Cover Designer: Joan O'Connor
Manufacturing Buyer: Al Dorsey
Printer and Binder: R.R. Donnelley & Sons Company/Harrisonburg
Cover Printer: Phoenix Color Corporation

For permission to use copyrighted material, grateful acknowledgment is
made to the copyright holders on p. 255, which is hereby made part of
this copyright page.

Library of Congress Cataloging-in-Publication Data
Williams, Joseph M.
    Style: ten lessons in clarity and grace / Joseph M. Williams.—7th ed.
    p.;   cm.
    Includes bibliographical references and index.
    ISBN 0-321-09517-0 (alk. paper)
    1. English language—Rhetoric.   2. English language—Technical
English.   3. English language—Business English.   4. English
language—Style.   5. Technical writing.   6. Business writing.   I. Title.
    PE1421.W545 2003
    808'.042—dc21   2002276821

Please visit our website at http://www.ablongman.com

ISBN 0-321-09517-0

3 4 5 6 7 8 9 10—DOH—05 04 03

To my mother and father

. . . English style, familiar but not coarse,
elegant, but not ostentatious . . .

—SAMUEL JOHNSON

CONTENTS

PREFACE

Most people won't realize that writing is a craft.
You have to take your apprenticeship in it like anything else.

—KATHERINE ANNE PORTER

WHAT'S NEW IN THE SEVENTH EDITION

Each of the last six editions has grown a bit. I've slimmed this one down to make it more compact, more direct, and, I hope, more usable. I have also added an Epilogue that addresses issues that go beyond local clarity to matters of global coherence, of making whole passages, even whole documents, hang together.

WHAT'S THE SAME

I aim at answering the same questions I asked in earlier ones:

- What is it in a sentence that makes readers judge writing as they do?
- How can we diagnose our own prose to anticipate their judgments?
- How can we revise a sentence so that readers will think better of it?

The standard advice about writing is well intentioned, but it doesn't address those questions. It consists mostly of truisms like "Make a plan" and "Think of your audience"—advice that most of us ignore in the act of wrestling ideas out onto the page. As I first drafted this paragraph, I wasn't thinking about you; I was struggling to get my own ideas straight; what I did know was that I would go back to this paragraph again and again, and that it was likely to be only then—as I revised—that I could think about you and discover the plan that fit my draft. I also knew that as I did so, there were some principles I could rely on. This book explains them.

PRINCIPLES, NOT PRESCRIPTIONS

Those principles may seem prescriptive, but that's not how I intend them. I offer them not as rules, but as ways to help you predict how readers will read and judge your prose and then help you decide whether and how to revise it. You may find that as you learn all those principles you write more slowly. That's inevitable. Whenever we reflect on what we do as we do it, we become self-conscious, sometimes to the point of paralysis. It passes. You can avoid some of that paralysis if you remember that these principles have little to do with how you write, much to do with how you revise. If there is a first principle of drafting, it is to forget advice about how to do it.

SOME PREREQUISITES

To learn how to revise efficiently, though, you have to know a few things:

- You need to know a few grammatical terms: SUBJECT, VERB, NOUN, ACTIVE, PASSIVE, CLAUSE, PREPOSITION, and COORDINATION. All key terms are capitalized the first time they appear and defined in the text or in the Glossary.
- You will have to learn new meanings for two familiar words: TOPIC and STRESS.
- You will have to learn five terms that you probably do not know at all. Two are important: NOMINALIZATION and METADISCOURSE; three are useful: RESUMPTIVE MODIFIER, SUMMATIVE MODIFIER, and FREE MODIFIER.

Finally, if you are reading this book on your own, go slowly. It is not an amiable essay that you can read in a sitting or two. Take the lessons a few pages at a time, up to the exercises. Do the exercises, edit someone else's writing, then some of your own written a few weeks ago, then something you've written that day.

An *Instructor's Manual* is available for those who are interested in some of the scholarly and pedagogical thinking that has gone into *Style*. It also provides suggested revisions for exercises not listed on pages 241–254.

ACKNOWLEDGMENTS

So many have offered support, suggestions, and criticisms over the last twenty years, that I cannot thank you all. But again I begin with those English 194 students (now in their forties!) who put up with faintly dittoed pages (that tells you how many years ago this book was born) and with a teacher who at times was as puzzled as they. I remain grateful to you all.

I have learned much from those undergraduate, graduate, and professional students, and post-docs who have gone through the Little Red Schoolhouse writing program here at the University of Chicago (a.k.a. Advanced Academic and Professional Writing). I am equally grateful to the graduate students who have taught these principles and offered important feedback.

I have intellectual debts to those who broke ground in psycholinguistics, text linguistics, and functional sentence perspective. Those who keep up with such matters will recognize the influence of Charles Filmore, Jan Firbas, Nils Enkvist, Michael Halliday, Noam Chomsky, Thomas Bever, Vic Yngve, and others. More recently, the work of Eleanore Rosch has provided a rich explanation for why verbs should be actions and characters should be subjects. Her work in prototype semantics is a powerful theoretical basis for the kind of style urged here.

I am indebted to colleagues who have taken time to read the work of another. For their especially thoughtful and careful reviews of this edition, I wish to acknowledge Nancy Barendse, Charleston Southern University; Darren Cambridge, University of Texas, Austin; Mark Canada, University of North Carolina, Pembroke; Paul J. Contino, Valparaiso University; Dr. Jim Garrett, Occidental College; Jill Gladstein, Swarthmore College; Karen Gocsik, Dartmouth University; Julie Kalish, Dartmouth University; Bernadette Longo, Clemson University; Joel Margulis, San Francisco State University; Linda C. Mitchell, San Jose State University; Ellen Moody, George Mason University; Ann M. Palkovich, George Mason University; Donna Burns Philips, Ohio State University; and Laura Bartlett Snyder, University of Louisville.

For reading earlier versions of this book, I must thank in particular Randy Berlin, Ken Bruffee, Douglas Butturff, Donald Byker, Bruce Campbell, Elaine Chaika, Avon Crismore, Constance Gefvert, Maxine Hairston, George Hoffman, Ted Lowe, Susan Miller, Neil Nakadate, Mike Pownall, Peter Priest, Margaret Shaklee, Nancy Sommers, Mary Taylor, and Stephen Witte. I am grateful for the feedback from the class taught by Stan Henning at the University of Wisconsin, Madison, and for the error in usage caught by Linda Ziff at Johns Hopkins University. I am also indebted to John Ruszkiewicz, Bill Vande Kopple, Margaret Batschelet, Theresa Ammirati, Yvonne Atkinson, Cheryl Brooke, Jeanne Gunner, Rebecca Moore Howard, Richard Jenseth, Elizabeth Bourque Johnson, Patricia Murray, John W. Taylor, Joseph F. Wappel, Alison Warriner, and Kevin S. Wilson. I am particularly indebted to an exchange with Keith Rhodes about Lesson 10. He made me think as hard as I should have about some claims that, as I think of them now, I am lucky to have escaped committing to print.

I am indebted to Christina Devlin for the Wesley quotation in Lesson Seven and to James Vanden Bosch for the Montaigne quotation in the Glossary. I gratefully acknowledge the assistance of Frederick C. Mish, editorial director, G & C. Merriam Company, in locating the best examples of three citations in Lesson Two, and Charles Bazerman, whose work on Crick and Watson led me to the first paragraph of their DNA paper.

I remain in the debt of the person who first urged me to write this book, Harriett Prentiss, and my current editor, Susan Kunchandy, who has sustained my faith in the competence of that profession.

I would also like to thank Betsy Webster, of Elm Street Publishing Services, who edited the manuscript. And finally, my thanks to my careful assistant, Alec MacDonald, who helped proof the text and assemble the index.

For several years, I have had the good fortune to work with two people who have been both good colleagues and good friends and whose careful thinking has helped me think better about many matters, both professional and personal: Don Freeman and Greg Colomb. Don's careful readings have saved me from more than a few howlers; I am indebted to him for the quote from William Blake in Lesson Eight. Greg has put up with more than most friends would, and I have benefited not only from his scrupulous critical thinking but from our shouting matches. It has been a pleasure and a privilege to work and hang out with him and Sandra for more than twenty years now.

And again, those who have contributed more to the quality of my life than I have let them know: Chris, Oliver, Megan and Phil, Dave and Patty, and Joe and Christine, and now the twins, Nicholas and Katherine. And at beginning and end still, Joan, whose patience, good judgment, and love still flow more generously than I deserve.

J. M. W.
South Haven, Michigan

PART ONE

Style as Choice

> *Have something to say,*
> *and say it as clearly as you can.*
> *That is the only secret of style.*
>
> —MATTHEW ARNOLD

Understanding Style

Style is the physiognomy of the mind.
—ARTHUR SCHOPENHAUER

*To me, style is just the outside of content,
and content the inside of style,
like the outside and inside of the human body—
both go together, they can't be separated.*
—JEAN-LUC GODARD

The great enemy of clear language is insincerity.
—GEORGE ORWELL

*In matters of grave importance,
style, not sincerity, is the vital thing.*
—OSCAR WILDE

PRINCIPLES AND AIMS

This book is based on two principles: It's good to write clearly, and anyone can. That first one is self-evident, especially to those who have to read sentences like this:

> An understanding of the causal factors involved in excessive drinking by students could lead to their more effective treatment.

But that second principle may seem optimistic to those writers who try to do better, but can't get close to this:

> We could more effectively treat students who drink excessively if we understood why they do.

Of course, writing fails for reasons more serious than unclear sentences. We bewilder our readers when we can't organize complex ideas coherently (I briefly address that issue in the Epilogue), and we cannot hope for their assent when we ignore their reasonable questions and objections. But once we've formulated our claims, organized their supporting reasons logically, and grounded those reasons on sound evidence, we still have to express it all in clear and coherent language, a difficult task for most writers, and a daunting one for many.

It is a problem that has afflicted generations of writers who, instead of communicating their ideas in clear and direct language, hide them not only from their readers, but sometimes even from themselves. When we read that kind of writing in government regulations, we call it *bureaucratese*; when we find it in legal documents, *legalese*; in scholarly writing that inflates small ideas into gassy abstractions, *academese*. Written deliberately or carelessly, it is a language of exclusion that a diverse and democratic society cannot tolerate. It is a problem with a history.

A SHORT HISTORY OF UNCLEAR WRITING

The Past

It was not until the middle of the sixteenth century that writers of English decided that our language was eloquent enough to replace Latin and French in intellectually respectable discourse. But their first efforts were written in a style so complex that it defeated easy understanding:

If use and custom, having the help of so long time and continuance wherein to [re]fine our tongue, of so great learning and experience which furnish matter for the [re]fining, of so good wits and judgments which can tell how to refine, have griped at nothing in all that time, with all that cunning, by all those wits which they will not let go but hold for most certain in the right of our writing, that then our tongue has no certainty to trust to, but write all at random.

—Richard Mulcaster, *The First Part of the Elementary,* 1582

Within a century, a complex style had spread to the writing of scientists (or, as they were then called, natural philosophers). As one critic complained,

Of all the studies of men, nothing may sooner be obtained than this vicious abundance of phrase, this trick of metaphors, this volubility of tongue which makes so great a noise in the world.

—Thomas Sprat, *History of the Royal Society,* 1667

When this country was settled, our writers had a chance to establish a new, more democratic prose style, not viciously voluble, but concise and direct. In fact, in 1776, the straightforward language of Thomas Paine's *Common Sense* helped inspire our Revolution:

In the following pages I offer nothing more than simple facts, plain arguments, and common sense.

Sad to say, he sparked no revolution in the style of our writing.

By the early nineteenth century, James Fenimore Cooper was complaining about the spread of turgid language:

The love of turgid expressions is gaining ground, and ought to be corrected. One of the most certain evidences of a man of high breeding, is his simplicity of speech: a simplicity that is equally removed from vulgarity and exaggeration. . . . Simplicity should be the firm aim, after one is removed from vulgarity. . . . In no case, however, can one who aims at turgid language, exaggerated sentiments, or pedantic utterances, lay claim to be either a man or a woman of the world.

—James Fenimore Cooper, *The American Democrat,* 1838

Unfortunately, in condemning that style, Cooper imitated it. Had he followed his own advice, he might have written,

We should discourage writers who love turgid language. A well-bred person speaks simply, in a way that is neither vulgar nor exaggerated. After we rid our language of vulgarity, we should aim at simplicity. No one can claim to be a man or woman of the world who exaggerates sentiments or deliberately speaks in language that is turgid or pedantic.

About fifty years later, Mark Twain wrote what we now think is classic American prose—easy, clear, and direct. He said this about Cooper's style:

> There have been daring people in the world who claimed that Cooper could write English, but they are all dead now—all dead but Lounsbury [an academic who praised Cooper's style] . . . . [He] says that *Deerslayer* is a "pure work of art." . . . [But] Cooper wrote about the poorest English that exists in our language, and . . . the English of *Deerslayer* is the very worst tha[t] even Cooper ever wrote.

We admire Twain's directness, but few of us consistently emulate it.

The Present

In the best-known essay on modern English style, "Politics and the English Language," George Orwell anatomized the pretentious language of today's politicians and academics:

> The keynote [of a pretentious style] is the elimination of simple verbs. Instead of being a single word, such as *break, stop, spoil, mend, kill,* a verb becomes a phrase, made up of a noun or adjective tacked on to some general-purposes verb such as *prove, serve, form, play, render.* In addition, the passive voice is wherever possible used in preference to the active, and noun constructions are used instead of gerunds (*by examination* of instead of *by examining*).

But just as Cooper did, in abusing that style Orwell modeled it. He could have written more directly:

> Those who write pretentiously eliminate simple verbs. Instead of using one word, such as *break, stop, kill,* they turn a verb into a noun or adjective and then tack it on to a general-purpose verb such as *prove, serve, form, play, render.* Wherever possible, they use the passive voice instead of the active and noun constructions instead of gerunds (*by examination* instead of *by examining*).

If the best known critic of that wordy style could not resist it, we ought not be surprised when politicians and academics embrace it: On the language of the social sciences:

> A turgid and polysyllabic prose does seem to prevail in the social sciences. . . . Such a lack of ready intelligibility, I believe, usually has little or nothing to do with the complexity of thought. It has to do almost entirely with certain confusions of the academic writer about his own status.
>
> —C. Wright Mills, *The Sociological Imagination*

On the language of medicine:

> It now appears that obligatory obfuscation is a firm tradition within the medical profession . . . . [Medical writing] is a highly skilled, calculated attempt to confuse the reader . . . . A doctor feels he might get passed over for an assistant professorship because he wrote his papers too clearly—because he made his ideas seem too simple.
>
> —Michael Crichton, *New England Journal of Medicine*

On the language of law:

> In law journals, in speeches, in classrooms and in courtrooms, lawyers and judges are beginning to worry about how often they have been misunderstood, and they are discovering that sometimes they cannot even understand each other.
>
> —Tom Goldstein, *New York Times*

On the language of science:

> There are times when the more the authors explain [about ape communication], the less we understand. Apes certainly seem capable of using language to communicate. Whether scientists are remains doubtful.
>
> —Douglas Chadwick, *New York Times*

Most of us first confront that kind of murky language in textbook sentences like this one:

> Recognition of the fact that systems [of grammar] differ from one language to another can serve as the basis for serious consideration of the problems confronting translators of the great works of world literature originally written in a language other than English.

That means, in about half as many words,

> When we recognize that languages have different grammars, we can consider the problems of those who translate great works of literature into English.

Generations of students have struggled to understand unnecessarily dense writing, many thinking they were not smart enough to grasp the writer's ideas. Some have been right about that, but more could have blamed the writer's inability to write clearly. Many students, sad to say, give up; sadder still, others learn not only to read that style but to imitate it, imposing more dense writing on the next generation of readers, thereby sustaining our 400-year-old tradition of opaque prose.

SOME PRIVATE CAUSES OF UNCLEAR WRITING

But if unclear writing has a long social history, it also has private causes. Michael Crichton mentioned one: Some writers plump up their prose to impress those who confuse a dense style with deep thinking. When we don't know what we're talking about (or have no confidence in what we do know) we typically throw up a screen of abstract words in long, complicated sentences.

Others write graceless prose not deliberately but because they are gripped by the idea that writing is good only when it is free of errors that only a grammarian can explain. They approach a blank page not as a space to try out new ideas, but as a minefield to cross gingerly. They creep from word to word, concerned less with their readers' understanding than with their own survival.

Others write unclearly because they just freeze up, especially when they are learning to think and write in a new academic or professional setting. Those afflicted include not just undergraduates taking their first course in economics or psychology, but graduate students, business people, doctors, lawyers—anyone writing on a new topic for unfamiliar and therefore intimidating readers. As we struggle to master new and complex ideas, most of us write worse than we can when we write about things we understand better. If that sounds like you, take heart. You will write more clearly once you more clearly understand your subject and readers.

But probably the biggest reason we write unclearly is ignorance. Our own writing always seems clearer to us than it does to our readers, because we read into it what we wanted to mean when we wrote it, an advantage our readers lack. And so instead of revising our writing to meet their needs, we just send it off if it has met ours.

In all of this, of course, there is a great irony: We are likely to confuse others when we write about a subject that confuses us, but when we are also reading prose written in a gratuitously difficult style, we can too easily assume that such complexity signals deep thought, and so we try to imitate it, compounding our already confused writing. This book aims at showing you how to read your writing as others will, and, when you should, revise it into something better.

On Writing and Rewriting

A warning: If you think about these principles *as you draft,* you may never draft anything at all. Most experienced writers get something down on paper (or up on the screen) as fast as they can, just to have something to revise. Then as they revise their early drafts into something clearer, they better understand their ideas. And when they understand their ideas better, they can express them more clearly, and when they can express them more clearly, they understand them even better . . . and so it goes, until they run out of energy, interest, or time.

For a fortunate few, that moment comes weeks, months, even years after they begin. (Over the last twenty years, I've pushed this book through dozens of drafts, and there are parts I still can't get right.) For most of us, though, the deadline is closer to tomorrow morning. And so we have to settle for prose that is less than perfect, but as good as we can make it. (Perfection is the ideal, but the enemy of done.) So use what you find here not as rules to impose to every sentence as you draft it, but as principles to help you quickly identify those sentences most likely to give your readers a problem, and then to revise them just as quickly.

As important as clarity is, though, some occasions call for more:

> Now the trumpet summons us again—not as a call to bear arms, though arms we need; not as a call to battle, though embattled we are; but a call to bear the burden of a long twilight struggle, year in

and year out, "rejoicing in hope, patient in tribulation," a struggle against the common enemies of man: tyranny, poverty, disease and war itself.

—John F. Kennedy, Inaugural Address, January 20, 1961

Few of us are called upon to write a presidential address, but in even our modest prose, some of us take a private pleasure in shaping a sentence well, regardless whether anyone will notice, like a cabinetmaker who sands the back of a drawer. Those who enjoy crafting sentences will find suggestions in Lesson Nine. Writing is also a social act with consequences that might or might not serve the best interests of readers, so in Lesson Ten, I address some ethical issues of style. In the Epilogue, I address some issues that go beyond simple clarity to larger issues of coherence.

Many years ago, H. L. Mencken wrote this:

With precious few exceptions, all the books on style in English are by writers quite unable to write. The subject, indeed, seems to exercise a special and dreadful fascination over school ma'ams, bucolic college professors, and other such pseudoliterates . . . Their central aim, of course, is to reduce the whole thing to a series of simple rules—the overmastering passion of their melancholy order, at all times and everywhere.

Mencken was right: No one can learn to write well by rule, especially those who cannot feel or think or see. But I know that many who do see clearly, feel deeply, and think carefully cannot write sentences that make their thoughts, feelings, and visions clear to others. I also know that the more clearly we write, the more clearly we see and feel and think. Rules help no one do any of that, but some principles can.

Here they are.

Correctness

No grammatical rules have sufficient authority to control the firm and established usage of language. Established custom, in speaking and writing, is the standard to which we must at last resort for determining every controverted point in language and style.
—HUGH BLAIR

English usage is sometimes more than mere taste, judgment, and education—sometimes it's sheer luck, like getting across the street.
—E. B. WHITE

God does not much mind bad grammar, but He does not take any particular pleasure in it.
—ERASMUS

CORRECTNESS, CHOICE, AND OBEDIENCE

To a careful writer, nothing is more important than choice, but in some matters, we have none—we can't put *the* after a NOUN, as in *street the* (capitalized words are defined in the Glossary). But we choose when we can. For example, which of these sentences would you choose to write if you wanted readers to think you wrote clearly?

1. Our lack of newspaper support caused our loss of the election.
2. We lost the election because newspapers didn't support us.

Both are grammatically "correct," but most of us would choose (2).

Unlike clarity, though, correctness seems a matter not of choice, but of obedience. When the *American Heritage Dictionary* says that *irregardless* is "never acceptable" (except, they say, for humor), our freedom to choose it seems at best academic. In matters of this kind, we choose not between better and worse, but between right and utterly, irredeemably, unequivocally Wrong, which is, of course, no choice at all.

But that lack of choice does seem to simplify things: "Correctness" requires not sound judgment, only a good memory. If we remember that *irregardless* is always Wrong, it ought not rise to even a subconscious level of choice. Some teachers and editors think we should memorize dozens of such "rules":

- Don't begin a sentence with *and* or *but*.
- Don't use double negatives.
- Don't split INFINITIVES.

Unfortunately, it's not that simple. Some rules alleged to govern good usage are less important than many think (indeed, some are not rules at all), and if you obsess over every one of them, you will hinder yourself from writing quickly and clearly. In fact, that's why I address "correctness" now, before clarity, because I want to put it where it belongs—behind us.

UNDERSTANDING THE SOCIAL LOGIC BEHIND RULES OF GRAMMAR

Opinion is split on the social role of grammatical rules. To some, they are just another device invented by the Ins to control the Outs by stigmatizing their speech and thereby limiting their social and political aspirations. To others, the rules of Standard English have been created by generations of educated speakers refining our language, rules now observed by the best writers of English, or at least should be.

Both views are correct, but only partly. For centuries, most of those who govern our affairs have indeed used grammatical "errors" to screen out those unwilling or unable to acquire the grammatical habits of the schooled middle class. But conservatives are also right that many rules of Standard English did originate in efficiencies of expression that everyone should know. For example, we no longer use the complex set of verb endings that English required a thousand years ago, allowing us to omit present tense endings in all but one context (in fact, we don't even need it there):

	1ST PERSON	2ND PERSON	3RD PERSON
Singular	I know + Ø.	You know + Ø.	She know + **S.**
Plural	We know + Ø.	You know + Ø.	They know + Ø.

Correctness as Historical Accident

But while the critics on the left are right to claim that the rules of Standard English have been used to discriminate, they are wrong to claim that they were *devised* for that end. Standard forms of a language always originate in accidents of geography and economic power. When a country has different regional dialects, that of the wealthiest region is likely to become most prestigious and the basis for that nation's standard form of writing. Thus if a thousand years ago, Scotland had by some geographical accident been closer to the European continent than was London, and its capital, Edinburgh, had been a great port and the center of Britain's economic, political, and literary life, we would write and speak less like Shakespeare and more like the Scottish poet Bobby Burns:

A ye wha are sae guid yourself	(All you who are so good yourselves
Sae pious and sae holy,	So pious and so holy,
Ye've nought to do but mark and tell	You've nothing to do but talk about
Your neebours' fauts and folly!	Your neighbors' faults and folly!)

Correctness as Unpredictability

But critics on the right are wrong when they claim that modern Standard English, refined, they claim, by the logic of generations of educated speakers and writers, must be intrinsically superior to nonstandard forms of speech. True, many rules of Standard English seem to reflect an evolution toward efficiency. But if by logical we mean systematic and therefore predictable, then Standard English is in some ways less "logical" than nonstandard English.

For example, the person who says *I **knowed*** makes the same logical "mistake" as the first person who said *I **climbed** the tree* instead of the originally "correct" *I **clum** the tree*. Both speakers logically regularize an inconsistency, an act that is usually taken as a sign of intelligence, unless the *in*consistency signals social prestige.

We could cite a dozen more examples where a nonstandard violation of a Standard rule reflects a logical mind smoothing out inconsistency and making English simpler. But it is, of course, the very *ir*regularity of Standard English that makes its rules so useful to those who want to discriminate: To speak and write Standard English, we must either be born into it or spend time learning its idiosyncrasies (and presumably the values of its speakers). Those determined to discriminate use any social difference available, of course. But since our language seems to reflect our quality of mind more directly than does our ZIP codes, it is easy for those inclined to discriminate to think that grammatical "errors" indicate mental or moral deficiency.

> ***Here's the point:***   We must reject the notion that observing the rules of Standard English makes anyone intellectually or morally superior. That belief is not just factually wrong; in a socially diverse democracy, it is destructive. Yet even if logic predicts *knowed,* so much greater is the power of social convention that we still avoid those words if we want to be taken seriously when we write for serious purposes.

THREE KINDS OF RULES

These corrosive attitudes about correctness have been encouraged by generations of grammarians who, in their zeal to codify "good" English, have confused three kinds of "rules":

1. Some rules define what makes English English—ARTICLES precede nouns: *the book,* not *book the.* These are the real rules that we violate only when we are tired or rushed. To be sure, these rules are occasionally violated by even the best writers. We all have used a singular verb distant from a plural subject, but when told about it, we fix it.

2. A few rules distinguish Standard English from nonstandard: *He doesn't have any money* versus *He don't have no money.* The only writers who *consciously* follow these rules are those striving to join the educated class. Schooled writers observe these rules as naturally as they observe the real rules and think about them only when they notice others violating them.

3. Finally, some grammarians have invented rules they think we all *should* observe. Most date from the last half of the eighteenth century:

> Don't split infinitives, as in *to **quietly** leave.*
>
> Don't use *than* after *different,* as in *This is different **than** that.* Use *from.*

A few date from the twentieth century:

> Don't use *hopefully* for *I hope,* as in ***Hopefully,** it won't rain.*
>
> Don't use *which* for *that,* as in *a car **which** I sold.*

But since grammarians have been accusing the best writers of violating such rules for the last 250 years, we have to conclude that for 250 years the best writers have been ignoring both the rules and grammarians. Which is lucky for grammarians, because if writers did obey all their rules, grammarians would have to keep inventing new ones, or find another line of work.

The fact is, none of the rules of this third kind reflects the consensus of unselfconscious usage of our best writers. In this lesson, we focus on just this third kind of rule, the invented ones, because only they really vex those who already speak and write Standard English.

Observing Rules Thoughtfully

It is, however, no simple matter if you want to be thought of as someone who writes both clearly and "correctly," but you don't want to feel that you have to follow every mindless rule ever concocted.

You could choose the worst-case policy: Follow all the rules all the time because sometime, someone will criticize you for something—for beginning a sentence with *and* or ending it with *up*. But if you mindlessly obey all the rules all the time, you surrender a measure of choice. Worse, you may become so obsessed with rules that you tie yourself into knots. And sooner or later, you will impose those rules—real or not—on others. After all, what good is learning a rule if all you can do is obey it?

The alternative to blind obedience is selective observance. But then you have to decide which rules to ignore. And then if you do ignore some alleged rule, you may have to deal with those whose passion (and memory) for "good" grammar seem to endow them with the ability to see in a split infinitive a symptom of moral corruption and social decay.

If you want to avoid being labeled "without standards," but also decline to submit to whatever "rule" someone can dredge up from memories of a ninth-grade English class, you have to know more about the rules than the rule-mongers do.

Two Kinds of Invented Rules

We can sort most of these invented rules into two groups: Folklore and Options.

1. *Folklore.* When you violate "rules" like these, few careful readers notice, much less care. So they are not rules at all, but folklore you can ignore (unless you are writing for someone with the power to demand that you observe even the folklore).

2. *Options.* When you ignore these rules, few readers notice. But paradoxically, some do when you observe them, because they detect in your observance signals of special formality. So you can observe these rules or not, depending on how you want your readers to respond.

1. Folklore

These rules include those whose observance or violation most careful readers and writers ignore. In what follows, the quotations that illustrate their "violations" are all from writers of intellectual and scholarly stature or who, on matters of usage, are reliable conservatives (some are both). You may not be familiar with some of these "rules," but even if you have not had one inflicted on you yet, chances are that one day you will. (A check mark indicates those sentences that are acceptable Standard English, despite what some grammarians claim.)

1. "Don't begin sentences with *and* or *but*." This passage ignores the "rule" twice:

> ✓**But,** it will be asked, is tact not an individual gift, therefore highly variable in its choices? **And** if that is so, what guidance can a manual offer, other than that of its author's prejudices—mere impressionism?
>
> —Wilson Follett, *Modern American Usage: A Guide,* edited and completed by Jacques Barzun et al.

On this matter, it is useful to consult the guide used by most conservative writers: the *second* edition of H. W. Fowler's *A Dictionary of Modern English Usage* (first edition, Oxford University Press, 1926; second edition, 1965; third edition, 1997, considered too permissive by archconservatives). The second edition was edited by Sir Ernest Gowers, who, to Fowler's original entry for *and* in the first edition, added this:

> That it is a solecism to begin a sentence with *and* is a faintly lingering superstition. (p. 29)

And to the original entry for *but*, he added "see *and*." To be sure, some inexperienced writers begin too many sentences with *and*, but that is an error not in grammar but in style.

Some insecure writers also think they should not begin a sentence with *because*. Not this:

> ✓**Because** we have access to so much historical fact, today we know a good deal about changes within the humanities which were not apparent to those of any age much before our own and which the individual scholar must constantly reflect on.
>
> —Walter Ong, S. J., "The Expanding Humanities and the Individual Scholar," *Publication of the Modern Language Association*

Though this folklore about *because* appears in no handbook, it is gaining currency. It must stem from advice intended to avoid sentence FRAGMENTS like this one:

> The plan was rejected. **Because** it was incomplete.

2. "Use the RELATIVE PRONOUN *that*—not *which*—for restrictive clauses." Allegedly, not this:

> ✓ Next is a typical situation **which** a practiced writer corrects "for style" virtually by reflex action.
>
> —Jacques Barzun, *Simple and Direct* (p. 69).

Yet just a few sentences earlier, Barzun himself (one of our most eminent intellectual historians and critics of style) had asserted,

> Us[e] *that* with defining [i.e. restrictive] clauses except when stylistic reasons interpose.

(No such reasons interposed in his sentence.) A rule can have no force when someone as eminent as Barzun asserts it on one page and unselfconsciously violates it on the next, and that "erroneous" *which* is never caught, not by his editors, not by his proofreaders, not even by Barzun himself.

This "rule" is relatively new. It first appeared in 1906 in Henry and Francis Fowler's *The King's English* (Oxford University Press; reprinted as an Oxford University Press paperback, 1973). The Fowlers thought that the random variation between *that* and *which* to introduce restrictive clauses was messy, so they just asserted that we should (with some exceptions) limit *which* to NONRESTRICTIVE clauses.

A nonrestrictive clause, you may recall, describes a noun that you can already identify unambiguously without the help of that clause. For example,

> ✓ ABCO Inc. ended its bankruptcy, **which** it had filed in 1997.

A company can have only one bankruptcy at a time, so we can unambiguously identify the bankruptcy mentioned without the help of the clause. We call that clause *nonrestrictive*, because it cannot "restrict" the meaning of the noun phrase *its bankruptcy* any more than it already is. We put a comma before the modifying clause and begin it with *which*. That rule is based on historical and contemporary usage.

But the Fowlers claimed that for *restrictive* clauses, we should use not *which* but only *that*: For example,

> ✓ABCO Inc. sold a product **that** [*not **which***] made millions.

Since ABCO presumably makes many products, the clause "restricts" which product the writer has in mind, and so, declared the Fowlers, it must begin with *that*.

Francis died in 1918, but Henry continued the family tradition with *A Dictionary of Modern English Usage*. In that landmark work, he discussed the finer points of *which* and *that*, then added this:

> Some there are who follow this principle now; but it would be idle to pretend that it is the practice either of most or of the best writers. (p. 635)

That wistful observation was kept in the second edition and again in the third. (For another example of this usage, see the passage by Walter Ong on p. 17.)

Having said that, I confess I follow Fowler's advice, not because I think that a restrictive *which* is an error, but because *that* is softer and because the Grammar Police subject those who write about language to withering (and often uninformed) scrutiny. I do choose a *which* when it is within a word or two of a *that*, because I don't like the sound of two *that's* close together:

> ✓We all have **that** one principle **that** we will not compromise.

> ✓We all have **that** one principle **which** we will not compromise.

3. "Use *fewer* with nouns you count, *less* with nouns you can't." Allegedly not this:

> ✓I can remember no **less** than five occasions when the correspondence columns of *The Times* rocked with volleys of letters . . .

> —Noel Gilroy Annan, Lord Annan, "The Life of the Mind in British Universities Today," *American Council of Learned Societies Newsletter*

No one uses *fewer* with mass nouns (*fewer sand*) but educated writers often use *less* with countable plural nouns
(*less resources*).

4. "Use *since* and *while* only to refer to time, not to mean
   because or *although*."

   Most careful writers use *since* with a meaning close to
   because but with an added sense of 'What follows *since* is
   information I assume you already know':

   ✓**Since** asbestos causes lung disease, it is a dangerous substance.

   Nor do most careful writers restrict *while* to its temporal
   sense (*We'll wait while you eat*), but use it as well with a
   meaning close to 'What I state in this clause I assume you
   know, but what I assert in the next qualifies it':

   ✓**While** we agree on a date, we disagree about the place.

   On the other hand, you might observe the advice to avoid
   as to signal cause, because it does so weakly:

   As the expenses are minor, we need not discuss them.

   Use *since* instead.

> ***Here's the point:***   If writers and readers we judge compe-
> tent think that a sentence beginning with *and* is not a prob-
> lem, then it is not those writers who should change their us-
> age but grammarians who should change their rules. A rule
> is folklore when vast numbers of otherwise careful readers
> and writers ignore it.

2. Options

These next bits of advice complement the Real Rules: Most readers do not notice when you follow a Real Rule, but do when you it
violate (like that). Few readers notice when you violate an op-
tional rule but some do when you observe it.

1. "Do not split infinitives." Purists condemn Dwight Mac-
   Donald, a linguistic arch-conservative, for this sentence
   (my emphasis in all the examples that follow).

✓One wonders why Dr. Gove and his editors did not think of labeling *knowed* as substandard right where it occurs, and one suspects that they wanted **to slightly conceal** the fact or at any rate to put off its exposure as long as decently possible.

—"The String Untuned," *The New Yorker*

They would require

. . . they wanted **to conceal slightly** the fact . . .

Infinitives are now split so commonly that when you avoid splitting one, careful readers may think you are trying to be especially correct, whether you are or not.

2. "Use *whom* as the OBJECT of a verb or preposition." Purists would condemn William Zinsser for this use of *who:*

> ✓Soon after you confront this matter of preserving your identity, another question will occur to you: "**Who** am I writing for?"
>
> —*On Writing Well*

They would insist on

. . . another question will occur to you: "For **whom** am I writing?"

Most readers take *whom* as a sign of self-conscious correctness. So when a writer uses it incorrectly, that choice is probably a sign of insecurity, as in this sentence:

The committee must decide **whom** should be promoted.

In that sentence, *whom* is the subject of the verb *should be promoted*, so that *whom* should be *who*. An actual rule: Use *who* when it is the subject of a verb *in its own clause*; use *whom* only when it is an object.

3. "Do not end a sentence with a preposition." Purists would condemn Sir Ernest Gowers, editor of Fowler's second edition, for this:

> ✓The peculiarities of legal English are often used as a stick to beat the official **with.**
>
> —*The Complete Plain Words*

and insist on this:

. . . a stick **with which** to beat the official.

The first is correct; the second formal. (Again, see the Ong passage on p. 17.) And when you choose to move both the preposition and its *whom* to the left, you make that sentence seem even more formal. Compare:

✓ The man I spoke **with** was the man I had written **to.**

✓ The man **with whom** I spoke was the man **to whom** I had written.

A final preposition can, however, end a sentence weakly (see pp. 164–165). George Orwell may have chosen to end this next sentence with *from* to make a sly point about English grammar, but I suspect *from* just landed there (and note the "incorrect" *which* six words from the end):

> [The defense of the English language] has nothing to do with . . . the setting up of a "standard English" **which** must never be departed **from.**
>
> —George Orwell, "Politics and the English Language"

This would have been less awkward and more emphatic:

> We do not defend the English language just to create a "standard English" whose rules we must always obey.

4. "Use the singular with *none* and *any.*"

Historically *none* and *any* were originally singular, but today most writers use them as plurals. Therefore, if you use them as singular, some readers will notice. The second is a bit more formal than the first:

✓ **None** of the reasons **are** sufficient to end the project.

✓ **None** of the reasons **is** sufficient to end the project.

On the most formal occasions, when you are under the closest public scrutiny, you might choose to observe these rules. Ordinarily, though, they are ignored by most careful writers, which is to say they are not rules at all. If you adopt the worst-case approach and observe them all, all the time—well, private virtues are their own reward.

Some Words That Attract Special Attention

There are a few words so often confused with others that when you distinguish them careful readers note it. For example, fewer writers distinguish *flaunt* from *flout* these days, so if you use either one correctly, those who think the difference matters are likely to note that at least *you* know that *flaunt* means 'to display conspicuously' and that *flout* means 'to scorn a rule or standard'. Thus if you chose to flout the rule about *flaunt* and *flout* scornfully, you would not flout your flaunting it, but flaunt your flouting it. Here are some others:

aggravate means 'to make worse.' It does not mean to **annoy**. You can aggravate an injury but not a person.

anticipate means 'to prepare for a contingency.' It does not mean just **expect**. You anticipate a question when you prepare its answer before it is asked; if you don't prepare, you only expect it.

anxious means 'uneasy.' It does not mean **eager**. You await good news eagerly; bad news anxiously,

blackmail means 'to extort by threatening to reveal damaging information.' It does not mean simply **coerce**. One country cannot blackmail another with nuclear weapons when it only threatens to use them.

cohort means 'a group who attends on someone.' It does not mean a single accompanying person. If Prince Charles marries his friend she will become his **consort**; his hangers-on will still be his *cohort*.

comprise means 'to include all parts in a single unit.' It does not mean on the one hand, to **constitute** a whole out of its parts nor on the other, merely "including" a few parts from among many.

continuous means 'without interruption.' It is not synonymous with **continual,** which means an activity extending over a period of time, possibly with interruptions. If you continuously interrupt, the person you interrupt will never say a word because your interruption will never stop. If you continually interrupt, you let the other person start sentences from time to time, but not finish them.

disinterested means 'neutral.' It does not mean **uninterested**. A judge should be disinterested in the outcome of a case, but not uninterested. (Incidentally, the original meaning of *disinterested* was 'to be uninterested.')

enormity means 'hugely bad.' It does not mean **enormous.** In private, a belch might be enormous, but at a state funeral, it would also be an enormity.

fortuitous means 'by chance.' It does not mean **fortunate**. You are fortunate when you fortuitously pick the right number in the lottery.

fulsome means 'sickeningly excessive.' It does not mean just 'much.' All of us enjoy full praise, except when it becomes fulsome.

notorious means 'well known for bad behavior.' It does not mean **famous**. Frank Sinatra was a famous singer but a notorious bully.

These days, truth be told, only a few readers care about these distinctions, but they may be just those readers whose judgment carries special weight. It takes only a few minutes to learn to use those words in ways that testify to your precision, so it may be worth your time to do so, especially if you also think that their distinctions are worth preserving.

On the other hand, you get no points for correctly distinguishing *imply* and *infer, principal* and *principle, accept* and *except, affect* and *effect, proceed* and *precede, discrete* and *discreet*. That's expected of schooled writers. Most careful readers also notice when a Latinate plural noun is used as a singular, so you might want to keep these straight, too:

Singular	datum	criterion	medium	stratum	phenomenon
Plural	data	criteria	media	strata	phenomena

Hobgoblins

For some reason, a few items of usage have become the object of particularly zealous abuse. There's no explaining why; none of them interferes with clarity or concision.

1. "Never use *like* for *as* or *as if*." Not this:

   > These operations failed **like** the earlier ones did.

   But this:

   > These operations failed **as** the earlier ones did.

   Like became a SUBORDINATING CONJUNCTION in the eighteenth century when some writers began to drop *as* from the phrase *like as*, leaving just *like* to serve as the conjunction. This process is called *elision* and is a common linguistic change. The editor of the second edition of Fowler deleted *like* for *as* from Fowler's original list of "Illiteracies" and moved it into the category of "Sturdy Indefensibles."

2. "Do not use *hopefully* to mean 'I hope'." Not this:

   > ✓ Hopefully, it will not rain.

   But this:

   > ✓ It is hoped that it will not rain.

   This "rule" dates from the twentieth century, but it has no basis in logic or grammar. It parallels the usage of other words that no one abuses, words such as *candidly, frankly, sadly,* and *happily:*

   > ✓ Candidly, we may fail. (That is, I am candid when I say we may fail.)

   > ✓ Seriously, we must go. (That is, I am serious when I say we must go.)

3. "Never use *finalize* to mean 'finish' or 'complete'."

   But *finalize* does not mean just 'finish.' It means 'to clean up the last few details,' a sense captured by no other word. Moreover, if we think *finalize* is bad because -*ize* is ugly, we would have to reject *nationalize, synthesize,* and *rationalize,* along with hundreds of other useful words.

4. "Never use *impact* as a verb, as in *The survey **impacted** our strategy*. Use it only as a noun, as in *The survey had an **impact** on our strategy*."

Impact has been a verb since the seventeenth century, but on some people, historical evidence has none.

5. "Do not modify absolute words such as *perfect, unique, final,* or *complete* with *very, more, quite,* and so on," a rule that would have ruled out this familiar sentence:

> ✓We the People of the United States, in order to form a **more perfect** union . . .

6. "Never ever use *irregardless* for *regardless* or *irrespective*." However arbitrary this rule is, it is a sound one that you should obey.

A Special Problem: Pronouns and Sexism

We expect literate writers to make verbs agree with subjects:

> ✓ Our **reasons are** based on solid evidence.

We also expect their pronouns to agree with antecedents. Not this:

> Early **efforts** to oppose the hydrogen bomb failed because **it** ignored political issues. **No one** wanted to expose **themselves** to anti-Communist hysteria.

But this:

> ✓ Early **efforts** to oppose the hydrogen bomb failed because **they** ignored political issues. **No one** wanted to expose **himself** to anti-Communist hysteria.

There are, however, two problems.

First, do we use a singular or plural pronoun when we refer to a noun that is singular in grammar but plural in meaning: When we refer to a *group, committee, staff, administration,* and so on, do we use *it* or *they?* Some writers use a singular pronoun when the group acts as a single entity:

> ✓ The **committee has** met but has not yet made **its** decision.

But they use a plural pronoun when members of the group act individually:

> ✓The **faculty have** the memo, but not all of **them** have read it.

These days the plural is used in both senses.

Second, what pronoun do we use to refer to *someone, everyone, no one* and to singular nouns that indicate no gender: *teacher, doctor, student?* We casually use *they:*

> **Everyone** knows **they** must take responsibility for **their** actions.
>
> When **a person** is on drugs, it is hard to help **them.**

More formal usage requires a singular pronoun:

> ✓ **Everyone** realizes that **he** must be responsible for **himself.**
>
> ✓ When **a person** is on drugs, it is hard to help **her.**

But the formal rule raises the problem of biased language.

Gender and Language

Common sense demands that we not gratuitously offend readers, but if we reject *he* as a generic pronoun because it is sexist and *they* because some readers consider it ungrammatical, we are left with bad choices among a clumsily intrusive *he or she,* a substantially worse *he/she,* or the worst, *s/he.*

> If **a writer** ignores the ethnic background of **his or her** readers, **s/he** may respond in ways **the writer** would not expect to words that to **him or her** are innocent of bias.

So we have to revise. We can begin by substituting plurals for singulars:

> ✓ When **writers** ignore the ethnicity of **their** readers, **they** may respond in ways that **they** might not expect to words that are to **them** innocent of bias.

But to the careful ear, plurals seem less precise than singulars, and *they* is ambiguous, when, as in that sentence, there are a lot of different plural referents. We can try a first person *we,* but *we* can be ambiguous as well.

> ✓ If **we** ignore the ethnic background of **our** readers, they may respond in ways **we** would not expect to words that to **us** are innocent of bias.

We can drop people altogether, but that encourages abstraction, a potentially bigger problem:

Failure to consider ethnic background may lead to an unexpected response to words considered innocent of bias.

Finally, we can alternately use *he* and *she,* as I have. But that is not a perfect solution either, because to some readers, *she* is as intrusive as *he/she.* A reviewer in the *New York Times*, for example, wondered what to make of an author whom the reviewer charged with attempting to

> right history's wrongs to women by referring to random examples as "she," as in "Ask a particle physicist what happens when a quark is knocked out of a proton, and she will tell you . . . ," which strikes this reader as oddly patronizing to women.

We might wonder how it struck women particle physicists.

For years to come, we will have a problem with the singular generic pronoun, and to some readers, any solution will be awkward. I suspect that eventually we will accept the plural *they* as a correct singular:

> ✓ **No one** should turn in **their** writing unedited.

In fact, the change has already been approved by the most highly respected style guide, *The Chicago Manual of Style.* Some claim, predictably, that in such compromises we surrender to imprecision. Until the issue is decided, the dispute gives us a choice, and that's not a bad thing, because our choices define who we are.

SUMMING UP

We must write correctly, but if in defining correctness we ignore the difference between truth and folklore, we risk overlooking what is important—the choices that make prose dense and wordy or clear and concise. We are not being precise when we merely get straight the *which*es and *that*s and eradicate *finalize* and *hopefully.* Many who obsess on such details are oblivious to this more serious kind of imprecise expression:

> Too precise a specification of information processing requirements incurs the risk of overestimation resulting in unused capacity or inefficient use of costly resources or of underestimation leading to ineffectiveness or other inefficiencies.

That means,

> ✓ When you specify too precisely the resources you need to process information, you may overestimate. If you do, you risk having more capacity than you need or using costly resources inefficiently.

Both are grammatically precise, but who would choose to go on reading more of the first?

I suspect that those who choose to observe all the rules all the time do so not because they think they are protecting the integrity of the language or the quality of our culture, but because they want to assert a style of their own. Some of us are straightforward and plain speaking; others take pleasure in a bit of elegance, in a touch of fastidiously self-conscious "class." It is an impulse we ought not scorn, but only so long as it is not a pretext for discrimination and includes a concern for the more important matters to which we now turn—the choices that define not "good grammar," but clarity and grace.

PART TWO
Clarity

*Everything that can be thought at all
can be thought clearly.
Everything that can be said can be said clearly.*

—Ludwig Wittgenstein

Actions

Suit the action to the word, the word to the action.
—WILLIAM SHAKESPEARE, *HAMLET,* 3.2

Words and deeds are quite different modes of
the divine energy. Words are also actions,
and actions are a kind of words.
—RALPH WALDO EMERSON

Action is eloquence.
—WILLIAM SHAKESPEARE, *CORIOLANUS,* 3.2

Whatever is translatable in other and simpler words of the same
language, without loss of sense or dignity, is bad.
—SAMUEL TAYLOR COLERIDGE

It takes less time to learn to write nobly than to
learn to write lightly and straightforwardly.
—FRIEDRICH NIETZSCHE

I am unlikely to trust a sentence that comes easily.
—WILLIAM GASS

Making Judgments

We have words enough to praise writing we like: *clear, direct, concise,* and more than enough to abuse writing (and writers) we don't: *unclear, indirect, wordy, confusing, abstract, dense, complex.* We could use those words to distinguish these two sentences:

1a. The cause of our schools' failure at teaching basic skills is not understanding the influence of cultural background on learning.

1b. Our schools have failed to teach basic skills because they do not understand how cultural backgrounds influence the way children learn.

Most of us would call (1a) a bit convoluted, (1b) clearer and more direct. But those words don't refer to anything *in* either sentence; they instead describe how those sentences make us *feel.* When we say that (1a) is *unclear,* we really say that *we* have a hard time understanding it; when we say it is *dense,* we really say that *we* have to struggle through it.

What we have to understand is *why* those two sentences make us feel as we do. Then you can predict when readers will think your own sentences are dense and unclear so that you can revise them. To do that, you have to understand what counts as a well-told story.

Telling Stories: Characters and Actions

Here's a story with a problem:

2a. Once upon a time, as a walk through the woods was taking place on the part of Little Red Riding Hood, the Wolf's jump out from behind a tree occurred, causing her fright.

We expect something closer to this:

✓2b. Once upon a time, Little Red Riding Hood was walking through the woods, when the Wolf jumped out from behind a tree and frightened her.

Why do we think that sentence (2b) tells its story so much more clearly than (2a)? Here's the brief answer:

- In (2a), the less clear sentence, the two main characters in the story, Little Red Riding Hood and the Wolf, are *not* SUBJECTS of any VERBS, and neither of the two verbs, *was taking* and *occurred*, names a key ACTION.

- In (2b), the clearer sentence, those two characters *are* subjects and the verbs *do* name their key actions, *walking*, *jump*, and *frightened*.

Here's the detailed explanation. (To get the most out of this lesson and the next one, you should be able to identify verbs, SIMPLE SUBJECTS and WHOLE SUBJECTS. See the Glossary.)

Principle of Clarity 1:   Characters as Subjects

Look at the subjects in (2a). The SIMPLE SUBJECTS (boldfaced) and main characters (italicized) are different words:

2a.   Once upon a time, as a **walk** through the woods was taking place on the part of *Little Red Riding Hood*, *the Wolf's* **jump** out from behind a tree occurred, causing *her* fright.

In that sentence, subjects are not characters; they are instead actions expressed as abstract NOUNS, *walk* and *jump*:

SUBJECT	VERB
a **walk** through the woods	was taking place
the *Wolf's* **jump** out from behind a tree	occurred

To be sure, the WHOLE SUBJECT of *occurred* has a character *in* it: *the Wolf's* jump, but *the Wolf* is only attached to the real subject: *jump*.

Contrast those abstract subjects with the concrete subjects in (2b). Notice how the subjects (boldfaced) and the main characters (italicized) are the same words:

SUBJECT	VERB
Little Red Riding Hood	was walking
the Wolf	jumped

Principle of Clarity 2: Actions as Verbs

Now compare how the actions and verbs differ. In (2a), the actions and verbs are also different words: The actions are not in verbs but in abstract nouns, and the verbs that are there (*was taking, occurred*) express little specific action (actions are boldfaced; verbs are capitalized):

> 2c. Once upon a time, as a **walk** through the woods WAS TAKING place on the part of Little Red Riding Hood, the Wolf's **jump** out from behind a tree OCCURRED, causing her **fright**.

In (2b), the clearer sentence, note how the actions and verbs are the same words:

> ✓2d. Once upon a time, Little Red Riding Hood WAS WALKING through the woods, when the Wolf JUMPED out from behind a tree and FRIGHTENED her.

Here's the point: In the version of Little Red Riding Hood that seems wordy and indirect the two main characters, Little Red Riding Hood and the Wolf, are *not* subjects and their actions—walk, jump, and fright—are *not* verbs. In the more direct version, (2b), the main characters *are* subjects and their main actions *are* verbs. In (2a), the story and the grammar of the sentence don't come together; in (2b), they do.

FAIRY TALES AND ACADEMIC WRITING

Fairy tales seem a long way from writing in college or on the job, but even there, sentences tell stories. Compare these two:

> 3a. The Federalists' argument in regard to the destabilization of government by popular democracy was based on their belief in the tendency of factions to further their self-interest at the expense of the common good.
>
> ✓3b. The Federalists argued that popular democracy destabilized government, because they believed that factions tended to further their self-interest at the expense of the common good.

Let's analyze those two sentences as we did the ones about Little Red Riding Hood.

Sentence (3a) feels dense for two reasons. First, its characters and subjects are different words. The subject is *argument*, but the main characters are Federalists, popular democracy, and factions (the characters are italicized, the simple subject is boldfaced):

> 3a. *The Federalists'* **argument** in regard to the destabilization of *government* by *popular democracy* was based on *their* belief in the tendency of *factions* to further *their* self-interest at the expense of the common good.

Second, the actions (boldfaced) are not verbs (capitalized), but rather abstract nouns (boldfaced):

> 3a. The Federalists' **argument** in regard to the **destabilization** of government by popular democracy WAS BASED on their **belief** in the **tendency** of factions to FURTHER their self-interest at the expense of the common good.

Notice in particular how long its whole subject is and how little meaning the main verb *was based* expresses:

WHOLE SUBJECT	VERB
The Federalists' argument in regard to the destabilization of government by popular democracy	was based

We think (3b) is clearer, first because its characters (italicized) *are* subjects (boldfaced):

> 3b. The ***Federalists*** argued that ***popular democracy*** destabilized government because ***they*** believed that ***factions*** tended to further *their* self-interest at the expense of the common good.

And second, all the actions are verbs (capitalized and boldfaced):

> 3b. The Federalists **ARGUED** that popular democracy **DESTABILIZED** government because they **BELIEVED** that factions **TENDED** to **FURTHER** their self-interest at the expense of the common good.

Notice too that all of those subjects are short and specific and that the verbs express specific meaning:

WHOLE SUBJECT/CHARACTER	VERB/ACTION
the Federalists	argued
popular democracy	destabilized
they	believed
factions	tended to further

In the rest of this lesson, we look in detail at actions and verbs; in the next, at characters and subjects.

VERBS AND ACTIONS

As we use the word here, *action* covers all literal or figurative movement, mental processes, relationships, and conditions. Our principle is this: Sentences seem clearer when actions are verbs. Look at how sentences (4a) and (4b) express their actions. In (4a), actions (boldfaced) are not verbs (capitalized) but nouns:

> 4a. Our **lack** of data PREVENTED **evaluation** of UN **actions** in **targeting** funds to areas most in **need** of **assistance.**

In (4b), on the other hand, the actions are almost all verbs:

> ✓4b. Because we LACKED data, we could not EVALUATE whether the UN had TARGETED funds to areas that most NEEDED **assistance.**

Your readers will think your writing is dense when you use lots of abstract nouns derived from verbs and ADJECTIVES, nouns ending in *-tion, -ment, -ence,* and so on, *especially when those nouns are subjects of verbs.*

Such nouns have a technical name: NOMINALIZATION. The word illustrates its meaning: When we nominalize *nominalize,* we create the nominalization *nominalization.* Here are a few examples:

VERB → NOMINALIZATION		ADJECTIVE → NOMINALIZATION	
discover	→ discovery	careless	→ carelessness
resist	→ resistance	different	→ difference
react	→ reaction	proficient	→ proficiency

We can also nominalize a verb by adding *-ing* (making it a GERUND):

She flies → her flying   We sang → our singing

Some nominalizations and verbs are identical:

hope → hope   result → result   repair → repair

We **REQUEST** that you **REVIEW** the data.

Our **request** IS that you DO a **review** of the data.

Actions in Adjectives

You can also hide action in adjectives. Such adjectives usually appear after a form of *be*:

The data ARE **indicative** of the problem.

The data **INDICATE** the problem.

Some examples:

is applicable → applies   is deserving → deserves   is dubious → doubts

No feature of style more characterizes abstract, indirect, difficult academic and professional writing than lots of nominalizations, especially when they are subjects of verbs.

Here's the point: In grade school, most of us learned that the order of Subject–Verb–Object is predictable, that subjects *are* characters (or "doers"), and that verbs *are* actions. That's true in a sentence like this:

subject	verb	object
We	discussed	the problem.
doer	action	

But it's not true for this almost synonymous sentence:

subject	verb	
The problem	was	the topic of our discussion.
		doer action

You can move characters and actions almost wherever you choose, and subjects and verbs don't have to be any particular thing at all. But readers prefer that most of your subjects be characters and most of your verbs be actions. When that's the case, they will describe your prose as clear and direct.

Exercise 3.1

Analyze the subject/character and verb/action patterns:

> There is opposition among many voters to nuclear power plants based on a belief of their threat to human health.
>
> Many voters oppose nuclear power plants because they believe that such plants threaten human health.

Exercise 3.2

If you are uncertain that you can reliably distinguish verbs, adjectives, and nominalizations, spend a few minutes turning the list of verbs and adjectives below into nominalizations and nominalizations into adjectives and verbs. Remember that some verbs and nominalizations have the same form:

> Poverty predictably CAUSES social problems.
>
> Poverty IS a predictable **cause** of social problems.

analysis	believe	attempt	conclusion	evaluate
suggest	approach	comparison	define	discuss
expression	failure	intelligent	thorough	appearance
decrease	improve	increase	accuracy	careful
emphasize	explanation	description	clear	

Exercise 3.3

Write some sentences using verbs and adjectives from Exercise 3.2. Then rewrite them using the corresponding nominalizations (try to express the same idea). For example, using *suggest, discuss,* and *careful,* write:

> I SUGGEST that we DISCUSS the issue in a CAREFUL manner.

Then rewrite that sentence into its nominalized form:

> My **suggestion** is that our **discussion** of the issue be done with **care.**

It may seem odd to ask you to ruin a good sentence, but only when you see how a clear sentence can be made less clear will you understand why it seemed clear in the first place.

From Diagnosis to Analysis to Revision

You can use the principles about characters as subjects and actions as verbs to explain why we judge a passage as we do. But more important, you can also use them to identify sentences that your readers probably would want you to revise.

Revising is a three-step process:

1. **Diagnose.** To predict how a reader will judge your writing, do this:

   a. Ignoring short (four- or five-word) introductory phrases, underline the first seven or eight words in each sentence.

   b. Look for two things:

   - Those underlined words include abstract nouns.
   - You have to read at least six or seven words before you get to a verb.

2. **Analyze.** If you find such sentences, do this:

   a. Decide who your cast of characters is, particularly flesh-and-blood characters.

   b. Find the actions that those characters perform.

3. **Revise.**

   a. If the actions are nominalizations, change them into verbs.

   b. Make the characters the subjects of those verbs.

   c. Rewrite the sentence with conjunctions like *because, if, when, although, why, how, whether,* or *that.*

Some Common Patterns

You can quickly spot and revise three common patterns of nominalizations.

1. The nominalization is the subject and an empty verb follows:

   The **intention** of *the committee* is to audit the records.

   a. Identify the characters:

   The intention of **the committee** is to audit the records.

   b. Change the nominalization to a verb: *intention → intend*

   c. Make the character the subject of the verb:

     The committee **INTENDS** *to audit the records.*

2. A nominalization follows *there is* or *there are:*

     There **IS** no **need** for *our* further **study** of this problem.

   a. Identify the characters:

     There is no need for **our** further study of this problem.

   b. Change the nominalization to a verb: *need → need, study → study*

   c. Make the character the new subject of the verb: *no need, our study → we need, we study:*

     We **NEED** *not* **STUDY** *this problem further.*

3. One nominalization appears in a subject and a second after a verb or phrase like *be, seems, has the result of,* etc.:

     Their **loss** in sales **WAS** a result of their competitors' **expansion** of outlets.

   a. Identify the characters:

     Their loss in sales was a result of their **competitors'** expansion of outlets.

   b. Revise the nominalizations into verbs:

     loss → lose   expansion → expand

   c. Make the characters subjects of those verbs:

     they lose   their competitors expand.

   d. Link the new clauses with a logical connection:
- To express simple cause: *because, since, when*
- To express conditional cause: *if, provided that, so long as*
- To contradict expected causes: *though, although, unless*

Their **loss** in sales	→ *They* **LOST** sales
was the result of	→ **because**
competitors' **expansion** in outlets.	→ *their competitors* **EXPANDED** outlets.

Two other patterns invite you to look for nominalizations after verbs. In these cases, the subject is often a character.

4. A nominalization follows a verb with little specific meaning:

> The *agency* CONDUCTED an **investigation** into the matter.

    a. Change the nominalization to a verb: *investigation* → *investigate*

    b. Replace the empty verb with the new verb: *conducted* → *investigated*

> ✓ The *agency* **INVESTIGATED** the matter.

5. Two or three nominalizations in a row are joined by prepositions:

> We did a **review** of the **evolution** of the brain.

    a. Turn the first nominalization into a verb: *review* → *review*

    b. Either leave the second nominalization as it is or turn it into a verb in a CLAUSE beginning with *how* or *why: evolution of the brain* → *how the brain evolved.*

> First, *we* **REVIEWED** the **evolution** of the *brain.*

> ✓ First, *we* **REVIEWED** how *the brain* **EVOLVED.**

Exercise 3.4

One sentence in each of these pairs is clear, expressing characters as subjects and actions as verbs; the other is indirect, with actions in nominalizations and characters not in subjects. First, identify which is which. Then circle nominalizations and highlight verbs. If you are good at grammar, underline subjects. Then put a "c" through characters.

1a. Some have argued that atmospheric carbon dioxide does not elevate global temperature.

1b. There has been speculation by educators as to the role of a good family environment in the improvement of educational achievement.

2a. Smoking during pregnancy may cause fetal injury.

2b. When we write concisely, readers understand easily.

3a. Researchers have identified the AIDS virus but failed to develop a vaccine to immunize those at risk.

3b. Attempts by economists at defining full employment have generally been met with failure.

4a. Complaints by editorial writers about voter apathy generally don't offer suggestions about dispelling it.

4b. Although many critics have claimed that children who watch television tend to become less able readers, no one has yet demonstrated that to be true.

5a. The loss of market share to Japan by domestic auto makers resulted in the disappearance of hundreds of thousands of jobs.

5b. When educators can discover how to use computer-assisted instruction, our schools can teach more complex subjects and students will learn faster.

6a. We need to know which parts of our national forests are being logged most extensively so that we can save virgin stands at greatest risk.

6b. There is a need for an analysis of library use to provide a reliable base for the projection of needed resources.

7a. Professional athletes often fail to realize that they are unprepared for life after stardom because their teams protect them from the problems that the rest of us adjust to every day.

7b. Many colleges have come to an understanding that continued tuition increases are no longer possible because of strong resistance from parents to the soaring costs of higher education.

Exercise 3.5

Now revise the nominalized sentences in Exercise 3.4 into verbal sentences. Use the verbal version as a model. For example, if the verbal sentence begins with *when*, begin your revision with *when:*

Sentence to revise: 2a. **Smoking** during pregnancy may lead
to fetal **injury.**

Model: 2b. When we WRITE concisely, readers
UNDERSTAND more easily.

Your revision: 2a. When pregnant women SMOKE . . .

Exercise 3.6

Revise these next sentences so that the nominalizations are
verbs and characters are their subjects. In (1) through (5),
characters are italicized and nominalizations are boldfaced.

1. *Lincoln's* **hope** was for the peaceful **preservation** of the
   Union, but the *South's* **attack** on Fort Sumter made war
   an **inevitability.**
2. **Attempts** were made on the part of the *President's aides*
   to assert *his* **immunity** from a *Congressional* subpoena.
3. There were **predictions** by *business executives* that the
   economy would experience a quick **revival.**
4. *Your* **analysis** of my report omits any data in **support**
   of *your* **criticism** of my **findings.**
5. The *health care industry's* **inability** to exert cost **controls** could lead to the *public's* **decision** that *congressional* **action** is needed.

In sentences 6 through 10, the agents are italicized; find
the actions.

6. A *papal* appeal was made to the *nations of the world* for
   assistance to those facing the threat of *African* starvation.
7. Attempts at explanations for increases in *voter* participation in this year's elections were offered by *several
   candidates.*
8. The agreement by the *class* on the reading list was based
   on the assumption that there would be tests on only certain selections.
9. There was no independent *business-sector* study of the
   cause of the sudden increase in the trade surplus.
10. An understanding as to the need for controls over
    drinking on campus was recognized by *fraternities.*

In 11 through 15, only the nominalizations are bold-faced; find or invent the characters.

11. There is **uncertainty** at the CIA about Korean **intentions** as to **cessation** of missile **testing**.

12. Thorough **physical conditioning** of the team is the **responsibility** of the coaching staff.

13. Any **contradictions** among the data requires an **explanation.**

14. The Dean's **rejection** of our proposal was a **disappointment** but not a **surprise** because our **expectation was** that a **decision** had been made.

15. Their **performance** of the play was marked by **enthusiasm** but lacked intelligent **staging**.

SOME HAPPY CONSEQUENCES

We began with two principles:

- Make central characters subjects of verbs.
- Use verbs to name the actions those characters are involved in.

When you apply those principles, your writing benefits in several ways:

1. Your sentences are more concrete. Compare:

> There WAS an affirmative **decision** for program **expansion.**

> ✓ *The Director* DECIDED to EXPAND the program.

2. Your sentences are more concise. When you use nominalizations, you usually have to add articles like *a* and *the* and prepositional phrases such as *of, by,* and *in.* You don't need them when you use verbs and conjunctions (italicized):

> A **revision** *of* the program WILL RESULT *in* **increases** *in* our **efficiency** *in* the **servicing** *of* clients.

> ✓ If we REVISE the program, we CAN SERVE clients more EFFICIENTLY.

3. Your sentences are more coherent. This next sequence of actions distorts their chronology. (The numbers refer to the real sequence of events.)

> Decisions[4] in regard to administration[5] of medication despite inability[2] of an irrational patient appearing[1] in a Trauma Center to provide legal consent[3] rest with the attending physician alone.

When we revise those actions into verbs and reorder them, we get something more coherent:

> ✓When a patient appears[1] in a Trauma Center and behaves[2] so irrationally that he cannot legally consent[3] to treatment, only the attending physician can decide[4] whether to administer[5] medication.

4. The logic of your sentences is clearer. When you nominalize verbs, you link actions with fuzzy prepositions and phrases such as *of, by,* and *on the part of.* But when you use verbs, you can link clauses with more precise SUBORDINATING CONJUNCTIONS like *because, although,* and *if:*

> Our more effective presentation of our study resulted in our success, despite an earlier start by others.

> ✓**Although** others started earlier, we succeeded **because** we presented our study more effectively.

A COMMON PROBLEM

Most of us can identify unclear writing by others, but we all have a harder time recognizing our own. You've probably had this experience: You write something you think is great, but your reader tells you that it is less than that. You wonder whether that person is just being difficult, but you bite your tongue and try to fix what you are certain should be clear to anyone who can read Dr. Seuss.

When that happens to me (regularly, I might add), I almost always realize—eventually—that my critics are right, that they can recognize where my writing is unclear better than I can.

How can we be right about the writing of others, and so wrong about our own? It is because all of us read into our own writing what we want readers to get out of it. That explains why two readers can disagree about the clarity of the same passage: Someone who understands its content is more likely to think the passage is clearly written than someone who knows less. Both are right.

Therefore, since you can never read as your readers will, you need to look at your own writing in a way that sidesteps your too-easy understanding of it. The quickest way is to underline the first seven or eight words of every sentence. If you don't see in those words a character as a subject and a verb as an action, you have a candidate for revision.

A final tip: Start looking for passages to revise by recalling where you struggled to express yourself. We all tend to write badly when we aren't certain of what we want to say.

USEFUL NOMINALIZATIONS

I have relentlessly urged you to revise nominalizations into verbs, but in fact, you cannot write well without them. The trick is to know which to keep and which to turn into verbs. Keep these:

1. A nominalization in a subject refers to a previous sentence:

   ✓ **These arguments** all depend on a single unproven claim.

   ✓ **This decision** can lead to positive outcomes.

   Those nominalizations link one sentence to another in a cohesive flow.

2. A succinct nominalization replaces an awkward *The fact that:*

   The fact that she ACKNOWLEDGED the problem impressed me.

   ✓ Her **acknowledgment** of the problem impressed me.

   But then, why not this:

   ✓ *She* IMPRESSED me when *she* ACKNOWLEDGED the problem.

3. A nominalization names what would be the object of the verb:

   I accepted *what she* REQUESTED.

   ✓ I accepted her **request.**

This kind of nominalization feels more concrete than an abstract one. However, contrast *request* above with this next sentence, where *request* is more of an action:

Her **request** for **assistance** CAME after the deadline.

✓ She REQUESTED **assistance** after the deadline.

4. A nominalization refers to a concept so familiar that it is almost a character (more about this in the next lesson):

> ✓ Few problems have so divided us as **abortion** on **demand.**
>
> ✓ The Equal Rights **Amendment** was an issue in past **elections.**
>
> ✓ **Taxation** without **representation** did not spark the American **Revolution.**

Those nominalizations name concepts familiar to all of us: *abortion on demand, amendment, election, taxation, representation, revolution.* You have to develop an eye for the nominalization that expresses one of these common ideas and one that can be revised into a verb:

> There is a **demand** for a **repeal** of the **inheritance** tax.
>
> ✓ We DEMAND that the government REPEAL the **inheritance** tax.

Exercise 3.7

Revise these sentences. At the end of each is a hint. For example:

> Congress's **reduction** of the deficit resulted in the **decline** of interest rates. [because]
>
> ✓ Interest rates DECLINED because Congress REDUCED the deficit.

1. The use of models in teaching prose style does not result in improvements of clarity and directness in student writing. [Although we use . . .]

2. Precision in plotting the location of building foundations enhances the possibility of accurate reconstruction of the village. [When we precisely plot . . .]

3. Any departures by the members from established procedures may cause termination of membership by the Board. [If members . . .]

4. A student's lack of socialization into a field may lead to writing problems because of her insufficient understanding about arguments by professionals in that field. [When . . . , ... , because . . .]

> 5. The successful implementation of a new curriculum depends on the cooperation of faculty with students in setting achievable goals within a reasonable time. [To implement . . . , ...]

CLARITY, NOT SIMPLEMINDEDNESS

Your readers will think that you write clearly to the degree you match actions to verbs and characters to subjects. But you also have to avoid Dick-and-Jane prose. This was written by a student aspiring to academic sophistication:

> After Czar Alexander II's emancipation of Russian serfs in 1861, many freed peasants chose to live on communes for purposes of cooperation in agricultural production as well as for social stability. Despite some communes' attempts at economic and social equalization through the strategy of imposing low economic status on the peasants, which resulted in their reduction to near poverty, a centuries-long history of social distinctions even among serfs prevented social equalization.

In his struggle to write clearly, he revised that paragraph into something that sounds like it was written by a 12-year old:

> In 1861, Czar Alexander II emancipated the Russian serfs. Many of them chose to live on agricultural communes. There they thought they could cooperate with one another in agricultural production. They could also create a stable social structure. The leaders of some of these communes tried to equalize the peasants economically and socially. As one strategy, they tried to impose on all a low economic status. That reduced them to near poverty. However, the communes failed to equalize them socially. This happened because even serfs had made social distinctions among themselves for centuries.

In Lessons 8 and 9 we look at ways to revise too-short, too-simple sentences into a style that is readable but still complex enough to communicate complex ideas. When that student applied those principles to his primer-style passage, he revised again:

> After the Russian serfs were emancipated by Czar Alexander II in 1861, many chose to live on agricultural communes, hoping they could cooperate in working the land and establish a stable social structure. At

first, those who led some of the communes tried to equalize the new peasants socially and economically by imposing on everyone a low economic status, a strategy that reduced them to near poverty. But the communes failed to equalize them socially because the serfs had for centuries been observing their own social distinctions.

Those sentences are long but clear because the writer consistently aligned major characters with subjects and actions with verbs.

SUMMING UP

We can represent these principles graphically. As we read, we integrate two levels of sentence structure. One is a relatively fixed grammatical sequence of subject and verb (the empty box is for everything that follows the verb):

Fixed	Subject	Verb	———

The other level of structure is based on the story it tells, on character, and on action. Character and action have no fixed order, but readers prefer that they occur in this order:

Variable	Character	Action	———

We can graphically combine those principles:

Fixed	Subject	Verb	———
Variable	Character	Action	———

Readers expect to see characters not just *in* a subject, as in these two:

> The *President's* **veto of the bill** infuriated Congress.
>
> The **veto of the bill** by *the President* infuriated Congress.

Instead, readers prefer to see the character *as* the subject, like this:

✓When ***the President***_{subject} VETOED_{verb} the bill, ***he***_{subject} INFURIATED_{verb} Congress.

When you frustrate your readers' expectations, you make them work harder than they have to. So keep these principles in mind as you revise:

1. When appropriate, express actions in verbs:

    The **intention** of the committee IS improvement of morale.

    ✓The committee **INTENDS** to improve morale.

2. When appropriate, make subjects of verbs the agents of actions.

    A decision by **the Dean** in regard to the funding by **the Department** of the program IS necessary for adequate **staff** preparation.

    ✓If **the staff** IS TO PREPARE adequately, **the Dean** MUST DECIDE whether **the Department** WILL FUND the program.

3. Don't revise nominalizations that do the following:

    a. Refer to a previous sentence:

       ✓**These arguments** all depend on a single unproven claim.

    b. Replace an awkward "The fact that":

       The fact that she strenuously objected impressed me.

       ✓**Her strenuous objections** impressed me.

    c. Name what would be the object of a verb:

       I do not know **what she INTENDS.**

       ✓I do not know **her intentions.**

Characters

*I have never had a thought which I could not set down in words,
with ever more distinctiveness than that which I conceived it.*
—EDGAR ALLAN POE

There is no artifice as good and desirable as simplicity.
—ST. FRANCIS DE SALES

Affected simplicity is refined imposture.
—LA ROCHEFOUCAULD

When character is lost, all is lost.
—ANONYMOUS

THE IMPORTANCE OF CHARACTERS

We generally judge writing to be clear and direct when we see crucial ACTIONS in VERBS. Compare (1a) with (1b):

1a. The CIA feared the president would recommend to Congress that it reduce its budget.

1b. The CIA had fears that the president would send a recommendation to Congress that it make a reduction in its budget.

Sentence (1a) is more concise than (1b), but some readers don't sense a big difference between them because they both have characters as subjects (boldfaced):

1a. **The CIA** FEARED **the president** would RECOMMEND to Congress that **it** REDUCE its budget.

1b. **The CIA** HAD fears that **the president** would SEND a recommendation to Congress that **it** MAKE a reduction in its budget.

But now compare the boldfaced subjects in (1b) and (1c):

1b. **The CIA** had fears that **the president** would send a recommendation to Congress that **it** make a reduction in its budget.

1c. **The fear on the part of the CIA** was that **a recommendation from the president to Congress** would be for a reduction in its budget.

Just about all readers think that (1c) is much less clear than either (1a) or (1b).

The reason is this: Unlike (1a) or (1b), the subjects in (1c) are not specific characters, but abstractions: *The fear on the part of the CIA* and *a recommendation from the president to Congress*. The main characters (CIA, the president, and Congress) are not subjects of verbs, but rather OBJECTS of PREPOSITIONS:

1c. The fear on the part *of* **the CIA** was that a recommendation *from* **the president** *to* **Congress** would be for a reduction in its budget.

Here's the point: Readers prefer to see actions in verbs, but they really want to see characters as their subjects. We give readers a problem when for no good reason we do not make characters subjects, or worse, delete them entirely, like this:

1d. There was fear that there would be a recommendation for a budget reduction.

Who fears? Who recommends? Who reduces? It is important to express actions in verbs, but if there is one key to a clear style it is this: Make the subjects of your verbs short, specific, and concrete.

FINDING AND RELOCATING CHARACTERS

To get characters into subjects, you have to know three things:

1. When you have not done that.
2. If you have not, where you should look for characters.
3. What you should do once you find them.

For example, this sentence feels indirect and impersonal.

> Governmental intervention in fast changing technologies has resulted in distortions of market evolution or interference in the development of new products.

Let's diagnose that sentence:

1. Skim the first seven or eight words:

   Governmental intervention in fast changing technologies has resulted in distortions of market evolution or interference in the development of new products.

   In those first few words, readers want to see characters as the subjects of verbs. But in that example, they don't.

2. Find the main characters.

   They may be POSSESSIVE PRONOUNS attached to a NOMINALIZATION, objects of prepositions, particularly *by* and *of*, or only implied:

   Governmental intervention in fast changing technologies has resulted in distortions of **market** evolution or interference in the development of new products.

   In this case, it looks like the characters are *government* and *market*.

3. Skim the passage for important actions, particularly those buried in nominalizations; then make them verbs and the relevant characters their subjects:

governmental **intervention**	→	The *government* **intervenes**
distortion	→	*[government]* **distorts**
market **evolution**	→	*markets* **evolve**
interference	→	*government* **interferes**
the **development** of new	→	*market* **develops** new products.

Now we can revise by reassembling those new subjects and verbs into a sentence, using words such as *if, although, because, that, when, how,* and *why*:

> ✓ When a *government* INTERVENES in fast changing technologies, *it* commonly DISTORTS how *markets* EVOLVE or INTERFERES with their ability to DEVELOP new products.

Be aware that just as actions can be in ADJECTIVES (*reliable* → *rely*), so can characters:

> Medieval *theological* debates often addressed issues considered trivial by modern *philosophical* thought.

When you find a character implied in an adjective, revise in the same way:

> ✓ Medieval *theologians* often debated issues that *modern philosophers* consider trivial.

Here's the point: Your first step in diagnosing your style is to look at your subjects. If you do not see your main characters there, your second step is to look for them. They can be in objects of prepositions, in possessive pronouns, in adjectives, or entirely missing. Once you find them, make them the subjects of verbs expressing their actions.

Reconstructing Absent Characters

You give readers their biggest problem when you delete *all* characters:

> A decision was made in favor of doing a study of the disagreements.

You may know who is doing what, but readers know less than you do and so usually need more help than you think. That sentence could mean either of these, and more:

> We decided that I should study why they disagreed.
>
> I decided that you should study why he disagreed.

Sometimes we omit characters to make a general statement.

> Research strategies that look for more than one variable are of more use in understanding factors in psychiatric disorder than strategies based on the assumption that the presence of psychopathology is dependent on a single gene or on strategies in which only one biological variable is studied.

But when we try to revise that into something clearer, we have to invent characters, then decide what to call them. Do we use *one* or *we,* or name a generic "doer?"

> ✓ If *one/we/researchers* are to understand what causes psychiatric disorder, *one/we/they* should use research strategies that look for more than one variable rather than assume that a single gene is responsible for psychopathology or adopt a strategy in which *one/we/they* study only one biological variable.

To most of us, *one* feels stiff, but *we* may be ambiguous because it can refer to the writer, to the writer and others but not the reader, to the reader and writer but not others, or to everyone. But when we avoid both nominalizations and vague pronouns, we can slide into PASSIVE verbs (we'll discuss them in a moment):

> To understand what makes patients vulnerable to psychiatric disorders, strategies that look for more than one variable SHOULD BE USED rather than strategies in which it IS ASSUMED that a gene causes psychopathology or only one biological variable IS STUDIED.

And in some cases, characters are so remote that you just have to start over:

> There are good reasons that account for the lack of evidence.

> ✓ I can explain why I have not found any evidence.

Here's the point: When you revise an abstract passage, you may have a problem if the hidden characters are "people in general." You can try *we* or a general term for whoever is doing the action, such as *researchers, social critics, one,* and so on, but the fact is, the English language has no good solution for this problem—that of naming a generic "doer."

A COMPLICATION: ABSTRACTIONS AS CHARACTERS

So far, I've discussed characters as if they were all flesh-and-blood. But we can tell stories whose main characters are abstractions, including nominalizations. Here's a story about a character called "freedom of speech," two nominalizations.

> ✓ No right is more fundamental to a free society than **freedom of speech. Free speech** served the left in the 1960s when it protested the Vietnam War, and **it** is now used by the right when it claims that speech includes political contributions. **The doctrine of free speech** has been embraced by all sides to protect themselves against those who would silence unpopular views. As a legal concept, **it** arose . . .

The phrase *free speech* (or its equivalents *freedom of speech* and *it*) is a virtual character because it is the subject of a series of sentences and seems to be involved in actions such as *served, is used, has been embraced,* and *arose.*

So here is a new definition of *character*:

A character is whatever can be the subject of a series of sentences that tell a story.

But when you do use abstract nominalizations as characters, you can create problems for your readers. Stories about abstractions as familiar as *free speech* are no problem, but if readers are not familiar with your abstractions, and especially if you use them with a lot of other abstractions, readers may well feel that your writing is terminally dense.

For example, most of us are unfamiliar with "prospective and immediate intention" as a philosophical concept, so we are likely to find it hard to understand a story about it, especially when that word *intention* is surrounded by lots of other nominalizations (actions are boldfaced; human characters are italicized):

> The **argument** is this. The cognitive component of **intention** exhibits a high degree of **complexity**. **Intention** is temporally divisible into two: prospective **intention** and immediate **intention**. The cognitive function of prospective **intention** is the **representation** of a *subject's* similar past **actions**, *his* current situation, and *his* course of future **actions**. That is, the cognitive component of prospective **intention** is a **plan**. The cognitive function of immediate **intention** is the **monitoring** and **guidance** of ongoing bodily **movement**.
>
> —Myles Brand, *Intending and Acting*

We can make that passage clearer to readers unfamiliar with such an abstract story if we tell it from the point of view of flesh-and-blood characters (they are italicized; "de-nominalized" verbs and one adjective are boldfaced and capitalized):

> ✓ *I* ARGUE this about intention. It has a complex cognitive component of two temporal kinds: prospective intention and immediate intention. *Prospective intention* lets *us* REPRESENT how *we* have ACTED in the past and in our present situation, and how *we* will ACT in the future. That is, *we* use the cognitive component of prospective intention to help *us* PLAN. *Immediate intention* lets *us* MONITOR and GUIDE *our* bodies as *we* MOVE them.

But have I made this passage say something that Professor Brand did not mean? Some argue that any change in form changes meaning. In this case, Professor Brand could offer an opinion, but only his readers could decide whether the two passages have different meanings, because at the end of the day, readers are always right.

Here's the point: Most readers prefer subjects of verbs to name the main characters in your story, and those main characters be flesh-and-blood characters. When you write about concepts, however, you can turn them into virtual characters by making them the subjects of verbs that communicate actions:

Intention **HAS** a complex cognitive component.
Prospective intention **LETS** us represent . . .
Immediate intention **LETS** us monitor and guide . . .

If readers are familiar with your special abstractions, no problem. But when they are not, avoid using lots of other nominalizations around them.

Exercise 4.1

Before you revise these next sentences, diagnose them. Look at the first six or seven words (ignore short introductory phrases). Then revise so that each has a specific character as subject of a specific verb. You may have to invent characters. Use *we, I,* or any other word that seems appropriate.

1. In recent years, the appearance of new interpretations about the meaning of the discovery of America has led to a reassessment of Columbus's place in Western history.

2. Decisions about forcibly administering medication in an emergency room setting despite the inability of an irrational patient to provide legal consent is usually an on-scene medical decision.

3. Tracing the transitions in a book or a well-written article will provide help in efforts at improving coherence in writing.

4. Resistance has been growing against building mental health facilities in residential areas because of a belief that the few examples of improper management are typical.

5. With the decline in network television viewing in favor of cable and rental cassettes, awareness is growing at the networks of a need to revise programming.

CHARACTERS AND PASSIVE VERBS

More than any other advice, you've probably heard "Don't write in the passive voice. Write in the active." That's not bad advice, but it's not always reliable. When you write in the active voice, you typically put

- a character as the agent of an action in the subject.
- the goal or receiver of an action in a DIRECT OBJECT:

	subject	verb	object
Active:	I	lost	the money.
	character/agent	action	goal

The passive differs in three ways:

1. The subject names the goal of the action.
2. A form of *be* precedes a verb in its PAST PARTICIPLE form.
3. The agent of the action is in a *by*-phrase or dropped:

	subject	be	+	verb	prepositional phrase
Passive:	The money	was		lost	[by me].
	goal			action	character/agent

The terms *active* and *passive* can, however, be confusing, because they can refer not only to those two grammatical constructions but also to how a sentence makes us *feel*. We often call a sentence passive if it feels flat, regardless of whether its verb is actually in the passive voice. For example, compare these two sentences.

> The project will succeed if we can effectively control costs.

> The success of the project depends on the effectiveness of cost control.

Both sentences are in the active voice, but the second *feels* passive, for two reasons:

- Neither of its actions—*success* and *control*—are verbs; both are nominalizations.
- It lacks an important character: *we*.

We compound that sense of passivity when we combine nominalizations with real passives:

Active-verbal:	We investigated why they interviewed so few minority applicants.
Active-nominalized:	We conducted an **investigation** into why they did so few **interviews** of minority applicants.
Passive-nominalized:	An **investigation** WAS CONDUCTED into why so few **interviews** WERE DONE.

Choosing between Active and Passive

Some critics of style relentlessly urge us to avoid the passive, but it is often the better choice. To choose between active and passive, you have to answer three questions:

1. *Must your readers know who is responsible for the action?*
   Often, we won't say who does an action, because our readers won't care or we don't know. For example, we naturally choose the passive in these sentences:

   ✓ The president **WAS RUMORED** to have considered resigning.

   ✓ Those who **ARE FOUND** guilty can **BE FINED.**

   ✓ Valuable records should always **BE KEPT** in a safe place.

   If we do not know who spread the rumors, we cannot say. And no one wonders who finds criminals guilty, fines them, or should keep records safe.
   Sometimes, of course, writers use the passive when they don't want readers to know who did an action, especially when the doer is the writer. For example,

   > Because the inspection was not done, the flaw was left uncorrected.

2. *Would the active or passive verb help your readers move smoothly from one sentence to the next?*
   We depend on the beginning of a sentence to give us a context of what we know before we follow the sentence to see what's new. If a sentence starts with information that is new and unexpected, it confuses us. For example, in this next short passage, the subject of the second sentence communicates new and complex information (italicized) before

it gives us information that is more familiar, information from the previous sentence:

> We must decide whether to improve education in the sciences alone or to raise the level of education across the whole curriculum. *The weight given to industrial competitiveness and the value we attach to the liberal* arts $_{\text{new information}}$ will influence **this decision** $_{\text{familiar information.}}$

In the second sentence, the verb *influence* is in the active voice. But we could follow the sentence more easily if it were passive, because the passive would put familiar information first and the new and complex information last, the order we all prefer:

> ✓We must decide whether to improve education in the sciences alone or raise the level of education across the whole curriculum. **This decision** $_{\text{familiar information}}$ WILL BE INFLUENCED$_{\text{passive verb}}$ by *the weight we give to industrial competitiveness and the value we attach to the liberal arts* $_{\text{new information.}}$

3. *Would the active or passive give your readers a more consistent and appropriate point of view?*

    The writer of this next passage reports the end of World War II in Europe from the point of view of the Allies. In so doing, she uses active verbs to make the Allies a consistent sequence of subjects:

> ✓By early 1945, *the Allies* HAD essentially DEFEATED$_{\text{active}}$ Germany; all that remained was a bloody climax. *American, French, British, and Russian forces* HAD BREACHED$_{\text{active}}$ its borders and WERE BOMBING$_{\text{active}}$ it around the clock. But *they* HAD not yet so DEVASTATED$_{\text{active}}$ Germany as to destroy its ability to resist.

But if she had wanted us to understand history from the point of view of Germany, she would have used passive verbs:

> ✓By early 1945, *Germany* HAD essentially BEEN DEFEATED$_{\text{passive}}$; all that remained was a bloody climax. *Its borders* HAD BEEN BREACHED$_{\text{passive}}$, and *it* WAS BEING BOMBED$_{\text{passive}}$ around the clock. *It* HAD not BEEN SO DEVASTATED$_{\text{passive}}$, however, that *it* could not RESIST.

Here's the point: Most writers depend on the passive verb too much, but it does have its uses. Use it in these circumstances:

- You don't know who did an action, your readers don't care, or you don't want them to know.
- You want to shift a long and complex bundle of information to the end of its sentence, especially when it also lets you move to its beginning information that is shorter and more familiar and therefore easier to understand.
- You want to focus your readers' attention on one or another character.

Exercise 4.2

In the following, change all active verbs into passives, and all passives into actives. Which sentences improve? Which do not? (In the first two, active verbs that could be passive are italicized; verbs already passive are boldfaced.)

1. Independence is **gained** by those on welfare when skills are **learned** that the marketplace *values*.

2. Different planes of the painting are immediately **noticed,** because their colors are **set** against a background of subtle shades of gray that are **laid** on in thin layers that cannot be **seen** unless the surface is **examined** closely.

3. In this article, it is argued that the Vietnam War was fought to extend influence in Southeast Asia and was not ended until it was made clear that the United States could not defeat North Vietnam unless atomic weapons were used.

4. Science education cannot be improved to a level sufficient to ensure that American industry will be supplied with skilled workers and researchers until more money is provided to primary and secondary schools.

5. The tone in the first part of Bierce's "An Occurrence at Owl Creek Bridge" is presented in a dispassionate way. In the first paragraph, two sentinels are described in detail, but the line, "It did not appear to be the duty of these two men to know what was occurring at the center of the bridge" takes emotion away from them. In paragraph 2, a description is given of the surroundings and spectators, but no feeling is betrayed because the language used is neutral and unemotional. This entire section is presented as devoid of emotion even though it is filled with details.

The "Objective" Passive

Scholarly writers, especially scientists, often allege that the passive creates an objective point of view by deleting the first person:

> Based on the writers' verbal intelligence, prior knowledge and essay scores, their essays **WERE ANALYZED** for structure and evaluated for richness of concepts. The subjects **WERE** then **DIVIDED** into a high- or low-ability group. Half of each group **WAS** randomly **ASSIGNED** to a treatment group or to a placebo group.

In truth, academic and scientific writers use the active voice and *I* and *we* regularly. These next passages come from articles in respected journals:

> ✓ This paper is concerned with two problems. How can **we** best handle in a transformational grammar certain restrictions that . . . . To illustrate, **we** may cite . . . .**we** shall show . . . .

> ✓ Since the pituitary-adrenal axis is activated during the acute phase response, **we** have investigated the potential role . . . . Specifically, **we** have studied the effects of interleukin-1 . . . .

Here are the first few words from several consecutive sentences from *Science*, a journal of considerable prestige:

> ✓ **We** examine . . . . **We** compare . . . . **We** have used . . . . Each has been weighted . . . . **We** merely take . . . . They are subject . . . . **We** use . . . . Efron and Morris describe . . . . **We** observed . . . . **We** might find . . . .

> —John P. Gilbert, Bucknam McPeek, and Frederick Mosteller, "Statistics and Ethics in Surgery and Anesthesia," *Science*

Here's the point: Some writers and editors resolutely avoid the first person by using the passive everywhere, but deleting an *I* or *we* does not make the science objective; it makes reports of it only seem so. We know that behind those impersonal sentences are flesh-and-blood researchers doing, thinking, and writing.

METADISCOURSE: WRITERS AND READERS AS CHARACTERS

When academic writers do use the first person, however, they use it in certain ways. Look at the verbs in the passages above. There are two kinds:

- One kind refers to research activities: *study, investigate, examine, observe, use.* These verbs are usually in the passive voice: *The subjects* WERE OBSERVED.
- The other kind of verb refers not to the subject matter or the research, but to the writer's own writing and thinking:, *cite, show, inquire.* These verbs are often active and in the first person: *We* WILL SHOW . . .

When you use this second kind of verb to refer to your own thinking and writing, you use what we call *metadiscourse.* Metadiscourse refers to

- the writer's thinking and writing: *We will explain, show, argue, claim, deny, suggest, contrast, add, expand, summarize . . .*
- the writer's degree of certainty: *it seems, perhaps, undoubtedly, I think* . . . (We call these HEDGES and INTENSIFIERS.)
- the readers' actions: *consider now, as you might recall, look at the next example . . .*
- the writing itself and logical connections among its parts: *first, second, third; to begin, finally; therefore, however, consequently . . .*

Metadiscourse appears most often in introductions, where we announce intentions: *I claim that . . . , I shall show . . . , We begin by . . .* and again at the end, when we summarize: *I have argued . . . , I have shown . . . , We have claimed . . . .*

On the other hand, we use the first person less often to describe specific actions that we perform as *part* of our research. We rarely find passages like this:

> To determine if monokines elicited an adrenal steroidogenic response, *I* ADDED a monocyte-conditioned medium and preparations of . . . .

The writer of the original sentence used the passive verb:

> To determine if monokines elicited a response, ***preparations*** . . . WERE ADDED . . .

But a problem lurks with a passive sentence: As did that writer, you risk dangling a modifier. You dangle a modifier when you create an introductory phrase whose *implied* subject differs from the *explicit* subject of the verb in the following main clause. In that example, the implied subject of the infinitive verb *determine* is *I* or *we: I determine* or *we determine.*

> [So that *I* could] determine if monokines elicited a response, ***preparations*** . . . WERE ADDED . . .

But that implied subject of *determine, I* or *we,* differs from the explicit subject of the clause it attaches to—*preparations: preparations* WERE ADDED. When that happens, you dangle a modifier. Writers of scientific prose use this pattern so often, however, that it has become standard usage in their community.

As a small historical footnote, we might note that this impersonal "scientific" style is a modern development. In his "New Theory of Light and Colors" (1672), Sir Isaac Newton wrote this charming first-person account of an early experiment:

> I procured a triangular glass prism, to try therewith the celebrated phenomena of colors. And for that purpose, having darkened my laboratory, and made a small hole in my window shade, to let in a convenient quantity of the sun's light, I placed my prism at the entrance, that the light might be thereby refracted to the opposite wall. It was at first a very pleasing diversion to view the vivid and intense colors produced thereby.

Here's the point: The first person *I* and *we* are common in scholarly prose. Some critics nevertheless frown on its use, particularly the expressions *I think . . . , I feel . . . , I believe . . . ,* probably because they see inexperienced writers use those words too often to introduce baseless opinion. But when used appropriately, the first person is entirely correct.

Exercise 4.3

The verbs in 1 through 4 below are passive, but two could be active because they are metadiscourse verbs that would take first-person subjects. Change the verbs that should be changed. Then go through each sentence again and revise nominalizations into verbs where appropriate.

1. It is believed that a lack of understanding about the risks of alcohol is a cause of student bingeing.
2. The model has been subjected to extensive statistical analysis.
3. Success in exporting more crude oil for hard currency is suggested here as the cause of the improvement of the Russian economy.
4. The creation of a database is being considered, but no estimate has been made in regard to the potential of its usefulness.

The verbs in 5 through 8 are active, but some of them should be passive because they are not metadiscourse verbs. Revise in other ways that seem appropriate.

5. In Section IV, I argue that the indigenous culture engaged in overcultivation of the land at the base of the mesa leading to its exhaustion as a food-producing area.
6. Our intention in this book is to help readers achieve an understanding not only of the differences in grammar between Arabic and English but also the differences in worldview as reflected by Arabic vocabulary.

7. To make an evaluation of changes in the flow rate, I made a comparison of the original flow rate on the basis of figures I had compiled with figures that Jordan had collected in a study of the diversion patterns of slow-growth swamps.

8. We performed the tissue rejection study on the basis of methods developed with our discovery of increases in dermal sloughing as a result of cellular regeneration.

Exercise 4.4

In these passages, change passive verbs into actives only where you think it will improve the sentence. If necessary, invent a rhetorical situation to account for your choice of active or passive. (There will be lots of different answers for this one.)

1. Your figures were reanalyzed to determine their accuracy. Results will be announced when it is judged appropriate.

2. Home mortgage loans now are made for thirty years. With the price of housing at inflated levels, those loans cannot be paid off in a shorter time.

3. The author's impassioned narrative style is abandoned and a cautious treatment of theories of conspiracy is presented. But the moment the narrative line is picked up again, he invests his prose with the same vigor and force.

4. Many arguments were advanced against Darwinian evolution in the nineteenth century because basic assumptions about our place in the world were challenged by it. No longer were we defined as privileged creatures but rather as a product of natural forces.

5. For many years, federal regulations concerning the use of wiretapping have been ignored. Only recently have tighter restrictions been imposed on the circumstances that warrant it.

In these sentences, change passives to actives where appropriate and edit nominalizations into a more direct character-action style. Invent characters where necessary.

6. It is my belief that the social significance of smoking receives its clearest explication through an analysis of peer interaction among adolescents. In particular, studies should be made of the manner in which interactive behavior is conditioned by social class.

7. These directives are written in a style of maximum simplicity as a result of an attempt at more effective communication with employees with limited reading skills.

8. The ability of the human brain to arrive at solutions of human problems has been undervalued, because studies have not been done that would be considered to have scientific reliability.

Exercise 4.5

The excerpt below is from a letter from the chancellor of a state university to parents of students. Why is the first part so impersonal, naming no flesh-and-blood characters at all after the second word, *you*? Why is the last part more personal? Change the first part so that you name in subjects whoever performs an action. Then change the second part to eliminate all characters. How do the two parts now differ?

> As you probably have heard, the U of X campus has been the scene of a number of incidents of racial and sexual harassment over the last several weeks. The fact that similar incidents have occurred on campuses around the country does not make them any less offensive when they take place here. Of the ten to twelve incidents that have been reported since early October, most have involved graffiti or spoken insults. In only two cases was any physical contact made, and in neither case was anyone injured.
>
> U of X is committed to providing its students with an environment where they can live, work, and study without fear of be-

ing taunted or harassed because of their race, gender, religion, or
ethnicity. I have made it clear that bigotry and intolerance will
not be permitted and that U of X's commitment to diversity is un-
equivocal. We are also taking steps to improve security in cam-
pus housing. We at U of X are proud of this university's tradition
of diversity . . .

NOUN + NOUN + NOUN

One more stylistic choice does not directly involve characters and
actions, but we include it here because it can distort the match
that readers expect between the form of an idea and the grammar
of a sentence. It is the long COMPOUND NOUN phrase:

> Early *childhood thought disorder misdiagnosis* often results from un-
> familiarity with recent *research literature* describing such conditions.
> This paper is a review of seven recent studies in which are findings of
> particular relevance to *pre-adolescent hyperactivity diagnosis* and to
> *treatment modalities* involving *medication maintenance level evalua-*
> *tion procedures.*

Some grammarians claim we should never use one noun to modify another, but that would rule out common phrases such as *stone
wall, student center, space shuttle,* and vast numbers of other useful terms.

But you should try revising a long series of nouns when it is
not familiar to your readers, and especially when it includes nominalizations. To revise, just reverse the order of words and find
prepositions to connect them:

1	2	3	4	5
early	childhood	thought	disorder	misdiagnosis
misdiagnose	disordered	thought	in early	childhood
5	4	3	1	2

Re-assembled, it looks like this:

> Physicians misdiagnose[5] disordered[4] thought[3] in young[1] children[2]
> because they are unfamiliar with recent literature on the subject.

Here's the point: When you write a string of nouns that you haven't seen before, revise them. Reverse their order, linking them with prepositions. If one of them is a nominalization, rewrite it into a full verb.

Exercise 4.6

Unpack the compound noun phrases in 1 through 4.

1. The plant safety standards committee discussed recent EPA air quality regulation announcements.
2. Diabetic patient blood pressure reduction may be brought about by renal depressor medication.
3. The main goal of this article is to describe text comprehension processes and recall protocol production.
4. On the basis of these principles, we may now attempt to formulate narrative information extraction rules.

In these next sentences, unpack compound nouns and revise nominalizations.

5. This paper is an investigation into information processing behavior involved in computer human cognition simulation.
6. Enforcement of guidelines for new automobile tire durability must be a Federal Trade Commission responsibility.
7. The Social Security program is a monthly income floor guarantee based on a lifelong contribution schedule.
8. Based on training needs assessment reviews and on office site visits, there was the identification of concepts and issues that can be used in our creation of an initial staff questionnaire instrument.

THE PROFESSIONAL VOICE

Every social group expects its members to show that they accept its values by adopting its voice and vocabulary. The apprentice banker must learn not only to think and look like one, but to sound like one as well. Too often, though, aspiring professionals think they sound authoritative only when they communicate in complex technical language. Whatever the cause, that exclusionary style erodes the trust that a civil society depends on, especially in a world where information and expert knowledge are increasingly the means to power and control.

It is true that some research can never be made clear to merely intelligent lay readers—but less often than many researchers think. Here is an excerpt from Talcott Parsons, a social scientist who was as influential in shaping his field as he was notorious for the opacity of his prose.

> Apart from theoretical conceptualization there would appear to be no method of selecting among the indefinite number of varying kinds of factual observation which can be made about a concrete phenomenon or field so that the various descriptive statements about it articulate into a coherent whole, which constitutes an "adequate," a "determinate" description. Adequacy in description is secured insofar as determinate and verifiable answers can be given to all the scientifically important questions involved. What questions are important is largely determined by the logical structure of the generalized conceptual scheme which, implicitly or explicitly, is employed.

We can make that clearer to moderately well-educated readers:

> When scientists lack a theory, they have no way to select from everything they could say about a subject only that which they can fit into a coherent whole and be "adequate" or "determinate." Scientists describe something "adequately" only when they can verify answers to questions they think are important, and they decide what questions are important based on their implicit or explicit theories.

And we could make even that more concise:

> Whatever you describe, you need a theory to fit its parts into a whole. You need a theory to decide even what questions to ask and to verify their answers.

My most concise version loses the nuances of Parsons' style. But the excruciating density of his style numbs all but his most masochistically dedicated readers.

Here's the point: Whether you are a reader or a writer, you must understand three things about a style that seems complex:

- It may needlessly complicate simple ideas.
- It may be necessary to express complex ideas precisely.
- It may needlessly complicate already complex ideas.

As a reader, your task is to distinguish these kinds of complexities so that you can know when a passage is needlessly complex. As a writer, your task is to recognize when you have committed that gratuitous complexity and, if you can, to revise it. It is just one more example of the Writer's Golden Rule: Write to others as you would have others write to you.

Summing Up

1. Readers judge prose to be clear when subjects of sentences name characters and verbs name actions.

Fixed	Subject	Verb	———
Variable	Character	Action	———

2. If you tell a story in which you make abstract nominalizations its main characters and subjects, use as few other nominalizations as you can:

> *A nominalization* IS a **transformation** of a verb into a noun, often resulting in **displacement** of characters from subjects by nouns.

> ✓ When *a nominalization* TRANSFORMS a verb into a noun, *that nominalization* often DISPLACES characters from subjects.

3. Use a passive if the agent of an action is self-evident:

> *The voters* **REELECTED** the president with 54 percent of the vote.
>
> ✓ *The president* **WAS REELECTED** with 54 percent of the vote.

4. Use a passive if it lets you replace a long subject with a short one:

> Research that demonstrated the soundness of our reasoning and the need for action **SUPPORTED** *this decision.*
>
> ✓ *This decision* **WAS SUPPORTED BY** research that demonstrated the soundness of our reasoning and the need for action.

5. Use a passive if it gives your readers a coherent sequence of subjects:

> ✓ By early 1945, *the Axis nations* had **BEEN** essentially **DEFEATED;** all that remained was a bloody climax. *The German borders* had **BEEN BREACHED,** and both *Germany and Japan* were being bombed around the clock. *Neither country,* though, had **BEEN** so **DEVASTATED** that *it* could not **RESIST.**

6. Use an active verb if it is a metadiscourse verb:

> The terms of the analysis must **BE DEFINED.**
>
> ✓ We must **DEFINE** the terms of the analysis.

7. When convenient, rewrite long compound noun phrases:

> We discussed the **board**[1] **candidate**[2] **review**[3] **meetings**[4] **schedule**[5].
>
> ✓ We discussed the **schedule**[5] of **meetings**[4] to **review**[3] **candidates**[2] for the **board**[1].

5

Cohesion and Coherence

*If he would inform, he must advance regularly from Things known to
things unknown, distinctly without Confusion, and the lower he
begins the better. It is a common Fault in Writers, to allow their
Readers too much knowledge: They begin with that which should be
the Middle, and skipping backwards and forwards, 'tis impossible for
any one but he who is perfect in the Subject before, to understand
their Work, and such an one has no Occasion to read it.*
—BENJAMIN FRANKLIN

*The two capital secrets in the art of prose composition are these: first,
the philosophy of transition and connection; or the art by which one
step in an evolution of thought is made to arise out of another: all
fluent and effective composition depends on the connections;
secondly, the way in which sentences are made to modify each other;
for the most powerful effects in written eloquence arise out of this
reverberation, as it were, from each other in a rapid succession of
sentences.*
—THOMAS DE QUINCEY

*"Begin at the beginning," the King said, gravely,
"and go on till you come to the end; then stop."*
—LEWIS CARROLL

CLARITY VERSUS COHERENCE

We've discussed clarity as if we could achieve it by mechanically mapping CHARACTERS and ACTIONS onto SUBJECTS and VERBS. But for a whole passage to seem clear, readers need more than individually clear sentences. These two passages, for example, say much the same thing, but they feel different:

1a. Since the discovery that one factor of its development might be genetic, great strides in the early and accurate diagnosis of Alzheimer's have been made in recent years. Senility in an older patient who seemed to be losing touch with reality was often confused with Alzheimer's. Genetic clues have become the basis of newer and more reliable tests in the last few years. The risk of human tragedy of another kind, though, has resulted from the increasing accuracy of these tests: Predictions about susceptibility to Alzheimer's have become possible, long before the appearance of any overt symptoms. An apparently healthy person could be devastated by such an early diagnosis at that point.

✓1b. In recent years, though researchers have have made great strides in the early and accurate diagnosis of Alzheimer's disease, those better diagnoses have raised a new problem in regard to informing those at risk. Not too long ago, when a physicians examined an older patient who seemed out of touch with reality, she had to guess whether that person had Alzheimer's or was senile. In the past few years, however, physicians have been able to use new and more reliable tests focusing on genetic clues. But in the accuracy of these new tests lies the risk of another kind of human tragedy: Physicians may be able to predict Alzheimer's long before its overt appearance, but such an early diagnosis could psychologically devastate an otherwise healthy person.

The first passage feels choppy, even disorganized. The second feels more cohesive and coherent.

Like the word *clarity*, however, the words *choppy* and *disorganized* refer not to what is on the page, but to how what is on the page makes us *feel*. What is it about the words in (1a) that makes us feel that it is unfocused; what makes (1b) feel more cohesive and coherent? We base judgments like that on two aspects of word order:

- We judge sequences of sentences to be *cohesive*, depending on how each sentence ends and the next one begins.

- We judge a whole passage to be *coherent*, depending on how all the sentences in a passage cumulatively begin.

Once you understand how we make those two judgments, you can diagnose and revise your sentences so that your readers will judge them to be not just individually clear, but collectively both cohesive and coherent.

COHESION: A SENSE OF FLOW

In Lesson 4, we devoted a few pages (61–64) to that familiar advice, "Avoid PASSIVES." If we always did, we would choose the ACTIVE verb in sentence (2a) below over the PASSIVE in (2b):

> 2a. The collapse of a dead star into a point perhaps no larger than a marble CREATES$_{active}$ a black hole.
> 2b. A black hole IS CREATED$_{passive}$ by the collapse of a dead star into a point perhaps no larger than a marble.

But we might choose otherwise if we wanted to put one of those sentences between these two:

> [1]Some astonishing questions about the nature of the universe have been raised by scientists studying black holes in space. [2a/b][———]. [3]So much matter compressed into so little volume changes the fabric of space around it in puzzling ways.

Here's the active sentence there:

> 1a. [1]Some astonishing questions about the nature of the universe have been raised by scientists studying black holes in space. [2a]The collapse of a dead star into a point perhaps no larger than a marble creates a black hole. [3]So much matter compressed into so little volume changes the fabric of space around it in puzzling ways.

And here's the passive:

> 1b. [1]Some astonishing questions about the nature of the universe have been raised by scientists studying black holes in space. [2b]A black hole is created by the collapse of a dead star into a point perhaps no larger than a marble. [3]So much matter compressed into so little volume changes the fabric of space around it in puzzling ways.

Our sense of "flow" should call not for (2a), the sentence with the active verb, but for (2b), the one with the passive.

The reason is clear: The last four words of the first sentence introduce an important character—*black holes in space:*

> [1]Some astonishing questions about the nature of the universe have been raised by scientists studying **black holes in space . . .**

If we follow it with (2a), the first concepts we hit in that sentence are collapsed stars and marbles, information that seems to come out of nowhere:

> [1] . . . universe have been raised by scientists studying black holes in space. [2a]**The collapse of a dead star into a point perhaps no larger than a marble** creates a black hole.

But if we follow sentence (1) with (2b), the sentence with the passive verb, we make a better connection between those two sentences, because now the first words we hit in (2b) pick up on words we just read at the end of (1):

> [1] . . . studying **black holes in space.** [2b]**A black hole** is created$_{passive}$ by the collapse of . . .

Note also that the passive lets us put at the *end* of sentence (2b) words that connect it to the *beginning* of sentence (3):

> [1] . . . black holes in space. [2b]A black hole is created by the collapse of a dead star into **a point perhaps no larger than a marble.** [3]**So much matter compressed into so little volume** changes the fabric of space around it in puzzling ways.

Here's the point: We feel one sentence is cohesive with the next when we see at the beginning of a second sentence information that appeared toward the end of the previous one. That's what creates our experience of "flow." And in fact, that's the main reason we have the passive in the language in the first place: to arrange sentences so that they flow from one to the next.

The First Principle of Cohesion: Old-to-New

That principle of reading suggests two principles of writing and revision that are mirror images of each other. The first is this:

> 1. Begin sentences with information familiar to your readers.

Readers get that familiar information from two sources: First, they remember information from the sentence or two before the one they are reading. That's why sentence (2b) about black holes coheres with (1) and why (3) coheres with (2b):

> [1]Some astonishing questions about the nature of the universe have been raised by scientists studying **[black holes in space.** [2b]**A black hole]** is created by the collapse of a dead star into **[a point perhaps no larger than a marble.** [3]**So much matter compressed into so little volume]** changes the fabric of space around it in puzzling ways.

Second, readers bring to a sentence general knowledge of its subject. We would not have been surprised, for example, if sentence (3) in that series about black holes had begun like this:

> 1b. . . . changes the fabric of space around it in puzzling ways.
> [3]**Astronomers have recently reported,** for example, that . . .

The word *Astronomers* did not appear in the previous sentence, but since we are reading about space, we shouldn't be surprised by a reference to them.

The second principle is the flip side of the first:

> 2. End sentences with information readers cannot anticipate.

Whatever is familiar and simple is easier to understand than what is new and complicated, and readers always prefer to read what is easy before they read what is hard.

It is easier to see how those two principles work—or don't—in the writing of others than in your own, because after you've worked on your own writing for a while, it all seems old—to you. But hard as it is to distinguish old from new in your own writing, you have to try, because readers want to begin sentences with information that is familiar to *them,* and only then move on to information that is new.

Here's the point: In every *sequence* of sentences you write, you have to balance principles that make individual sentences clear and principles that make a series of them cohesive. *But in that tradeoff, you must give priority to helping readers create a sense of cohesive flow.* You create that sense of flow by opening sentences with information that readers are familiar with. Fortunately, this principle about old and new information cooperates with the principle of characters as subjects. Once you mention your characters, they become familiar information to your readers. So when you regularly get characters up front, you also get up-front familiar information.

Exercise 5.1

Revise these two passages to improve their old-new flow. In (1), I boldface the words that seem to me to be old information. Revise the sentences so that old information appears first.

1. Two aims—the recovery of the American economy and the modernization of America into a military power— were **in Reagan's mind when he assumed the office of the presidency.** The drop in unemployment figures and inflation, and the increase in the GNP testifies to **his success in the first.** But our increased involvement in international conflict without any clear set of political goals indicates **less success with the second.** Nevertheless, vast increases in the military budget and a good deal of saber rattling **pleased the American voter**.

2. The various components of Abco's current profitability, particularly growth in Asian markets, will be highlighted in our report to demonstrate its advantages versus competitors. Revenue returns along several dimensions—product type, end-use, distribution channels, distributor type, etc.—will provide the basis for this analysis. Likely growth prospects of Abco's newest product lines will depend most on its ability in regard to

the development of distribution channels in China, according to our projections. A range of innovative strategies will be needed to support the introduction of new products.

COHERENCE: A SENSE OF THE WHOLE

When you create cohesive flow, you take the first of two steps toward helping readers think your prose hangs together. But they must feel that your writing is not only cohesive but *coherent*, a quality different from cohesion. It's easy to confuse the words *cohesion* and *coherence*, because they sound so much alike.

- Think of *cohesion* as the experience of seeing pairs of sentences fit neatly together, the way two Lego® pieces do.
- Think of *coherence* as the experience of recognizing what all the sentences in a piece of writing add up to, the way lots of Lego® pieces add up to a building, bridge, or boat.

In ordinary prose, that larger whole usually consists of some point or claim along with all the other sentences that support it. (For more on this point, see the Epilogue.)

This next passage, for example, has great cohesive "flow," because we move from the end of each sentence to the next without a hitch:

> Sayner, Wisconsin, is the snowmobile capital of the world. The buzzing of snowmobile engines fills the air, and their tanklike tracks crisscross the snow. The snow reminds me of Mom's mashed potatoes, covered with furrows I would draw with my fork. Her mashed potatoes usually make me sick, that's why I play with them. I like to make a hole in the middle of the potatoes and fill it with melted butter. This behavior has been the subject of long chats between me and my analyst.

Though we connect each sentence to the one before and after, the passage is incoherent. (It was created by six different writers, one of whom wrote the first sentence, with the other five sequentially adding one sentence to fit just the immediately preceding one.)

Here's the principle of coherence briefly stated: Readers judge a passage to be coherent when the words beginning each sentence in it *cumulatively* constitute a limited and related *set* of words. Those words are usually subjects of sentences, but not always. (There is a second principle that we will discuss in the next lesson.)

Subjects, Topics, Grammar, and Coherence

For 500 years, English teachers have defined *subject* in two ways:

1. the "doer" of the action.
2. what a sentence is "about."

In Lessons 3 and 4, we saw why that first definition is not reliable.

Also flawed is that second schoolbook definition: "A subject is what a sentence is about," because often, the subject of a sentence does not state its topic; that function can be performed by other parts. For example:

- The subject of this next sentence is *it*, but its topic (bold-faced) is *your claims,* the OBJECT of the PREPOSITION *for:*

    It is impossible for **your claims** to be proved conclusively.

- The subject of this next sentence is *I*, but its topic is *these questions,* the object of *to.*

    In regard to **these questions,** I believe there is a need for more research.

- The subject of this next sentence is *it*, but its topic is *our proposals,* the subject of a verb in a SUBORDINATE CLAUSE.

    It is likely that **our proposals** will be accepted.

- The subject of this next sentence is *no one,* but its topic is *results like these,* a direct object shifted to the front for emphasis.

    Results like these *no one* could have predicted.

> ***Here's the point:***   We use the term *topic* to mean what a sentence is "about," but that topic is not always its grammatical subject. *But we expect it to be.* We judge writing to be clear and direct when we quickly see subjects and topics in the same words.

Topics and Coherence

Readers judge a passage coherent to the degree that they quickly and easily see two things:

- the topics of individual sentences and clauses.
- how the topics in a whole passage constitute a related set of concepts.

How does this passage strike you?

1a. The particular ideas toward the beginning of sentences define what a passage is "about" for a reader. Moving through a paragraph from a cumulatively coherent point of view is made possible by a sequence of topics that seem to constitute a limited set of related ideas. A seeming absence of context for each sentence is one consequence of making random shifts in topics. Feelings of dislocation, disorientation, and lack of focus in a passage occur when that happens.

Most readers find that passage close to incoherent, because its string of topics is inconsistent and diffuse; they do not focus our attention on a limited set of related ideas:

The particular ideas toward the beginning of sentences . . .

Moving through a paragraph from a cumulatively coherent point of . . .

A seeming absence of context for each sentence . . .

Feelings of dislocation, disorientation, and lack of focus . . .

Now compare the topic/subjects in this passage:

Readers look for the topics of sentences to tell them what a whole passage is "about." If **they** feel that its sequence of topics focuses on a limited set of related topics, then **they** will feel they are moving through that passage from a cumulatively coherent point of view. But if **topics** seem to shift randomly, then **readers** have to begin each sentence from no coherent point of view, and when that happens, **readers** feel dislocated, disoriented, and the **passage** seems out of focus.

The subject/topics in that passage focus on just two concepts: *topics* and *readers,* and so we judge that passage to be more focused, more *coherent.*

Diagnosis, Analysis, and Revision

Here's how to diagnose, analyze, and revise your writing to make it coherent.

1. Diagnose:
   a. Underline the first seven or eight words of every sentence in a passage.
   b. If you can, underline the first five or six words of every CLAUSE, both SUBORDINATE and MAIN.

2. Analyze:
   a. Have you underlined words that constitute a relatively small set of related ideas? Even if *you* see connections among them, think hard about whether your readers will.
   b. Do those words name your most important characters, real or abstract?
   c. Give the passage a title. Its words are likely to identify what should be the topics of most of the sentences.

3. Revise:
   a. In most of your sentences, use subjects to name topics.
   b. Put those subjects close to the beginning of your sentences. Avoid opening sentences with long introductory clauses or phrases.

Alleged Monotony

At this point, you may recall the advice "Vary how you begin your sentences." When you reread your own prose, you may think that a sequence of the same topics is monotonous, but your readers are less likely to notice it because they will be focusing on your ideas. On the other hand, you might revise if you find you have used the same words for the same topics in the same positions. This passage goes over the top in that kind of consistency:

> "**Moral climate**" is created when an objectivized moral standard for treating people is accepted by others. **Moral climate** results from norms of behavior which are accepted by society whereby if people conform they are socially approved of, or if they don't they are shunned. In this light, **moral climate** acts as a reason to refrain from

saying or doing things that the community does not support. **A moral climate** encourages individuals to conform to a moral standard and apply that standard to their own circumstances.

Be cautious, though: Most writers change topics too often.

Integrating the Principles

We can integrate all these principles about old and new and a consistent topic string with the principles about characters as subjects and actions as verbs (I'll fill in the empty box in Lesson 6):

Fixed	Topic	
Variable	Short, simple, familiar	Long, complex, new
Fixed	Subject	Verb	———
Variable	Character	Action	———

No unit of information is shorter and simpler than the name of a character. So when you create a sequence of subjects out of a limited set of characters, real or abstract, you create a sequence of topics that your readers will think is consistent and therefore coherent.

Exercise 5.2

Revise these passages to give them consistent topic strings. First determine the characters, then their actions. Then start each sentence with a character, and let the sentence take you where it wants to go. In (1), words that could be consistent subject/topics are boldfaced.

1. **Vegetation** covers the earth, except for those areas continuously covered with ice or utterly scorched by continual heat. Richly fertilized plains and river valleys are places where **plants** grow most richly, but also at the

edge of perpetual snow in high mountains. The ocean and its edges as well as in and around lakes and swamps are **densely vegetated.** The cracks of busy city sidewalks have **plants** in them as well as in seemingly barren cliffs. Before humans existed, the earth was covered with **vegetation,** and the earth will have **vegetation** long after evolutionary history swallows us up.

2. The power to create and communicate a new message to fit a new experience is not a competence animals have in their natural states. Their genetic code limits the number and kind of messages that they can communicate. Information about distance, direction, source, and richness of pollen in flowers constitutes the only information that can be communicated by bees, for example. A limited repertoire of messages delivered in the same way, for generation after generation, is characteristic of animals of the same species, in all significant respects.

3. The importance of language skills in children's problem-solving ability was stressed by Jones (1985) in his paper on children's thinking. Improvement in nonverbal problem solving occurred as a result of improvements in language skills. The use of previously acquired language habits for problem articulation and activation of knowledge previously learned through language is thought to be the cause of better performance. Therefore, systematic practice in the verbal formulation of nonlinguistic problems prior to attempts at their solution might be an avenue for exploration in the enhancement of problem solving in general.

THE DIFFICULT CRAFT OF BEGINNING A SENTENCE WELL

It's hard to begin a sentence well, because in its first few words you may have to juggle several elements that keep your readers from getting to its topic/subject. It's called *throat-clearing*.

Throat-clearing typically begins with METADISCOURSE that connects a sentence to the previous one, with transitions such as *and, but, therefore:*

> And therefore . . .

We then add a second kind of metadiscourse that expresses our attitude toward what is coming, words such as *fortunately, perhaps, allegedly, it is important to note, for the most part,* or *politically speaking:*

> And therefore, politically speaking . . .

Then we can indicate time, place, or manner:

> And therefore, politically speaking, in Eastern states since 1980 . . .

Only then do we get to the topic/subject:

> And, therefore, politically speaking, in Eastern states since 1980, **acid rain** has become a serious problem.

When you open several sentences with that kind of "throat-clearing," your readers have a hard time seeing not just what individual sentences are "about," but the cumulative focus of a whole passage. When you find a sentence with several words before its subject/topic, revise:

> ✓ Since 1980, therefore, **acid rain** has become a serious political problem in Eastern states.

Faked Coherence

Some writers try to fake coherence by lacing their prose with conjunctions like *thus, therefore, however,* and so on, regardless of whether they signal real logical connections. An example:

> Because the press is the major medium of interaction between the president and the people, how it portrays him influences his popularity. **Therefore**, it should report on the president objectively. Both reporters and the president are human, **however**, subject to error and favoritism. **Also**, people act differently in public than they do in private. **Hence**, to understand a person, it is important to know the whole person, his environment, upbringing, and education. **Indeed**, from the correspondence with his family, we can learn much about Harry S. Truman, our thirty-third president.

Experienced writers rely less on connecting devices like these than on the intrinsic logical flow of their prose. They are especially careful not to overuse words like *and, also, moreover, another,* and so on, words that say simply "Here's one more thing." You need a *but* or *however* when you contradict or qualify what you just said, and you can use a *therefore, consequently,* or *as a result* to wind up a line of reasoning. But avoid using words like those more than a few times a page. Your readers don't need them when your logic is sound.

Here's the point: Get to your subject/topic quickly. Avoid piling up introductory elements ahead of it, especially conjunctions that don't do any real work.

Exercise 5.3

Revise these passages to give them more consistent topic strings. First, decide who you think the main characters should be, then make those characters the subjects of as many sentences as you can. In the first example, I boldface topics so that you can see how inconsistent they are. Begin revising by identifying the main characters and making them topic/subjects of verbs expressing important actions.

1. **Some potential threats** exist in the modern mass communications media, though there are many significant advantages. If **a powerful minority** should happen to control it, **public opinion** could be manipulated through biased reporting. And while **a wide knowledge of public affairs** is a great advantage that results from national coverage, **divisiveness and factionalism** can be accentuated by connecting otherwise isolated, local conflicts into a single larger conflict as a result of showing that **conflicts about the same issues** are occurring in different places. It will always be true, of course, that **human nature** produces differences of opinion, but **the threat of faction and division** may be reinforced when **national coverage** publicizes uninformed opinions. According to some, **education** can suppress faction when **the true nature of conflicts** reaches the public through the media, but **history** has shown that as **much**

coverage is given to people who encourage conflict as to people who try to remove conflict.

2. Some sort of palace revolt or popular revolution plagued seven out of eight reigns of the Romanov line after Peter the Great. In 1722, achievement by merit was made the basis of succession when the principle of heredity was terminated by Peter. This resulted in many tsars' not appointing a successor before dying, including Peter. Ivan VI was less than two months old when appointed by Czarina Anna, but Elizabeth, daughter of Peter the Great, defeated Anna and ascended to the throne in 1741. Succession not dependent upon authority resulted in the boyars' regularly disputing who was to become sovereign. Male primogeniture became the law in 1797 when Paul I codified the law of succession. But conspirators strangled him, one of whom was probably his son, Alexander I.

3. Many issues other than science, domestic politics in particular, faced Truman when he was considering the Oppenheimer committee's recommendation to stop the hydrogen bomb project. A Sino-Soviet bloc had been proclaimed by Russia and China, so the Cold War was becoming an issue. Support for Truman's foreign policy was shrinking among Republican leaders in Congress. And the first Russian atom bomb test made the public demand a strong response from him. Truman's conclusion that he could not afford letting the public think that Russia had been allowed to be first in developing the most powerful weapon yet was an inevitable one. In retrospect, the risk in the Oppenheimer recommendation was worth taking according to some historians, but the political issues that Truman had to face were too powerful to ignore.

Exercise 5.4

The point of this exercise is to demonstrate that simply by changing subjects, you can change the "feel" of a passage quite a bit. In his essay, "Stranger in the Village," James Baldwin, an influential African-American writer, reflects on the relationship he feels to European Christianity. In the first sentence of that essay, he makes the cathedral at Chartres the topic and metaphorical agency:

> **The cathedral at Chartres,** I have said, says something to the people of this village which **it** cannot say to me, but it is important to understand that **this cathedral** says something to me which **it** cannot say to them.

But in the second sentence, he switches the topic/subjects to the villagers and then to himself:

> Perhaps **they** are struck by the power of the spires, the glory of the windows; but **they** have known God, after all, longer than **I** have known him, and in a different way, and **I** am terrified . . .

He wasn't forced by the nature of things to make those choices. For example, he could have written this:

> **I** have said that **I** hear something from the cathedral at Chartres that **the people** of this village do not hear, but it is important to understand that . . .

Experiment on Baldwin's passage by changing the topics. First, focus the whole passage on Baldwin. Then revise a second time, focusing on the people of Chartres as topics, then a third time focusing on the architecture. What are the consequences? Why did he make the choices he did, do you think? (There is no one right answer.) Here is the original passage:

> The cathedral at Chartres, I have said, says something to the people of this village which it cannot say to me, but it is important to understand that this cathedral says something to me which it cannot say to them. Perhaps they are struck by the power of the spires, the glory of the windows; but they have known God, after all, longer than I have known him, and in a different way, and I am terrified by the slippery bottomless well to be found in the crypt, down which heretics were hurled to death, and by the obscene, inescapable gargoyles jutting out of the stone and seeming to say that God and the devil can never be divorced. I doubt that the villagers think of the devil when they face a cathedral because they have never been identified with the devil. But I must accept

the status which myth, if nothing else, gives me in the West before I can hope to change the myth.

What does this exercise suggest about "natural" connections between characters and subjects? What does this imply about how we understand who's responsible for what actions? How much can a writer control how the reader decides who's responsible? We return to this matter in Lesson 10.

SUMMING UP

We can sum up this Lesson in this model:

Fixed	Topic		
Variable	Short, simple, familiar	Long, complex, new	
Fixed	Subject	Verb	———
Variable	Character	Action	———

It represents two principles:

1. Begin sentences with subjects consisting of short simple words and phrases communicating information that your readers are familiar with:

   > The number of dead in the Civil War exceeded all other wars in American history combined. A reason for the lingering animosity between North and South today is **the memory of this terrible carnage.**

   > ✓ Of all the wars in American history, none has exceeded the Civil War in the number of dead. **The memory of this terrible carnage** is one reason for the lingering animosity between North and South today.

2. Through a series of sentences, keep your topics short and reasonably consistent:

> **Competition by Asian companies with American companies in the Pacific** is the first phase of this study. **Labor costs and the ability to introduce new products quickly in particular** are examined. **A plan that will show American industry how to restructure its facilities** will be developed from this study.

> ✓ In the first phase of this study, **we** examine how **Asian companies** compete with American companies in the Pacific region. **We** examine in particular their labor costs and ability to introduce new products quickly. **We** develop from this study a **plan that** will show **American industry** how to restructure its facilities.

Emphasis

Beginning and end shake hands with each other.
—GERMAN PROVERB

One of the most difficult things is the first paragraph. I have spent many months on a first paragraph, and once I get it, the rest just comes out very easily. In the first paragraph you solve most of the problem with your book. The theme is defined, the style, the tone.
—GABRIEL GARCIA MARQUEZ

All's well that ends well.
—WILLIAM SHAKESPEARE

In the end is my beginning.
—T. S. ELIOT

CLARITY IN EMPHASIS

If you consistently write sentences with short SUBJECT/TOPICS that name a few central CHARACTERS and then join them to strong VERBS, you'll likely get the rest of the sentence right, and in the process create a passage that seems both cohesive and coherent. But if the first few words of a sentence are important, so are the last few, because how you end a sentence determines how readers judge both its clarity and its strength. In this lesson, we address clarity first, then emphasis, then how emphasis contributes to a kind of coherence that is even more global than the coherence we gain from consistent topics.

Clarity

As we've seen when readers get up momentum in the first few words of a sentence, they can more easily get through complicated material that follows. Compare:

> 1a. A sociometric and actuarial analysis of Social Security revenues and disbursements for the last six decades to determine changes in projecting deficits is the subject of this study.

> ✓1b. In this study, we analyze Social Security's revenues and disbursements for the last six decades, using sociometric and actuarial criteria to determine changes in projecting deficits.

As we start (1a), we must not only struggle with technical terms, but read a 23-word subject before we get to a verb. In (1b), we go through sixteen words before we hit a term that might slow us up, and by that point we have enough momentum to carry us through the complexity to the end. In short, in (1a), we hit the complexity—syntactic and semantic—at the beginning; in (1b), we don't hit complexity until near the end, where we can handle it better.

There are two kinds of complexity.

Complex Grammar   Which of these two sentences do you prefer?

> 2a. Lincoln's claim that the Civil War was God's punishment of both North and South for slavery appears in the last part of the speech.

✓2b. In the last part of his speech, Lincoln claims that God gave the Civil War to both North and South as a punishment for slavery.

Most of us dislike (2a) because it begins with a complex subject. We prefer (2b) because it begins simply and moves toward complexity.

Complex Terms   Readers also have a problem with unfamiliar technical terms. Compare:

3a. The role of calcium blocker drugs in the control of cardiac irregularity can be seen through an understanding of the role of calcium in the activation of muscle groups. The regulatory proteins actin, myosin, tropomyosin, and troponin make up the sarcomere, the basic unit of muscle contraction. ATPase, the energy-producing protein myosin, makes up its thick filament, while actin, tropomyosin, and troponin make up its thin filament. Interaction of myosin and actin triggers muscle contraction . . .

✓3b. When a muscle contracts, it uses calcium. We must therefore understand how calcium influences the contraction of muscles to understand how cardiac irregularity is controlled by drugs called "calcium blockers." The basic unit of muscle contraction is the sarcomere. It has two filaments, one thin and one thick. Those filaments consist of four proteins that regulate contraction: actin, myosin, tropomyosin, and troponin. Muscles contract when the protein in the thin filament, actin, interacts with the protein in the thick filament, the energy-producing or ATPase protein myosin . . .

Both passages use the same technical terms, but (3b) is clearer to those who know nothing about muscle chemistry.

Those passages differ in two ways. First, information that is implicit in (3a) is stated explicitly in (3b):

3a. . . . and troponin make up the sarcomere, the basic unit of muscle contraction. Its thick filament is made up of . . .

✓3b. The basic unit of muscle contraction is the sarcomere. It has two filaments, one thick and one thin . . .

More important, I moved the technical terms at the beginning of the sentences in (3a) to the end of the sentences in (3b). Here in (3a) its technical terms are boldfaced; note that almost all are at the beginning of their sentences:

3a. The role of **calcium blocker drugs** in the control of **cardiac ir-regularity** can be seen through an understanding of the role of calcium in the activation of muscle groups.

The regulatory proteins actin, myosin, tropomyosin, and troponin make up the **sarcomere,** the basic unit of muscle contraction.

ATPase, the energy-producing protein myosin, makes up its thick filament, while **actin, tropomyosin, and troponin** make up its thin filament.

Interaction of myosin and actin triggers muscle contraction.

These principles apply to prose intended even for professional readers. In this next passage from the *New England Journal of Medicine*, the writer deliberately constructs the second sentence to get a new technical term at its end (introduced by metadiscourse):

The incubation of peripheral-blood lymphocytes with a lymphokine, interleukin-2, generates lymphoid cells that can lyse fresh, noncultured, natural-killer-cell-resistant tumor cells but not normal cells. *We term these cells* **lymphokine-activated killer (LAK) cells.**

Here's the point: Your readers want you to use the end of your sentences to communicate two kinds of difficulty:

* long and complex PHRASES and CLAUSES; and
* new information, particularly unfamiliar technical terms.

THE NUANCES OF EMPHASIS AND STRESS

In the last lesson, we said that an important position in the *psychological* geography of a sentence is its first few words, because they announce the topic of a sentence, its psychological subject (see pp. 84–85). Its other important position is its last few words. You can sense their role when you hear your voice rise and stress one syllable more strongly than you do the others:

. . . more strongly than you do the $^{o-}$-thers.

We have the same experience when reading silently. We'll call this climactic part of a sentence its STRESS and add it to our last box.

Fixed	Topic		Stress	
Variable	Short, simple, familiar		New, long, complex	
Fixed	Subject	Verb	———	
Variable	Character	Action	———	

How you manage the words in that stress position helps establish the voice readers hear through your prose.

Compare these passages. One was written to blame an American president for being weak with Russia on arms control. The other is my revision; it seems to blame Russia. You can tell which is which if you thump your finger as you read the different bold-face words at the ends of the sentences:

1a. The administration has blurred an issue central to arms control, **the issue of verification.** Irresponsible charges, innuendo, and leaks have submerged **serious problems with Soviet compliance.** The objective, instead, should be not to exploit these concerns in order to further poison our relations, repudiate existing agreements, or, worse still, terminate arms control altogether, but to **insist on compliance and clarify questionable Soviet behavior.**

1b. The issue of verification—so central to arms control—has been **blurred by the administration.** Serious problems with Soviet compliance have been submerged in **irresponsible charges, innuendo, and leaks.** The objective, instead, should be to clarify questionable Soviet behavior and insist on compliance—not to exploit these concerns in order to **further poison our relations, repudiate existing agreements, or, worse still, terminate arms control altogether.**

Here's the point: Just as we look at the first few words of your sentences for coherence, we look at the last few words for rhetorical emphasis. We assign emphasis to words we hear under this final stress, and what we hear emphasized, we expect to be significant.

MANAGING ENDINGS FOR EMPHASIS

Here are some ways to get emphasis on words that deserve it.

Three Tactical Revisions

1. Trim the end.

> Some sociobiologists claim that our genes control our social behavior **in the way we act in situations we are in every day.**

> Since *social behavior* means *the way we act in situations . . .* , we drop everything after *behavior:*

> ✓ Some sociobiologists claim that our genes **control our social behavior.**

2. Shift peripheral ideas to the left.

> The data offered to prove ESP are too weak **for the most part.**

> ✓ **For the most part,** the data offered to prove ESP are **too weak.**

> Particularly avoid ending with anticlimactic METADISCOURSE:

> Job opportunities are getting better in computer programming, **it must be remembered.**

> ✓ **It must be remembered** that job opportunities in computer programming are getting better.

3. Shift new information to the right.

    A more common way to manage stress is by moving new information to the end of a sentence.

> Questions about the ethics of withdrawing intravenous feeding are **more difficult** [than something just mentioned].

> ✓ **More difficult** [than something just mentioned] are questions about the ethics of withdrawing intravenous feeding.

Six Syntactic Devices

1. Passives (for the last time)

    A passive verb lets you flip a subject and OBJECT. Compare these next two sentences. To stress the concept of genes influencing behavior, we revise the active verb into a passive to get that idea closer to the stress position:

Some sociobiologists claim that **our genes** influence_{active} aspects of behavior that we think are learned. **Our genes,** for example, seem to determine . . .

✓Some sociobiologists claim that aspects of behavior that we think are learned are in fact influenced_{passive} **by our genes. Our genes,** for example, seem to determine . . .

2. *There*

Some editors discourage *there is/there are* constructions, but if you avoid them entirely, you lose a device that lets you shift a phrase toward the end of its sentence and thereby stress it. Compare:

Several syntactic devices let you manage where in a sentence you locate units of new information.

✓**There are** several syntactic devices that let you manage where in a sentence you locate units of new information.

Experienced writers regularly use *there* at the beginning of a paragraph to introduce concepts that they develop in sentences that follow.

3. *What-shift*

This is another device that shifts a part of the sentence to the right:

We need a monetary policy that would end fluctuations in money supply, unemployment, and inflation.

✓*What* we need *is* a monetary policy that would end fluctuations in money supply, unemployment, and inflation.

4. *It*-shift

When you have a subject consisting of a long NOUN CLAUSE, you can move it to the end of the sentence and start with an *it:*

That oil prices would be set by OPEC once seemed inevitable.

✓*It* once seemed inevitable **that oil prices would be set by OPEC.**

The cost of these five devices is a few extra words, so use them sparingly.

5. *Not only X, but Y* (as well)

In this next pair, note how the *but* emphasizes the last element of the pair:

We must clarify these issues and **develop trust.**

✓ We must *not only* clarify these issues, *but* **develop trust**.

Unless you have reason to emphasize the negative, end with the positive:

The point is to highlight our success, **not to emphasize our failures.**

✓ The point is not to emphasize our failures but **to highlight our success.**

6. Repeated words and pronoun substitution

This is a fine point: A sentence can end flatly if you repeat at its end a word used just a few words before, because the voice we hear in our mind's ear drops off at the end of a sentence. You can hear that drop if you read aloud this sentence and the previous two sentences. To avoid that kind of flatness, rewrite or use a pronoun instead of repeating the word at the end of the sentence. For example:

A sentence will seem to end flatly if you use a word at its end that you used just a few words before, because when you repeat that word, your voice **drops.** Instead of repeating the noun, use a **pronoun**. The reader will at least hear emphasis on the word just **before** *it*.

Exercise 6.1

Revise these sentences to emphasize the right words. In the first three, I boldfaced what I think should be stressed. Then eliminate wordiness, nominalizations, etc.

1. The judiciary's tendency **to rewrite the Constitution** is the biggest danger to the nation, in my opinion, at least.

2. A new political philosophy that could affect our society **well into the twenty-first century** may emerge from these studies.

3. There are **limited** opportunities for teachers to work with individual students in large American colleges and universities.

4. Building suburban housing developments in flood-plains has led to the existence of extensive and wide-spread flooding and economic disaster in parts of our country in recent years, it is now clear.

5. The teacher who makes an assignment of a long final term paper at the end of the semester and who then gives only a grade and nothing else such as a critical comment is a common object of complaint among students at the college level.

6. Renting textbooks rather than buying them for basic required courses such as mathematics, foreign languages, and English, whose textbooks do not go through yearly changes, is feasible, however, economically speaking.

Exercise 6.2

Revise these passages so that their sentences begin with appropriate topics and end with appropriate emphasis.

1. The story of King Lear and his daughters was a popular one during the reign of Queen Elizabeth. At least a dozen available books offered the story to anyone wishing to read it, by the time Elizabeth died. The characters were undeveloped in most of these stories, however, making the story a simple narrative that stated an obvious moral. When he began work on Lear, perhaps his greatest tragedy, Shakespeare must have had several versions of this story available to him. He turned the characters into credible human beings with complex motives, however, even though they were based on the stock figures of legend.

2. Whether the date an operation intends to close down might be part of management's "duty to disclose" during contract bargaining is the issue here, it would appear. The minimization of conflict is the central rationale for the duty that management has to bargain in good faith. In order to allow the union to put forth proposals on behalf of its members, companies are obligated to disclose

major changes in an operation during bargaining, though the case law is scanty on this matter.

3. Athens' catastrophic Sicilian Invasion is the most important event in Thucydides' *History of the Peloponnesian War*. Three-quarters of the history is devoted to setting up the invasion because of this. Through the step-by-step decline in Athenian society that Thucydides describes, we can see how he chose to anticipate the Sicilian Invasion. The inevitability that we associate with the tragic drama is the basic reason for the need to anticipate the invasion.

This next passage will seem difficult because it deals with a strange subject. But even if you don't understand the words, you can still make it more readable.

4. Mucosal and vascular permeability altered by a toxin elaborated by the vibrio is a current hypothesis to explain this kind of severe condition. Changes in small capillaries located near the basal surface of the epithelial cells, and the appearance of numerous microvesicles in the cytoplasm of the mucosal cells are evidence in favor of this hypothesis. Hydrodynamic transport of fluid into the interstitial tissue and then through the mucosa into the lumen of the gut is believed to depend on altered capillary permeability.

Revise this next passage so that the most important data are stressed.

5. Changes in revenues are as follows. An increase to $56,792 from $32,934, a net increase of approximately 73 percent, was realized July 1–August 31 in the Ohio and Kentucky areas. In the Indiana and Illinois areas there was in the same period a 10 percent increase of $15,370, from $153,281 to $168,651. However, a decrease to $190,580 from $200,102, or 5 percent, occurred in the Wisconsin and Minnesota regions in almost the same period of time.

TOPICS, STRESS, AND THEMES

There is one more function that the stress of certain sentences performs, one that is important in helping us sense the coherence of a whole passage. As we saw in the last lesson, readers take the clearest topic to be a short noun phrase that comes early in a sentence, usually as its subject. That's why most of us judge this next paragraph to be unfocused: Its sentences do not open from any consistent point of view. After you read this passage, skim the boldfaced topics:

> 1a. **Great strides in the early and accurate diagnosis** of Alzheimer's disease have been made in recent years. Not too long ago, **senility in an older patient who seemed to be losing touch with reality** was often confused with Alzheimer's. **Genetic clues** have become the basis of newer and more reliable tests in the last few years, however. **The risk of human tragedy of another kind,** though, has resulted from the increasing accuracy of these tests: **Predictions about susceptibility to Alzheimer's** have become possible, long before the appearance of any overt symptoms. At that point, **an apparently healthy person** could be devastated by such an early diagnosis.

If we revise that passage to make the topics more consistent, we make it more coherent:

> ✓1b. In recent years, through **researchers** have made great strides in the early and accurate diagnosis of Alzheimer's disease, **those better diagnoses** have raised a new problem in regard to informing those most at risk. Not too long ago, when **a physician** examined an older patient who seemed out of touch with reality, **she** had to guess whether **that person** had Alzheimer's or was only senile. In the past few years, however, **they** have been able to use new and more reliable tests focusing on genetic clues. But in **the accuracy of these new tests** lies the risk of another kind of human tragedy: **Physicians** may be able to predict Alzheimer's long before its overt appearance, but **such an early diagnosis** could psychologically devastate an apparently healthy person.

Those topics now focus on researcher/physicians and testing.

But I made another revision that is just as important. I revised the *first* sentence so that its end stressed those words expressing the particular concepts that the rest of the paragraph would develop:

> In recent years, though researchers have made great strides in the early and accurate diagnosis of Alzheimer's disease, those better **diagnoses** have raised **a new problem** in regard to **informing those most at risk.**

We can call those key words that run through a passage its *themes.*

Look at the passage again to see how these themes run through it:

- Look first at just the boldfaced words; they are all associated with "testing."
- Then look at the italicized words; they all refer to concepts associated with Alzheimer's.
- Then look at the capitalized words; they all have to do with a new problem.

✓1b. In recent years, though researchers have made great strides in the early and accurate diagnosis of *Alzheimer's disease*, those better **diagnoses** have raised A NEW PROBLEM in regard to INFORMING THOSE MOST AT RISK. Not too long ago, when a physician examined an older patient who seemed out of touch with reality, she had to **guess** whether that person had *Alzheimer's* or was only senile. In the past few years, however, they have been able to use **new and more reliable tests** focusing on genetic clues. But in the accuracy of these **new tests** lies the RISK OF ANOTHER KIND OF HUMAN TRAGEDY: Physicians may be able to **predict** *Alzheimer's* long before its overt appearance, but such an early **diagnosis** could PSYCHOLOGICALLY DEVASTATE AN APPARENTLY HEALTHY PERSON.

That passage now "hangs together" not for just one reason, but for three:

- It has a consistent topic string consisting of physicians and diagnosis.
- Running through it are other strings of words that focus our attention on the themes of (1) tests, (2) concepts related to Alzheimer's disease, and (3) a new problem.

- *And no less important, the opening sentence prepares us to notice those particular themes by emphasizing them in its stress position.*

And that's a third function of the stress position in a sentence that opens a passage: The stress of that opening sentence highlights themes that we want readers to notice in what follows. This principle applies not just to sentences that introduce individual paragraphs, but to sentences that introduce passages of any length: *Locate at the ends of those sentences, in their stress position, the words that announce the key concepts that you intend to develop in the rest of the passage.*

Here's the point: We depend on themes running through a passage to create a sense of coherence. You help readers identify those themes in two ways:

- Repeat them as topics of sentences, usually as subjects.
- Repeat them elsewhere in a passage, as nouns, verbs, and adjectives.

Readers are more likely to notice those themes if you state them at the end of the sentence that introduces a passage, in its stress position.

WHAT'S THE POINT?

One last point about coherence: In the paragraph about diagnosing Alzheimer's, the writer used the opening sentence not just to signal the key terms in what would follow, but expressed in that opening sentence *the main point of the paragraph*, the claim that the rest of the paragraph developed, supported, explained. When we can see the main point of a paragraph, a section, or the whole piece of writing, *particularly at the end of a short segment introducing it*, we are better able to see the relevance of everything that follows.

Compare this version of the Alzheimer's paragraph with (1b) on p. 105.

1c. In recent years, researchers have made great strides in the early and accurate diagnosis of Alzheimer's disease. Not too long ago, when a physician examined an older patient who seemed out of touch with reality, she had to guess whether that person had Alzheimer's or was only senile. In the past few years, however, they have been able to use new and more reliable tests focusing on genetic clues. The accuracy of these new tests could psychologically devastate an apparently healthy person.

If the point of that paragraph is how an early diagnosis of Alzheimer's could damage an otherwise healthy person, we are misled by the opening sentence. It sounds as if we are going to read nothing but good in early and better diagnosis, but that turns out not to be the case.

A last suggestion: When you write a title for your piece, use words that state the key themes. Those words should also be in your point sentence. Do the same thing if your paper is long enough to have section headings: Create them out of the words you use in the point sentence for each section.

Here's the point: Every paragraph, section, and whole in a piece of writing has to have a point that the rest supports, explains, or develops. State that point at the end of a short segment introducing that paragraph, section, or whole.

Exercise 6.3

Here are three opening sentences and the rest of a paragraph that each of those sentences might introduce. Which introductory sentence best sets up the ideas that follow? Assume that the reader would be already familiar with the characters—Russian rulers. The best of the three sentences will in its last few words highlight the new concepts that we associate with those rulers.

1. The next century the situation changed, because disputes over succession to the throne caused some sort of palace revolt or popular revolution in **seven out of eight reigns of the Romanov line after Peter the Great.**

2. The next century the situation changed, because after Peter the Great seven out of eight reigns of the Romanov line were **plagued by turmoil over disputed succession to the throne.**

3. Because turmoil over disputed succession to the throne plagued seven out of eight reigns of the Romanov line after Peter the Great, **the situation changed in the next century.**

The problems began in 1722, when Tsar Peter the Great passed a law of succession that terminated the principle of succession by heredity and required the sovereign to appoint a successor when he died. But because many of the Tsars, including Peter, died before they named successors, those who aspired to rule had no authority by appointment, and so their succession was often disputed by the boyars, lower-level aristocrats. There was turmoil even when successors were appointed. In 1740, Ivan VI was adopted by Czarina Anna Ivanovna and named as her successor at age two months, but his succession was challenged by Elizabeth, daughter of Peter the Great. In 1741, she defeated Anna and ascended to the throne herself. In 1797 Paul tried to eliminate these disputes by codifying a law: primogeniture in the male line. But turmoil continued. Paul was strangled by conspirators, one of whom was probably his son, Alexander I.

SUMMING UP

1. Use the stress position of a sentence to introduce long, complex, or otherwise difficult-to-process material, particularly unfamiliar technical terms and new information.

> **A determination of involvement of lipid-linked saccarides in the assembly of the oligasaccaride chains of ovalbumin in vivo** was the principal aim of this study. ***In vitro* and *in vivo* studies utilizing oviduct membrane preparations and oviduct slices and the antibiotic tunicamycin** were undertaken to accomplish this.

✓The principal aim of this study was to determine how **lipid-linked saccarides are involved in the assembly of the oligasaccaride chains of ovalbumin** *in vivo.* To accomplish this, studies were undertaken *in vitro* **and** *in vivo,* **utilizing the antibiotic tunicamycin on preparations of oviduct membrane and on oviduct slices.**

2. Use the stress position for words that you want your readers to hear emphasized in their minds' ear.

The administration has blurred an issue central to arms control, **the issue of verification.** Irresponsible charges, innuendo, and leaks have submerged **serious problems with Soviet compliance.**

The issue of verification—so central to arms control—has been **blurred by the administration.** Serious problems with Soviet compliance have been submerged in **irresponsible charges, innuendo, and leaks.**

3. Use the stress of a sentence that introduces a passage to announce the key concepts that the rest of the passage will develop:

✓1b. In recent years, though researchers have made great strides in the early and accurate diagnosis of *Alzheimer's disease*, those better **diagnoses** have raised A NEW PROBLEM in regard to INFORMING THOSE MOST AT RISK.

Not too long ago, when a physician examined an older patient who seemed out of touch with reality, she had to **guess** whether that person had *Alzheimer's* or was only senile. In the past few years, however, they have been able to use **new and more reliable tests** focusing on genetic clues. But in the accuracy of these **new tests** lies the RISK OF ANOTHER KIND OF HUMAN TRAGEDY: Physicians may be able to **predict** *Alzheimer's* long before its overt appearance, but such an early **diagnosis** could PSYCHOLOGICALLY DEVASTATE AN APPARENTLY HEALTHY PERSON.

S U M M A R Y :   P A R T   2

A simple English sentence is more than the sum of its parts; it is a system of systems.

Fixed	Topic		Stress
Variable	Short, simple, familiar	New, long, complex	
Fixed	Subject	Verb	———
Variable	Character	Action	———

We prefer sentences that reflect those principles.

1. We want to get to the subject of your main clause quickly, so avoid opening more than a few sentences with long, complex phrases and subordinate clauses.

2. We want to get past the subject of your main clause to a verb quickly, so:

   a. keep your subjects short and, if you can, concrete—ideally flesh-and-blood characters;

   b. open your sentences with information that is familiar to us.

3. We deal with complexity more easily at the end of a sentence, so put there information that you think we will find least familiar, most complex, most difficult to understand.

4. We are confused when in a series of sentences each opens with a different subject, so through a passage, focus on just those few topics that define what that passage or paragraph is centrally "about."

PART THREE

Grace

There are two sorts of eloquence; the one indeed scarce
deserves the name of it, which consists chiefly in
laboured and polished periods, an over-curious and
artificial arrangement of figures, tinseled over with a
gaudy embellishment of words. . . . The other sort of
eloquence is quite the reverse to this, and which may be
said to be the true characteristic of the holy Scriptures;
where the eloquence does not arise from a laboured and
farfetched elocution, but from a surprising mixture of
simplicity and majesty.

—LAURENCE STERNE

Concision

I believe more in the scissors than I do in the pencil.
—TRUMAN CAPOTE

*Often I think writing is sheer paring away of oneself leaving always
something thinner, barer, more meager.*
—F. SCOTT FITZGERALD

*If you require a practical rule of me, I will present you with this:
Whenever you feel an impulse to perpetrate a piece of exceptionally
fine writing, obey it—wholeheartedly—and delete it before sending
your manuscript to press. Murder your darlings.*
—ARTHUR QUILLER-COUCH

*I write for those who judge of books, not by the quantity, but by the
quality of them: who ask not how long, but how good they are? I
spare both my reader's time and my own, by couching my sense in as
few words as I can.*
—JOHN WESLEY

*The ability to simplify means to eliminate the unnecessary
so that the necessary may speak.*
—HANS HOFMANN

To a Snail: If "compression is the first grace of style," you have it.
—MARIANNE MOORE

115

CLARITY, GRACE, AND CONCISION

You are close to clarity when you match CHARACTERS and ACTIONS to SUBJECTS and VERBS, and closer yet when you get the right characters into TOPICS and the right words under STRESS. But your readers may still think your prose is a long way from graceful if it looks like this:

> In my personal opinion, it is necessary that we should not ignore the opportunity to think over each and every suggestion offered.

That writer matched characters with subjects, and actions with verbs, but in too many words: Opinion is personal, so we don't need *personal,* and since this whole statement is opinion, we don't need *in my opinion. Think over* means *consider. Each and every* is redundant. A suggestion is by definition offered, and *not ignore* means *consider.* In other, fewer, words,

✓ We should consider each suggestion.

Though not elegant, that sentence has at least style's first grace— that of compression, or as we'll call it, concision. Concision, though, is only a good beginning. We must still make our sentences shapely. In this lesson, we focus on concision; in the next, on shape.

FIVE PRINCIPLES OF CONCISION

When I edited that sentence about suggestions, I applied five principles:

1. Delete words that mean little or nothing.
2. Delete words that repeat the meaning of other words.
3. Delete words implied by other words.
4. Replace a phrase with a word.
5. Change negatives to affirmatives.

These principles are easy to state but hard to follow, because you have to inch your way through every sentence you write, cutting here, compressing there, and that's labor-intensive. Those five principles, though, can guide you in that work.

1. Delete Meaningless Words

Some words are verbal tics that we use as unconsciously as we clear our throats:

kind of   actually   particular really   certain various
virtually individual basically   generally given   practically

> Productivity **actually** depends on **certain** factors that **basically** involve psychology more than **any particular** technology.

> ✓ Productivity depends on psychology more than on technology.

2. Delete Doubled Words

Early in the history of English, writers paired a French or Latin word with a native English one, because foreign words sounded more learned. Now they are just redundant. Among the common pairs:

full and complete   hope and trust   any and all
true and accurate   each and every   basic and fundamental
hopes and desires   first and foremost various and sundry

3. Delete What Readers Can Infer

This is a common redundancy but hard to identify, because it comes in so many forms.

Redundant Modifiers   Often, the meaning of a word implies its modifier:

> Do not try to predict those **future** events that will **completely** *revolutionize* society because **past** *history* shows that it is the **final** *outcome* of minor events that **unexpectedly** *surprises* us more.

> ✓ Do not try to predict revolutionary events because history shows that the outcome of minor events surprises us more.

Some common redundancies:

terrible tragedy   various different free gift
basic fundamentals future plans   each individual
final outcome   true facts   consensus of opinion

Redundant Categories   Every word implies its general category, so you can usually cut a word that names it. Compare:

> During that *period* **of time,** the *membrane* **area** became *pink* **in color** and *shiny* **in appearance.**

> ✓ During that *period,* the *membrane* became *pink* and *shiny.*

When you do that, you may have to change an ADJECTIVE into an ADVERB:

> The holes must be aligned in an *accurate* **manner.**

> ✓ The holes must be aligned *accurately.*

Sometimes you change an adjective into a NOUN:

> The county is responsible for the *educational* **system** and *public recreational* **activities**.

> ✓ The county is responsible for *education* and *public recreation.*

Here are some general nouns (boldfaced) often used redundantly:

large in **size**	round in **shape**	honest in **character**
unusual in **nature**	of a strange **type**	**area** of mathematics
of a bright **color**	at an early **time**	in a confused **state**

General Implications   This kind of wordiness is even harder to spot because it can be so diffuse:

> Imagine someone trying to learn the rules for playing the game of chess.

Learning implies *someone trying, playing a game* implies *rules, chess* is a kind of *game.* So, more concisely,

> Imagine learning the rules of chess.

4. Replace a Phrase with a Word

This redundancy is especially difficult to fix, because you need a big vocabulary and the wit to use it. For example:

> As you carefully read what you have written to improve wording and catch errors of spelling and punctuation, the thing to do before anything else is to see whether you could use sequences of subjects and verbs instead of the same ideas expressed in nouns.

That is,

✓ As you edit, first replace nominalizations with clauses.

I compressed five phrases into five words:

carefully read what you have written	→	edit
the thing to do before anything else	→	first
use X instead of Y	→	replace
nouns instead of verbs	→	nominalizations
sequences of subjects and verbs	→	clauses

I can offer no principle to tell you when to replace a phrase with a word, much less give you the word. I can point out only that you often can, and that you should be alert for opportunities to do so—which is to say, try.

Here are some common phrases (boldfaced) to watch for. Note that some of these let you revise a nominalization into a verb (both italicized):

We must explain **the reason for** the *delay* in the meeting.
✓ We must explain **why** the meeting is *delayed*.

Despite the fact that the data were checked, errors occurred.
✓ **Even though** the data were checked, errors occurred.

In the event that the information is ready early, contact this office.
✓ **If** the information is ready early, contact this office.

In a situation in which a class is closed, you may petition for admission.
✓ **When** a class is closed, you may petition for admission.

I should now like to say a few words **concerning the matter of** money.
✓ I should now like to say a few words **about** money.

There is a need for more careful *inspection* of all welds.
✓ You **must** *inspect* all welds more carefully.

We **are in a position** to make you a firm offer.
✓ We **can** make you a firm offer.

It is possible that nothing will come of these preparations.

✓ Nothing **may** come of these preparations.

Prior to the *end* of the training, you should apply for your license.

✓ **Before** your training *ends,* you should apply for your license.

We have noted a **decrease/increase in** the number of errors.

✓ We have noted *fewer/more* errors.

5. Change Negatives to Affirmatives

When you express an idea in its negative form, not only do you have to use an extra word: *same → not different,* but you also force readers to do a kind of algebraic factoring. These two sentences, for example, mean much the same thing, but the affirmative is more direct:

Do not write in the negative. → Write in the affirmative.

Do not translate a negative into an affirmative if you want to emphasize the negative. (Is that such a sentence? I could have written, *Keep a negative sentence when . . .*) But you can rewrite most negatives, some formulaically:

not different	→	similar	not many	→	few
not the same	→	different	not often	→	rarely
not allow	→	prevent	not stop	→	continue
not notice	→	overlook	not include	→	omit

Some verbs, conjunctions, and prepositions are implicitly negative:

Verbs	*preclude, prevent, lack, fail, doubt, reject, avoid, deny, refuse, exclude, contradict, prohibit, bar*
Conjunctions	*except, unless*
Prepositions	*without, against, lacking, but for*

You can baffle readers if you combine *not* with these negative words. Compare these:

Except when applicants have **failed** to submit applications **without** complete documentation, benefits will **not** be **denied.**

✓ You will receive benefits only if you submit all your documents.

✓ To receive benefits, submit all your documents.

And you baffle readers thoroughly when you combine explicitly and implicitly negative words with passives and nominalizations:

> There should be **no** submission of payments **without** notification of this office, **unless** the payment does **not** exceed $100.

> Do not **submit** payments if you have not **notified** this office, unless you are **paying** less than $100.

Now revise the negatives into affirmatives:

> ✓ If you pay more than $100, notify this office first.

Here's the point: Readers think you write clearly when you use no more words than necessary to say what you mean.

1. Delete words that mean little or nothing.
2. Delete words that repeat the meaning of other words.
3. Delete words implied by other words.
4. Replace a phrase with a word.
5. Change negatives to affirmatives.

Exercise 7.1

Prune the redundancy from these sentences.

1. Critics cannot avoid employing complex and abstract technical terms if they are to successfully analyze literary texts and discuss them in a meaningful way.
2. Scientific research generally depends on fully accurate data if it is to offer theories that will allow us to predict the future in a plausible way.
3. In regard to desirable employment in teaching positions, prospects for those engaged in graduate school level studies are at best not certain.
4. In spite of the fact that the educational environment is a very significant facet to each and every one of our children, some groups do not support reasonable and fair

tax assessments that are required for providing an educational experience at a high level of quality.

5. Most likely, a majority of all patients who appear at a public medical clinical facility do not expect special medical attention or treatment, because their particular health problems and concerns are often not major and for the most part can usually be adequately treated without much time, effort, and attention.

6. Notwithstanding the fact that all legal restrictions on the use of firearms are the subject of heated debate and argument, it is necessary that the general public not stop carrying on discussions pro and con in regard to them.

Exercise 7.2

Where appropriate, change the following negatives to affirmatives. Do any additional editing you think useful.

1. There is no possibility in regard to a reduction in the size of the federal government if reductions in federal spending are not introduced.

2. Do not discontinue medication unless symptoms of dizziness and nausea are not present for six hours.

3. No one should be prevented from participating in cost-sharing educational programs without a full hearing into the reasons for his or her not being accepted.

4. No agreement exists on the question of an open or closed universe, a dispute about which no resolution is likely as long as a computation of the total mass of the universe has not been done.

5. So long as taxpayers do not engage in widespread refusal to pay taxes, the government will have no difficulty in paying its debts.

6. No alternative exists in this country to the eventual development of tar sand, oil shale, and coal as sources of fuel, if we wish to stop being energy dependent on imported oil.

7. Not until a resolution between Catholics and Protestants in regard to the authority of papal supremacy is reached will there be a start to a reconciliation between these two Christian religions.

8. Except when such expenses do not exceed $250, the Insured may not refuse to provide the Insurer with all relevant receipts, checks, or other evidence of costs, when requested.

Exercise 7.3

Here are two actual sentences from two allegedly "free" offers.

> You will not be charged our first monthly fee unless you don't cancel within the first thirty days.

> To avoid being charged your first monthly fee, cancel your membership before your free trial ends.

Which one did you have to read twice? Why might the less clear one have been written like that? Revise it.

A PARTICULAR KIND OF REDUNDANCY: METADISCOURSE

In Lesson 4, I described METADISCOURSE as language we use to refer to

- our intentions: *to sum up, candidly, I believe*
- the reader's responses: *note that, consider now, as you see*
- the structure of our text: *first, second, finally, therefore, however*

You need metadiscourse in everything you write, but you can bury your ideas under it:

> The last point I would like to make is that in regard to men-women relationships, it is important to keep in mind that the greatest changes have occurred in the way they now work with one another.

Only a few words in that sentence address men-women relationships:

> men-women relationships . . . greatest changes . . . the way they work with one another.

The rest is metadiscourse:

> The last point I would like to make is that in regard to . . . it is important to keep in mind that . . .

If we prune that, we can tighten the sentence:

> The greatest changes in men-women relationships have occurred in the way that they work with one another.

Now that we see what the sentence says, we can make it yet more direct:

> ✓ Men and women have changed their relationships most in the way they work with one another.

Some teachers and editors urge us to cut all metadiscourse, but everything we write needs some. You have to read with an eye to how it is used in your field by writers who you think are clear and concise, then do likewise. There are, however, some types that you can usually cut.

Metadiscourse That Attributes Your Ideas to a Source

You announce that something has been anonymously *observed* or found to *exist*, or *seen, noticed, noted,* and so on; it is more direct just to state the fact:

> High divorce rates **have been observed** to occur in areas that **have been determined to have** low population density.
> ✓ High divorce rates occur in areas with low population density.

Metadiscourse That Announces Your Topic

The boldface phrases tell your reader what your sentence is "about":

> **This section introduces** another problem, that of noise pollution. **The first thing to say about it is** that noise pollution exists not only . . .

You help readers catch a topic more easily if you cut the metadiscourse:

✓ Another problem is noise pollution. First, it exists not only . . .

You can use two other constructions to call attention to a word or phrase, usually mentioned at least once before:

> **In regard to** a vigorous style, the most important feature is a short, concrete subject followed by a forceful verb.

> **So far as** China's industrial development **is concerned,** it will take decades to equal that of Japan.

But you can usually get those topics into a subject:

✓ The most important feature of a vigorous style is a short, concrete subject followed by a forceful verb.

✓ China will take decades to equal Japan's industrial development.

Look hard at a sentence opening with a metadiscourse subject and verb that merely announce a topic:

> In this essay, **I will discuss** Robert Frost's bird imagery.

I write that kind of sentence when I have little idea where I am going, saying in effect, "I have a topic to write about and hope I eventually think of something to say about it." On the other hand, that kind of sentence in a professional journal promises to develop that topic.

Excessive Hedging and Intensifying

This kind of metadiscourse can not only be redundant, but influence what your readers infer about your character, because it signals your confidence and caution. Between hedging and intensifying, you have to find the middle way.

Hedges   Here are some common hedges:

Adverbs	*usually, often, sometimes, almost, virtually, possibly, perhaps, apparently, in some ways, to a certain extent, somewhat, in some/certain respects*
Adjectives	*most, many, some, a certain number of*
Verbs	*may, might, can, could, seem, appear, suggest, indicate*

Some readers think all hedging is not just redundant, but mealy-mouthed:

> There **seems to be** some evidence that **may suggest** that **certain** differences between Japanese and Western rhetoric **could** derive from historical influences **possibly** traceable to Japan's long cultural isolation and Europe's equally long history of cross-cultural contacts.

On the other hand, only a fool or someone with massive historical evidence would make an assertion as flatly confident as this:

> This evidence **proves** that Japanese and Western rhetorics differ because of Japan's long cultural isolation and Europe's equally long history of cross-cultural contacts.

In thoughtful academic writing, we more often state claims closer to this (and look at what you just read for my own hedging):

> ✓This evidence **suggests** that **aspects** of Japanese and Western rhetoric differ because of Japan's long cultural isolation and Europe's equally long history of cross-cultural contacts.

This next paragraph introduced the article announcing the most significant breakthrough in the history of genetics, the discovery of the double helix of DNA. If anyone was entitled to be assertive, it was Crick and Watson. But they chose diffidence (note, too, the first person *we*; hedges are boldfaced):

> We **wish to suggest a** [note: not *the*] structure for the salt of deoxyribose nucleic acid (D.N.A.) . . . A structure for nucleic acid has already been proposed by Pauling and Corey . . . **In our opinion,** this structure is unsatisfactory for two reasons: (1) **We believe** that the material which gives the X-ray diagrams is the salt, not the free acid . . . (2) **Some** of the van der Waals distances **appear** to be too small.
>
> —J. D. Watson and F. H. C. Crick,
> "Molecular Structure of Nucleic Acids"

Without the hedges, their claim would be more concise, but more aggressive. Compare this (I boldface my stronger words, but most of the more aggressive tone comes from the absence of hedges):

> We **announce** here **the** structure for the salt of deoxyribose nucleic acid (D.N.A.) . . . A structure for nucleic acid has already been proposed by

Pauling and Corey . . . Their structure is unsatisfactory for two reasons: (1) The material which gives their X-ray diagrams is the salt, not the free acid . . . (2) Their van der Waals distances **are** too small.

You can use the verbs *suggest* and *indicate* instead of *prove* or *show* to make a claim about which you are less than 100 percent certain, but confident enough to propose:

> ✓ The evidence **indicates** that some of these questions remain unresolved.

> ✓ These data **suggest** that further studies are necessary.

Intensifiers   Some common intensifiers:

Adverbs	*very, pretty, quite, rather, clearly, obviously, undoubtedly, certainly, of course, indeed, inevitably, invariably, always*
Adjectives	*key, central, crucial, basic, fundamental, major, principal, essential*
Verbs	*show, prove, establish, as you/we/everyone knows/can see, it is clear/obvious that*

Confident writers use intensifiers less often than hedges because they do not want to sound this smug:

> For a century now, **all** liberals have argued against **any** censorship of art, and **every** court has found their arguments so **completely** persuasive that **not a** person **any** longer remembers how they were countered. As a result, today, censorship is **totally** a thing of the past.

Some inexperienced writers think that kind of aggressive style is persuasive. Quite the opposite: If we state claims moderately, our readers are more likely to consider them thoughtfully:

> For **about** a century now, **many** liberals have argued against censorship of art, and **most** courts have found their arguments persuasive **enough** that **few** people **may** remember **exactly** how they were countered. As a result, today, censorship is **virtually** a thing of the past.

Some will claim that a passage hedged that much is both wordy and weak. Perhaps. But it does not come at us like a bulldozer. It leaves room to imagine a reasoned and equally moderate response. In fact, in some academic areas, readers adopt the rule of thumb that if you begin with *It is obvious . . .* , what you then say is not.

The most common intensifier is the absence of a hedge. In this case, less is more. The first sentence below has no intensifiers where the blank lines appear, but neither does it have any hedges there, and so it seems like a strong claim:

> _____ Americans believe that the federal government is _____ intrusive and _____ authoritarian.
>
> **Many** Americans believe that **certain branches** of the federal government are **often** intrusive and **increasingly** authoritarian.

Here's the point: You need some metadiscourse in everything you write, especially metadiscourse that guides readers through your whole text, words such as *first, second, therefore, on the other hand,* and so on. You also need some metadiscourse that hedges your certainty, words such as *perhaps, seems, could,* and so on. The problem is that you can too easily use too many.

Exercise 7.4

Here are sentences that announce a topic rather than state a thesis. Delete the metadiscourse and rewrite what remains into a full statement. Then decide whether the full statement seems to make an interesting claim. For example:

> In this study, I examine the history of Congressional legislation regarding the protection of children in the workplace.

First, delete the metadiscourse:

> . . . the history of Congressional legislation regarding the protection of children in the workplace.

Then rewrite what is left into a full sentence:

> ✓ Congress has legislated the protection of children in the workplace.

That appears to be a self-evident, not particularly interesting claim.

1. This essay will survey recent research in schemata theory as applied to the pedagogy of mathematical problem solving.

2. I will analyze Frost's use of imagery of seasons in his longer poems published at the end of his career.

3. The methodological differences between English and American histories of the War of 1812 that resulted in radically differing interpretations of the cause of the conflict are the topic of this study.

4. In this study, I analyze the mistaken assumption underlying Freud's interpretation of dreams.

5. We will consider scientific thinking and its historical roots in connection with the influence of Egypt on Greek thought.

6. This article discusses needle sharing among drug users.

7. The relationship between birth order and academic success will be explored.

8. I intend to address the problem of the reasons for the failure and success of trade embargoes in this century.

Exercise 7.5

Edit these for both unnecessary metadiscourse and redundancy.

1. But on the other hand, we can perhaps point out that there may always be TV programming to appeal to our most prurient and, therefore, lowest interests.

2. In this particular section, I intend to discuss my position about the possible need to dispense with the standard approach to plea bargaining. I believe this for two reasons. The first reason is that there is the possibility of letting hardened criminals avoid receiving their just punishment. The second reason is the following: Plea bargaining seems to encourage a growing lack of respect for the judicial system.

3. Turning now to the next question, there is in regard to wilderness area preservation activities one basic principle when attempting to formulate a way of approaching decisions about unspoiled areas to be set aside as not open to development for commercial exploitation.

4. It is my belief that in regard to terrestrial-type snakes, an assumption can be made that there are probably none in unmapped areas of the world surpassing the size of those we already have knowledge of.

5. Depending on the particular position that one takes on this question, the educational system has taken on a degree of importance that may be equal to or perhaps even exceed the family as a major source of transmission of social values.

PRODUCTIVE REDUNDANCY

Learning by Writing

Some teachers look upon any redundancy as a sign of mental laziness. But we inevitably fall into some redundancy when we write about a subject that we are just learning. We signal membership in a community by what we say and how we say it, but a surer sign is what we know to leave unsaid—our community's common knowledge. Unfortunately, learning what not to say takes time.

Here, for example, is a paragraph by a student who was a good undergraduate writer (I checked). But he was writing his first paper in a new community, law school:

> It is my opinion that the ruling of the lower court concerning the case of *Haslem* v. *Lockwood* should be upheld, thereby denying the appeal of the plaintiff. The main point supporting my point of view on this case concerns the tenet of our court system which holds that in order to win his case, the plaintiff must prove that he was somehow wronged by the defendant. The burden of proof rests on the plaintiff. He must show enough evidence to convince the court that he is in the right.

To his legal writing teacher, everything after the first sentence was redundant: *Obviously* if a court upholds a ruling, it denies the appeal; *obviously* the plaintiff can win only if he proves a defendant has wronged him; *obviously* the plaintiff has the burden of proof; *obviously* the plaintiff has to provide evidence. But at this stage in his career, this writer was an outsider learning his community's tacit common knowledge, and so could not resist stating it.

Autobiographical Metadiscourse

Just as "belaboring the obvious" signals a writer starting out in a field, so does some metadiscourse. When we are comfortable thinking through familiar problems, we can suppress the narrative of our mental processes. But when we are inexperienced in a subject, we often feel compelled to give a running commentary about what we thought and did:

Look again at that paragraph by the first-year law student. Not only did he "belabor the obvious," he made the machinery of his thinking visible. I boldface metadiscourse and italicize the self-evident:

> **It is my opinion that** *the ruling of the lower court concerning the case of Haslem v. Lockwood* should be upheld, *thereby denying the appeal of the plaintiff.* **The main point supporting my point of view on this case concerns** *the tenet of our court system which holds that in order to win his case, the plaintiff must prove that he was somehow wronged by the defendant. The burden of proof rests on the plaintiff. He must show enough evidence to convince the court that he is in the right.*

When we delete autobiographical narrative and commonplaces that knowledgeable readers assume, we are left with something leaner:

> *Haslem* should be affirmed because the plaintiff failed to meet his burden of proof.

Having emphasized concision so relentlessly, I must now qualify what I have urged: Readers dislike graceless redundancy, but they also dislike a style so concise that it is all sharp edges. Here, for example, is a paragraph of good advice from the most widely sold book on style, Strunk and White's *The Elements of Style* (I recommend its 2nd edition):

> Revising is part of writing. Few writers are so expert that they can produce what they are after on the first try. If the work merely needs shortening, a pencil is the most useful tool, but quite often the writer will discover, on examining the completed work, that there are serious flaws in the arrangement of the material, calling for re-arrangement. When that is the case, he can save himself much labor and time by using scissors on his manuscript, cutting it to pieces and fitting the pieces together in a better order. Do not be afraid to seize whatever you have written and cut it to ribbons; it can always be restored to its original condition in the morning, if that course seems best. Remember, it is no sign of weakness or

defeat that your manuscript needs major surgery. This is a common occurrence in all writing, and among the best writers.

If we run that through a style-compactor, we can squeeze out a lot of redundancy:

> Most writers revise because few are expert enough to write perfect first drafts. If you want to shorten, erase. If you misarrange, cut and reorder; you can always restore it. Even great writers revise, so if your manuscript needs surgery, it signals no weakness or failure.

But we've also squeezed out its garrulous charm. I can't tell you how to know when you write too concisely. That's why you must listen to your readers, because they know something you never can: They know how it feels to be your reader.

SUMMING UP

Concision does not guarantee grace, but it clears away deadwood so that you can see the shape of a sentence more clearly.

1. Redundant pairs

> If and when we can define our final aims and goals, each and every member of our group will be ready and willing to offer aid and assistance.
>
> ✓ If we define our goals, we will all be ready to help.

2. Redundant modifiers

> In the business world of today, official governmental red tape seriously destroys initiative among individual businesses.
>
> ✓ Government red tape destroys business initiative.

3. Redundant categories

> In the area of education, tight financial conditions are forcing school boards to cut nonessential expenses.
>
> ✓ Tight finances are forcing school boards to cut nonessentials.

4. Meaningless modifiers

> Most students generally find some kind of summer work.
>
> ✓ Most students find summer work.

5. Obvious implications

> Energy used to power industries and homes will in years to come cost more money.
>
> ✓ Energy will eventually cost more.

6. Excessive detail

> A microwave oven that you might buy in any department store uses less energy that is so expensive than a conventional oven that uses gas or electricity.
>
> ✓ Microwave ovens use less energy than conventional ones.

7. A phrase for a word

> A sail-powered craft that has turned on its side or completely over must remain buoyant enough so that it will bear the weight of those individuals who were aboard.
>
> ✓ A capsized sailboat must support those on it.

8. Excessive metadiscourse

> It is almost certainly the case that totalitarian systems cannot allow a society to have what we would define as stable social relationships.
>
> ✓ Totalitarianism blocks stable social relationships.

9. Indirect negatives

> There is no reason not to believe that engineering malfunctions in nuclear energy systems cannot be anticipated.
>
> ✓ Malfunctions in nuclear energy systems will surprise us.

10. Hedges and intensifiers

> The only principle here is the Goldilocks rule: Not too much, not too little, but just right. Not much help, but this is a matter where you have to develop and then trust your ear.

> **Too certain:**   In my research, **I prove** that people with a gun in their home use it to kill themselves or a family member instead of to protect themselves from an intruder.
>
> **Too uncertain:**   **Some** of my recent research **seems** to **imply** that there **may** be a **risk** that **certain** people

with a gun in their homes **could** be **more prone** to use it to kill themselves or a family member than to protect themselves from **possible** intruders.

Just right?   My research **indicates** that people with a gun in their homes **are more likely** to use it to kill themselves or a family member than they are to protect themselves from an intruder.

Shape

The structure of every sentence is a lesson in logic.
—John Stuart Mill

Sentences in their variety run from simplicity to complexity,
a progression not necessarily reflected in length: a long sentence
may be extremely simple in construction—indeed must be simple
if it is to convey its sense easily.
—Sir Herbert Read

A long complicated sentence should force itself upon you,
make you know yourself knowing it.
—Gertrude Stein

Long sentences in a short composition are like
large rooms in a little house.
—William Shenstone

Something that looks like a bad sentence
can be the germ of a good one.
—Ludwig Wittgenstein

You never know what is enough until you know
what is more than enough.
—William Blake

CLEAR COMPLEXITY

If you can write clear and concise sentences, you have achieved a good deal, and much more if you can assemble them into flowing, coherent passages. But if you can't write a clear sentence longer than twenty words or so, you'd be like a composer who could write only jingles. Despite those who tell us not to write long sentences, you cannot communicate every complex idea in a short one, so you have to know how to assemble a sentence that is both long and clear.

Consider, for example, (1a):

> 1a. In addition to differences in ethnicity or religion that have for centuries plagued Bosnians, Serbs, and Croats, explanations seeking causes of their hatred must include all of the other social, economic, and cultural conflicts that have plagued them that are rooted in a troubled history that extends 1000 years into the past.

Even if that idea needed all those words (which it didn't), they could certainly be arranged into a more shapely sentence.

We can start revising by editing the abstractions into CHARACTER/SUBJECTS and ACTION/VERBS and then break the sentence into shorter ones:

> 1b. Historians have tried to explain why Bosnians, Serbs, and Croats hate one another today. Many have claimed that the sources of conflict are age-old differences in ethnicity or religion. But they must study all the other social, economic, and cultural conflicts that have plagued them through their 1000 years of troubled history.

But if (1a) is shapeless, (1b) is fragmented. We need something closer to this:

> ✓1c. To explain why Bosnians, Serbs, and Croats hate one another today, historians must study not only age-old differences of ethnicity and religion, but all the other social, economic, and cultural conflicts that have plagued them through their 1000 years of troubled history.

That sentence is long but does not sprawl. So it can't be length alone that makes a sentence ungainly. In this lesson, I focus on how to write sentences that are not only long and complex but clear and shapely.

Diagnosing Two Kinds of Problems

It's easier to see sprawl in the writing of others than in our own because we know what we want our sentences to mean even before we read them. So you have to diagnose your prose in ways that sidestep your intractable subjectivity.

Start by putting a slash mark after every PUNCTUATED SENTENCE./Then pick out sentences longer than two typed lines and read them aloud./If in reading one of your long sentences you get the feeling that you are about to run out of breath before you come to a place where you can pause to integrate all of its parts into a whole that communicates a single conceptual structure [breathe], you have found a sentence your readers are likely to want you to revise, like this one./Or if your sentence, because of one interruption after another, seems to stop and start, your readers are, if they are typical, likely to make a judgment that your sentence, as this one does, lurches from one part to the next.

Our sense of shapeless length usually results from two things:

- It takes us too long to get to the verb in the MAIN CLAUSE.
- After the verb, we have to slog through a shapeless sprawl of SUBORDINATE CLAUSES.

Revising Long Openings

Some sentences seem to take forever to get to the point:

> Since most undergraduate students change their fields of study at least once during their college careers, many more than once, first-year students who are not certain about their program of studies should not load up their schedules to meet requirements for a particular program.

That sentence takes 31 words to get to its main verb, *should not load up*. Since the point of a sentence is usually in the subject and verb of its main clause, here are two rules of thumb:

1. Get to the subject of the main clause quickly; avoid long introductory PHRASES and clauses.
2. Get to the verb of the main clause quickly; avoid long, abstract subjects and interruptions between subjects and verbs.

Rule of Thumb 1: Get to the Subject Quickly

We have a problem with sentences that open with long introductory phrases and clauses, because as we read them, we have to hold in mind that the subject and verb of the main clause are still to come, and that frustrates easy understanding. Compare these:

> 2a. **Since most undergraduate students change their major fields of study at least once during their college careers,** *first-year students* who are not certain about the program of studies they want to pursue SHOULD NOT LOAD UP their schedules to meet requirements for a particular program.

> ✓2b. **Most undergraduate students** CHANGE their major fields at least once during their college careers, so **first-year students** SHOULD NOT LOAD UP their schedules with requirements for a particular program if they are not certain about the program of studies they want to pursue.

As we read the first 21 words in (2a), we have to keep in mind that the subject of a main clause is still coming. In (2b), we get to subjects and verbs of the first two clauses immediately. If you open with a long introductory clause, try moving it to the end of its sentence or turning it into a sentence of its own.

Rule of Thumb 2: Get Past the Subject to Its Verb Quickly

We also want to get past the main subject to its verb. That means:

- keep subjects short
- avoid interrupting the subject–verb connection.

Revise Long Subjects into Short Ones. Start by underlining your WHOLE SUBJECTS. If you find a long subject (more than six or seven words) including NOMINALIZATIONS, try turning a nominalization into a verb and finding a subject for it:

> **Abco Inc.'s *understanding* of the drivers of its profitability in the Midwest market for small electronics** helped it pursue opportunities on the West Coast.

> ✓**Abco Inc.** was able to pursue opportunities on the West Coast because it understood what drove profitability in the Midwest market for small electronics.

A subject can also be long if it has attached to it a long RELATIVE CLAUSE:

> *A company* **that focuses on hiring the best personnel and then trains them not just for the work they are hired to do but for higher-level jobs** IS likely to earn the loyalty of its employees.

Try turning the relative clause into an introductory SUBORDINATE CLAUSE:

> ✓**When** *a company* FOCUSES **on hiring the best personnel and then trains them not just for the work they are hired to do but for higher-level jobs,** it is likely to earn the loyalty of its employees.

If the clause turns out to be as long as that one, move it to the end of its sentence or turn it into an INDEPENDENT CLAUSE:

> ✓A company is likely to earn the loyalty of its employees **when** it focuses on hiring the best personnel and then trains them not just for the work they are hired to do but for higher-level jobs.

> ✓Some companies focus on hiring the best personnel and then train them not just for the work they are hired to do but for higher-level jobs later. Such companies are likely to earn the loyalty of their employees.

Remove Interruptions between Subjects and Verbs.   You also frustrate readers when you interrupt the connection between a subject and verb. Compare these:

> Some scientists, **because they write in a style that is impersonal and objective,** do not easily communicate with laypeople.

That *because*-clause after the subject forces us to hold our mental breath until we reach the verb, *do not easily communicate.* Move the interruption to the beginning or end of its sentence, depending on whether it connects more closely to what came before or comes after. (Review pp. 81–82):

> ✓Because some scientists write in a style that is impersonal and objective, they do **not easily communicate with laypeople. This lack of communication** damages . . .

> ✓Some scientists do not easily communicate with laypeople because they write in **a style that is impersonal and objective. It is a kind of style** filled with passives and . . .

We mind short interruptions less:

> ✓ Some scientists **deliberately** write in a style that is impersonal and objective.

Remove Interruptions between Verbs and Objects   We also like to get past the verb to its object quickly. This sentence doesn't let us do that:

> We must develop, **if we are to become competitive with other companies in our region,** a core of knowledge regarding the state of the art in operationally effective industrial organizations.

Move the interrupting element to the beginning or end of its sentence, depending on what comes next:

> ✓ **If we are to compete with other companies in our region,** we must develop a core of knowledge about the state of the art in **effective industrial organizations. Such organizations provide . . .**
>
> ✓ **We** must develop a core of knowledge about the state of the art in effective industrial organizations **if we are to compete with other companies in our region. Increasing competition . . .**

Here's the point: Readers read most easily when you get them quickly

- to the subject of your main clause and
- past a short subject to its verb.

At that point, you can give readers longer and more complicated material. Therefore, avoid long introductory phrases and clauses, long subjects, and interruptions between subjects and verbs.

Exercise 8.1

These sentences have long introductory phrases and clauses. Revise.

1. Since workfare has not yet been shown to be a successful alternative to welfare because evidence show-

ing its ability to provide meaningful and regular employment for welfare recipients is not yet available, those who argue that all the states should make a full-scale commitment to workfare are premature in their recommendations.

2. While grade inflation has been a subject of debate by teachers and administrators and even in newspapers, employers looking for people with high levels of technical and analytical skills have not had difficulty identifying desirable candidates.

3. Although one way to prevent foreign piracy of videos and CDs is in the criminal justice systems of foreign countries and for cases to move faster through their systems and for stiffer penalties to be imposed, no improvement in the level of expertise of judges who hear these cases is expected any time in the immediate future.

4. Since school officials responsible for setting policy about school security have said that local principals may require students to pass through metal detectors before entering a school building, the need to educate parents and students about the seriousness of bringing onto school property anything that looks like a weapon can be made a part of the total package of school security.

5. If the music industry ignores the problem of how a rating system applied to offensive lyrics could be applied to music broadcast over FM and AM radio, then even if it were willing to discuss a system that could be used in the sale of music in retail stores, the likelihood of any significant improvement in its image with the public is nil.

These sentences have long subjects. Revise.

6. Explaining why Shakespeare decided to have Lady Macbeth die off stage rather than letting the audience see her die has to do with understanding the audience's reactions to Macbeth's death.

7. An agreement by the film industry and by television producers on limiting characters using cigarettes, even

if carried out, would do little to discourage young people from smoking.

8. A student's right to have access to his or her own records, including medical records, academic reports, and confidential comments by advisers, will generally take precedence over an institution's desire to keep those records private, except when limitations of those rights under specified circumstances were agreed to by the student during registration.

These sentences are unfortunately interrupted. First, eliminate wordiness, then correct the interruption.

9. The construction of the Interstate Highway System, owing to the fact that Congress, on the occasion when it originally voted funds for it, did not anticipate the rising cost of inflation, ran into serious financial problems.

10. Such prejudicial conduct or behavior, regardless of the reasons offered to justify it, is rarely not at least to some degree prejudicial to good order and discipline.

11. TV "reality" shows, because they have an appeal to our fascination with real-life conflict because of our voyeuristic impulses, are about the most popular shows that are regularly scheduled to appear on TV.

12. Insistence that there is no proof by scientific means of a causal link between tobacco consumption and various disease entities such as cardiac heart diseases and malignant growth, despite the fact that there is a strong statistical correlation between smoking behavior and such diseases, is no longer the officially stated position of cigarette companies.

13. The continued and unabated emission of carbon dioxide gas into the atmosphere, unless there is a marked reduction, will eventually result in serious changes in the climate of the world as we know it today.

Reshaping Sprawl

Once we make the subject–verb–object connection, we can deal with longer, more complex information. But we don't want to wade through sprawl like this:

> Of the areas of science important to our future, few are more promising than genetic engineering, which is a new way of manipulating the elemental structural units of life itself, which are the genes and chromosomes that tell our cells how to reproduce to become the parts that constitute our bodies.

A sentence seems to sprawl when after the verb, it tacks on a series of clauses of the same kind. It looks like this:

> Of the areas of science important to our future [opening phrase]
>> few are more promising than genetic engineering,
>> [subject–verb core]
>>> **which** is a new way of manipulating the elemental structural units of life itself, [tacked-on clause]
>>>> **which** are the genes and chromosomes [tacked-on clause]
>>>>> **that** tell our cells how to reproduce to become the parts [tacked-on clause]
>>>>>> **that** constitute our bodies. [tacked-on clause]

Diagnose this problem by having someone read your prose aloud to you. If that person seems to run out of breath before getting to the end of a sentence, so will your silent reader. You can revise in three ways:

Cut

1. Try reducing some of the relative clauses to phrases by deleting *who/that/which+is/was*, etc.:

> ✓ Of the many areas of science important to our future, few are more promising than genetic engineering, ~~which is~~ a new way of manipulating the elemental structural units of life itself, ~~which are~~ the genes and chromosomes that tell our cells how to reproduce to become the parts that constitute our bodies.

Occasionally, you have to rewrite the remaining verb into an *-ing* form:

> The day is coming when we will all have numbers **that will identify** our financial transactions so that the IRS can monitor all activities **that involve** economic activity.

> ✓ The day is coming when we will all have numbers ~~that will~~ **identifying** our financial transactions so that the IRS can monitor all activities ~~that~~ **involving** economic activity.

2. Or break the subordinate clauses out into their own sentences.

> ✓ Many areas of science are important to our future, but few are more promising than genetic engineering. It is a new way of manipulating the elemental structural units of life itself, the genes and chromosomes that tell our cells how to reproduce to become the parts that constitute our bodies.

If none of that works, you have to do some major restructuring.

Change Clauses to Phrases

You can write a long sentence but still avoid sprawl if you change clauses to one of three kinds of modifying phrases: resumptive, summative, or free. You have probably never seen those terms before, but we need them to name what they refer to.

Resumptive Modifiers   These two examples contrast a relative clause and a resumptive modifier:

> Since mature writers often use resumptive modifiers to extend a sentence, we need a word to name what I have not done in this sentence, which I could have ended after the word *sentence* but extended to show you a relative clause attached to a noun.

> ✓ Since mature writers often use resumptive modifiers to extend a sentence, we need a word to name what I am about to do in this sentence, **a sentence that I could have ended at that comma, but extended to show you how resumptive modifiers work.**

The boldface resumptive modifier repeats a key word and starts again. To create a resumptive modifier, find a key word, usually a noun, then pause after it with a comma:

> Since mature writers often use resumptive modifiers to extend a sentence, we need a word to name what I am about to do in this **sentence,**

Then repeat it:

> Since mature writers often use resumptive modifiers to extend a sentence, we need a word to name what I am about to do in this **sentence,**
>> **a sentence . . .**

Then after that repeated word add a relative clause:

> Since mature writers often use resumptive modifiers to extend a sentence, we need a word to name what I am about to do in this sentence,
>> a sentence **that I could have ended at that comma, but extended to show you how resumptive modifiers work.**

You can also resume with an ADJECTIVE or verb. In that case, you don't add a relative clause; you just continue.

> ✓It was American writers who found a voice that was both **true** and **lyrical,**
>> **true** to the rhythms of the working man's speech and **lyrical** in its celebration of his labor.

> ✓All who value independence should **resist** the trivialization of government regulation,
>> **resist** its obsession with administrative tidiness and compulsion to arrange things not for our convenience but for theirs.

Summative Modifiers   Here are two sentences that contrast relative clauses and summative modifiers. Notice how the *which* in the first one feels "tacked on":

> Economic changes have reduced Russian population growth to less than zero **which will have serious social implications.**
> ✓Economic changes have reduced Russian population growth to less than zero, **a demographic event that will have serious social implications.**

To create a summative modifier, end a grammatically complete segment of a sentence with a comma:

Economic changes have reduced Russian population growth to less than zero,

Find a noun that sums up the substance of the sentence:

Economic changes have reduced Russian population growth to less than zero,

a demographic event . . .

Then continue with a relative clause:

Economic changes have reduced Russian population growth to less than zero,

a demographic event **that will have serious social implications.**

Free Modifiers   Compare these:

Socrates questioned the foundations of political behavior **and encouraged youth to question the authority of their elders while maintaining that he wanted only to puzzle out the truth.**

✓Socrates questioned the foundations of political behavior,

encouraging youth to question the authority of their elders, claiming all the while that he wanted only to puzzle out the truth_{free modifier}•

Like the other modifiers, a free modifier can appear at the end of a clause, but instead of repeating a key word or summing up what went before, it says something about the subject of the closest verb:

✓Free modifiers resemble resumptive and summative modifiers, **letting you** [i.e., the free modifier lets you] **extend the line of a sentence while avoiding a train of ungainly phrases and clauses.**

Free modifiers usually begin with an *-ing* PRESENT PARTICIPLE, as those did, but they can also begin with a PAST PARTICIPLE verb, like this:

✓Leonardo da Vinci was a man of powerful intellect,

driven **by** [i.e., da Vinci was driven by] **an insatiable curiosity and** *haunted* **by a vision of artistic perfection.**

A free modifier can also begin with an adjective:

✓ In 1939, we began to assist the British against Germany,

    aware [i.e., we were aware] **that we faced another world war.**

We call these modifiers "free" because they can both begin and end a sentence:

  ✓ **Driven by an insatiable curiosity,** Leonardo da Vinci was . . .

  ✓ **Aware that we faced another world war,** in 1939 we began . . .

Dangling Modifiers   Create a free modifier, however, and you risk dangling a modifier. A modifier "dangles" when its implied subject differs from the explicit subject of the clause it attaches to. (Review p. 67):

> Hoping to find some cause of the flaw, the results of the tests were reviewed.

The modifier, *hoping to find,* dangles because its implicit subject (whoever hopes) differs from the explicit subject of the clause it attaches to (*the results of the tests*). To revise, make the implied and explicit subjects identical:

  ✓ **Hoping** to find some cause of the flaw, **we** reviewed the results of the tests.

Most readers ignore dangling modifiers when the modifier is METADISCOURSE.

  ✓ **To summarize,** it is clear that . . .

  ✓ **Turning now to our financial resources,** our first question is . . .

Here's the point: When you have to write a long sentence, don't just add one phrase or clause after another, willy-nilly. Particularly avoid tacking one relative clause onto another onto another. Try extending the line of a sentence with resumptive, summative, and free modifiers. When you create a free modifier, however, be sure its implied subject matches the explicit subject of the verb closest to it.

Coordinate

It's harder to create good coordination than good modifiers, but when done well, it is more pleasing to the reader. Coordination is in fact the foundation of a gracefully shaped sentence. Compare these. My version is first; the original is second:

> The aspiring artist may find that even a minor, unfinished work which was botched may be an instructive model for how things should be done, while for the amateur spectator, such works are the daily fare which may provide good, honest nourishment, which can lead to an appreciation of deeper pleasures that are also more refined.

> ✓ For the aspiring artist, the minor, the unfinished, or even the botched work, may be an instructive model for how things should—and should not—be done. For the amateur spectator, such works are the daily fare which provide good, honest nourishment—and which can lead to appreciation of more refined, or deeper pleasures.

> —Eva Hoffman, "Minor Art Offers Special Pleasures"

My revision sprawls through a string of tacked-on clauses:

> The aspiring artist may find that even a minor, unfinished work
> **which** was botched may be an instructive model for
> **how** things should be done,
> **while** for the amateur spectator, such works are the daily fare
> **which** may provide good, honest nourishment,
> **which** can lead to an appreciation of deeper pleasures
> **that** are also more refined.

Hoffman's original gets its shape from its multiple coordinations. Structurally, it looks like this:

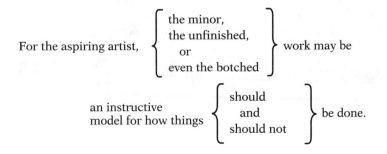

For the amateur spectator, such works are

$$
\text{the daily fare}
\begin{cases}
\text{which provide }
\begin{cases}
\text{good,} \\
\text{honest}
\end{cases}
\text{nourishment—} \\
\qquad\qquad\text{and} \\
\text{which can} \\
\text{lead to} \\
\text{appreciation} \\
\text{of}
\quad
\begin{cases}
\text{more refined,} \\
\qquad\text{or} \\
\text{deeper}
\end{cases}
\text{pleasures.}
\end{cases}
$$

That second sentence in particular shows how elaborate a coordination can get.

Some inexperienced writers just add on element after element with *and*:

> Grade inflation is a problem at many universities, ***and*** it leads to a devaluation of good grades earned by hard work ***and*** will not be solved simply by grading harder.

Those *and*'s obscure the relationships among those claims:

> ✓ Grade inflation is a problem at many universities, **because** it devalues good grades that were earned by hard work, **but** it will not be solved simply by grading harder.

A General Design Principle: Short to Long   We should note one feature that distinguishes well-formed coordination from ill-formed. You can hear it if you read this next passage aloud:

> We should devote a few final words to a matter that reaches beyond the techniques of research to the connections between those subjective values that reflect our deepest ethical choices and objective research.

That sentence seems to end too abruptly with *objective research*. Structurally, it looks like this:

$$
\ldots\text{between}
\begin{cases}
\text{those subjective values that reflect our} \\
\text{deepest ethical choices} \\
\qquad\qquad\text{and} \\
\text{objective research.}
\end{cases}
$$

This next revision moves from shorter to longer by reversing the two coordinate elements and by adding a parallelism to the second one to make it longer. Read this one aloud:

> We should devote a few final words to a matter that reaches beyond the techniques of research to the connections between objective research and those values that reflect our deepest ethical choices and strongest intellectual commitments.

Structurally, it looks like this:

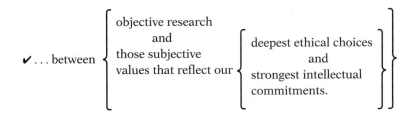

✔ ... between {
  objective research
  and
  those subjective
  values that reflect our {
    deepest ethical choices
    and
    strongest intellectual
    commitments.
  }
}

Here's the point: Coordination lets you extend the line of a sentence more gracefully than tacking on one element to another. When you can coordinate, try to arrange the elements so that they go from shorter to longer.

Exercise 8.2

In these sentences, create resumptive, summative, and free modifiers. In the first five, start a resumptive modifier with the word in italics. Then use the word in brackets to create another sentence with a summative modifier. For example:

> ✓ Within ten years, we could meet our *energy needs* with solar power. [a possibility]

Resumptive:

> ✓ Within ten years, we could meet our *energy needs* with solar power, **needs** that will soar as our population grows.

Summative:

> ✓ Within ten years, we could meet our energy needs with solar power, **a possibility** that few anticipated ten years ago.

Free:

> ✓ Within ten years, we could meet our energy needs with solar power, **freeing** ourselves of dependence on foreign oil.

But before you begin adding resumptive and summative modifiers, edit these sentences for redundancy, wordiness, nominalizations, and other problems.

1. Many different school systems are making a return back to traditional *education* in the basics. [a change]

2. Within the period of the last few years or so, automobile manufacturers have been trying to meet new and more stringent-type quality control *requirements*. [a challenge]

3. The reasons for the cause of aging are a *puzzle* that has perplexed humanity for millennia. [a mystery]

4. The majority of young people in the world of today cannot even begin to have an understanding of the *insecurity* that a large number of older people had experienced during the period of the Great Depression. [a failure]

5. The successful accomplishment of test-tube fertilization of embryos has raised many *issues* of an ethical nature that continue to trouble both scientists and laypeople. [an event]

6. Many who lived during the period of the Victorian era were appalled when Darwin put forth the suggestion that their ancestry might have included creatures such as apes.

7. In the period known to scholars and historians as the Renaissance, increases in affluence and stability in the area of political affairs had the consequence of allowing streams of thought of different kinds to merge and flow together.

8. The field of journalism has to an increasing degree placed its focus on the kind of news stories and events that at one time in our history were considered to be only gossip of a salacious and sexual nature.

Exercise 8.3

The best way to learn coordination is by imitating it. Try imitating any of the passages laid out above. For example, imitating the Eva Hoffman passage (page 148), you might write this:

> For the serious student, the library sometimes provides a chance to be alone and to think through problems that may be too complex or too painful to think about in a noisy and crowded dormitory.

TROUBLESHOOTING LONG SENTENCES

Even when you manage their internal structures, though, long sentences can still go wrong.

Faulty Coordination

Ordinarily, we coordinate elements only of the same grammatical structure: clause and clause, PREPOSITIONAL PHRASE and prepositional phrase, etc. When you coordinate different grammatical structures, readers may feel you have created an offensive lack of PARALLELISM. Careful writers avoid this:

The committee recommends { **revising the curriculum** to recognize trends in local employment and **that the division be reorganized** to reflect the new curriculum. }

They would correct that to this:

$$
\boldsymbol{\checkmark}\text{. . . recommends}\;\left\{
\begin{array}{c}
\textbf{that the curriculum be revised} \\
\text{to recognize . . .} \\
\text{and} \\
\textbf{that the division be reorganized} \\
\text{to reflect. . . .}
\end{array}
\right\}
$$

Or to this:

$$
\boldsymbol{\checkmark}\text{. . . recommends}\;\left\{
\begin{array}{c}
\textbf{revising the curriculum} \\
\text{to recognize . . .} \\
\text{and} \\
\textbf{reorganizing the division} \\
\text{to reflect. . . .}
\end{array}
\right\}
$$

Certain nonparallel coordinations occur in well-written prose. For example, careful writers coordinate a noun phrase with a *how*-clause:

$$
\boldsymbol{\checkmark}\text{ We will attempt to delineate}\;\left\{
\begin{array}{c}
\textbf{the problems} \text{ of education} \\
\text{in developing nations} \\
\text{and} \\
\textbf{how coordinated efforts} \\
\textbf{can address} \text{ them in} \\
\text{economical ways.}
\end{array}
\right\}
$$

Or they coordinate an ADVERB with a prepositional phrase:
Careful readers do not blink at either.

$$
\begin{array}{c}
\boldsymbol{\checkmark}\text{ The proposal appears} \\
\text{to have been written}
\end{array}
\;\left\{
\begin{array}{c}
\textbf{quickly,} \\
\textbf{carefully,} \\
\text{and} \\
\textbf{with the help} \text{ of many.}
\end{array}
\right\}
$$

We respond to coordination best when the elements are coordinate not only in grammar but in thought. This seems "off":

Many voters [believe that elected officials are abusing their office], [are calling for term limits], **and** [in that way think that they can get rid of them].

Those three elements are grammatically coordinate, but not logically. They are a sequence of cause-effect/cause-effect:

✓ Many voters believe **so** strongly that elected officials are abusing their office **that** they are calling for term limits **in order to** get rid of them.

Unfortunately, I can't tell you how to recognize when elements are not coordinate in thought.

> *Here's the point:* When you extend a sentence, consciously try to coordinate elements that are both grammatically and logically parallel.

Unclear Connections

Readers are also bothered by a coordination so long that they lose track of its internal connections and pronoun references:

Teachers should remember that students are vulnerable and uncertain about those everyday, ego-bruising moments that adults ignore, and that they do not understand that one day they will become as confident and as secure as the adults that bruise them.

We sense a flicker of hesitation about where to connect:

. . . and that they do not understand that one day they . . .

To revise a sentence like that, shorten the first half of the coordination, then start the second half closer to the point where the coordination began:

✓ Teachers should remember that students are vulnerable to ego-bruising moments that adults ignore and that they do not understand that one day . . .

If you can't do that, repeat a word that reminds the reader where the coordination began (thereby creating a resumptive modifier):

✓ Teachers should try to remember that students are vulnerable to ego-bruising moments that adults ignore, **to remember** that they do not understand that . . .

Misplaced or "Squinting" Modifiers

Another problem with modifiers is that sometimes we are unsure what they modify:

> Overtaxing oneself in physical activity too frequently results in injury.

What happens too frequently, overtaxing or injuries? We can make its meaning unambiguous by moving *too frequently:*

> ✓Overtaxing oneself too frequently in physical activity results in injury.

> ✓Overtaxing oneself in physical activity results too frequently in injury.

A modifier at the end of a clause can ambiguously modify either a neighboring or a more distant phrase:

> Scientists have learned that their observations are as subjective as those in any other field **in recent years.**

We can move the modifier to a less ambiguous position:

> ✓**In recent years,** scientists have learned that . . .

> ✓Scientists have learned that **in recent years** their . . .

> *Here's the point:* Even well-constructed long sentences can give readers a problem if they can't connect the second part of a coordination to its starting point or if they are unsure about what a phrase actually modifies.

INTRINSIC SENSE

You can use these devices to shape a long yet clear sentence, but not even the best syntax can salvage one if its content is incoherent. This next sentence appeared in a Sunday *New York Times* travel section. The sentence before had introduced the professional women of Amsterdam's red-light district:

> They are so unself-conscious about their profession that by day they can be seen standing naked in doorways, chatting with their neighbors in the shadow of the Oudekerstoren Church, which offers Saturday carillon concerts at 4 P.M. and a panoramic view of the city from its tower in summer.

This syntactically well-formed sentence opens with a coherent clause:

> They are so unself-conscious about their profession that by day they can be seen standing naked in doorways . . .

It continues with a free modifier:

> chatting with their neighbors in the shadow of the Oudekerstoren Church . . .

then concludes with a relative clause containing a balanced pair of direct objects:

. . . which offers
{
Saturday carillon concerts at 4 P.M.
and
a panoramic view of the city from its tower in the summer.
}

But the movement of ideas is goofy (or evidence of a sly sense of humor).

SUMMING UP

Here are the principles for giving sentences a coherent shape:

1. Get quickly to the first word of the subject, then to the verb and its object.

   a. Avoid long introductory phrases and clauses. Revise them into their own independent clauses:

   > Since most undergraduate students change their major fields of study at least once during their college careers, many more than once, **first-year students w**ho are not certain about their program of studies they want to pursue should not load up their first-year schedules to meet requirements for a particular program.

   > ✓**Undergraduate students** change their major fields at least once during their college careers, so **first-year students** should not load up their schedules with requirements for a particular program if they are not certain about the program of studies they want to pursue.

   b. Avoid long subjects. Revise a long subject either into an introductory subordinate clause:

   > **A company that focuses on hiring the best personnel and then trains them not just for the work they are hired to do**

but for higher-level jobs is likely to earn the loyalty of its employees.

✓**When a company focuses on hiring the best personnel and then trains them not just for the work they are hired to do but for higher-level jobs later,** it is likely to earn the loyalty of its employees.

If the new introductory clause is very long, try shifting it to the end of its sentence:

✓A company is likely to earn the loyalty of its employees **when it focuses on hiring the best personnel and then trains them not just for the work they are hired to do but for higher-level jobs later.**

Or just break it out in a sentence of its own:

✓**Some companies focus on hiring the best personnel and then train them not just for the work they are hired to do but for higher-level jobs later.** Such companies are likely to earn the loyalty of their employees.

c. Avoid interrupting subjects and verbs, and verbs and objects. Move the interrupting element either to the beginning or end of the sentence, depending on what the next sentence is about:

Some scientists, **because they write in a style that is impersonal and objective,** do not easily communicate with laypeople.

✓**Because some scientists write in a style that is impersonal and objective,** they do *not easily communicate with laypeople. This lack of communication* damages . . .

✓Some scientists do not easily communicate with laypeople **because they write in a style that is impersonal and objective. It is a kind of style filled with passives . . .**

2. After the main clause, avoid adding one subordinate clause to another to another to another . . .

   a. Trim relative clauses and break the sentences into two:

   Of the areas of science **that** are important to our future, few are more promising than genetic engineering, **which** is a new way of manipulating the elemental structural units of life itself,

which are the genes and chromosomes **that** tell our cells how to reproduce to become the parts **that** constitute our bodies.

✓Many areas of science are important to our future but few are more promising than genetic engineering. It is a new way of manipulating the elemental structural units of life itself, **which** are the genes and chromosomes **that** tell our cells how to reproduce to become the parts that constitute our bodies.

✓Of the many areas of science ~~that are~~ important to our future, few are more promising than genetic engineering, ~~which is~~ a new way of manipulating the elemental structural units of life itself, ~~which are~~ the genes and chromosomes that tell our cells how to reproduce to become the parts ~~that~~ constituting our bodies.

b. Extend the line of a sentence with resumptive, summative, and free modifiers:

✓**Resumptive:**   When we discovered that the earth was not the center of the universe, it reshaped our understanding of who we are, **an understanding that was changed again by Darwin, again by Freud, and again by Einstein.**

✓**Summative:**   After a period of uncertainty, American productivity has risen to new heights, **an achievement that only a decade ago was considered an impossible dream.**

✓**Free:**   Global warming will become a central political issue of the 21st century, **raising questions whose answers will affect the standard of living in every Western nation.**

c. Coordinate elements that are parallel not only in grammar but in sense:

Besides the fact that no civilization has experienced such rapid alterations in their spiritual and mental lives, the material conditions of their daily existence have changed greatly too.

✓No civilization has experienced such rapid alterations in their spiritual and mental lives and in the material conditions of daily existence.

A last note: To write complex sentences clearly, you need good punctuation. See the Appendix.

9

Elegance

In literature the ambition of the novice is to acquire the literary language; the struggle of the adept is to get rid of it.
—GEORGE BERNARD SHAW

Anything is better than not to write clearly. There is nothing to be said against lucidity, and against simplicity only the possibility of dryness. This is a risk well worth taking when you reflect how much better it is to be bald than to wear a curly wig.
—SOMERSET MAUGHAM

But clarity and brevity, though a good beginning, are only a beginning. By themselves, they may remain bare and bleak. When Calvin Coolidge, asked by his wife what the preacher had preached on, replied "Sin," and, asked what the preacher had said, replied "He was against it," he was brief enough.
But one hardly envies Mrs. Coolidge.
—FRANK L. LUCAS

Read over your compositions, and wherever you meet with a passage which you think is particularly fine, strike it out.
—SAMUEL JOHNSON

LEARNING WHAT CANNOT BE TAUGHT

Anyone who can write clearly, concisely, and coherently should rejoice to achieve so much. But while most of us prefer bald clarity to the density of typical institutional prose, we may feel that relentless simplicity is dry, even arid. It has the spartan virtue of unsalted meat and potatoes, but such fare is rarely memorable. A flash of elegance can not only fix a thought in our minds, but give us a flicker of pleasure every time we recall it. This lesson is for those of you who aim at more than clear and coherent prose, who like to write not just for its utility, but for the pleasure it can give both your reader and yourself.

Unfortunately, I can't tell you how to do that. In fact, I incline toward those who think the best eloquence is disarming simplicity—and so when you think you have written something particularly fine, I would second Samuel Johnson's advice to strike it out. Nevertheless, there are a few devices that express thoughts in ways that are both elegant and clear.

Just knowing them, however, is about as helpful as just knowing the ingredients in the bouillabaisse of a great cook and then thinking you can make it. Knowing ingredients and knowing how to combine them distinguishes reading cookbooks and Cooking. Maybe it's a gift. But even a gift has to be educated and practiced.

BALANCE AND SYMMETRY

What most makes a sentence graceful is a balance and symmetry among its parts so that one echoes another in sound, rhythm, structure, and meaning. A skilled writer can balance almost any two parts of a sentence, but the most common balance comes from COORDINATION.

Balanced Coordination

Here is a balanced passage and my revision. A tin ear can distinguish them:

1a. The national unity of a free people depends upon a sufficiently even balance of political power to make it impracticable for the administration to be arbitrary and for the opposition to be revolutionary and irreconcilable. Where that balance no longer exists, democracy perishes. For unless all the citizens of a state are forced by circumstances to compromise, unless they feel that they can affect policy but that no one can wholly dominate it, unless by habit and necessity they have to give and take, freedom cannot be maintained.

—Walter Lippmann

1b. The national unity of a free people depends upon a sufficiently even balance of political power to make it impracticable for an administration to be arbitrary against a revolutionary opposition that is irreconcilably opposed to it. Where that balance no longer exists, democracy perishes, because unless all the citizens of a state are habitually forced by necessary circumstances to compromise in a way that lets them affect policy with no one dominating it, freedom cannot be maintained.

My sentences lurch from one part to the next. In Lippmann's, we hear one CLAUSE and PHRASE echo another in word order, sound, and meaning, giving the whole passage an intricate architectural symmetry.

If we extend the concepts of TOPIC and STRESS from a sentence to its parts, we can see how he balances even short segments. Note how each significant word in one phrase echoes another in its corresponding one. (I boldface topics of phrases and italicize stresses.):

The national unity of a free people depends upon a sufficiently even balance of political power to make it impracticable

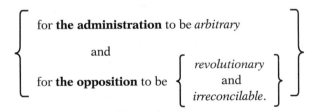

Lippmann balances the phrasal topics of *administration* and *opposition,* and closes by balancing the stressed sounds and meanings of *arbitrary, revolutionary,* and *irreconcilable.*

He follows with a short concluding sentence whose stressed words are not coordinated, but still balanced (I use square brackets to indicate noncoordinated balance):

Where [**that balance** *no longer exists,*
democracy *perishes.*]

Then he creates an especially intricate design, balancing many sounds and meanings:

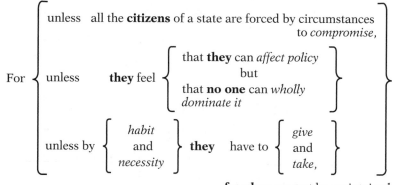

For { unless all the **citizens** of a state are forced by circumstances to *compromise,*

unless **they** feel { that **they** can *affect policy* but that **no one** can *wholly dominate it* }

unless by { *habit and necessity* } **they** have to { *give and take,* } }

freedom cannot be *maintained.*

- He repeats *citizens* as the SUBJECT/topic of each clause: *all the citizens, they, they* (note the passive in the first one: *citizens are forced*).

- He balances the sound and sense of *force* against *feel,* and the meaning of *affect policy* against the meaning of *dominate it.*

- In the last *unless*-clause, he balances the meaning of *habit* against *necessity,* and the stressed *give* against *take.*

- Then to balance the clauses of that short preceding sentence, *balance no longer exists—democracy perishes,* he concludes with an equally short clause, *freedom cannot be maintained,* whose meaning and structure echo the corresponding pair in the preceding sentence:

  balance   no longer exists
  democracy   perishes
  freedom   cannot be maintained

For those who care, it is an impressive construction.

Uncoordinated Balance

We can also balance structures that are not grammatically coordinate. In this example, the subject balances the OBJECT:

> **Scientists** whose research *creates revolutionary views of the universe*
>
> invariably upset
>
> **those of us** who *construct our vision of reality out of our common sense experience of it.*

Here, the PREDICATE of a RELATIVE CLAUSE in a subject balances the predicate of the sentence:

> A government
> > that is unwilling to *listen* to the *moderate* hopes of its *citizenry*
> >
> > must eventually *answer* to the *harsh* justice of its *revolutionaries.*

Here a direct object balances the object of a PREPOSITION:

Those of us concerned with our school systems will not sacrifice

> the *intellectual growth* of   our *innocent children*
> > to
> the *social engineering* of   *incompetent bureaucrats.*

A more complicated balance:

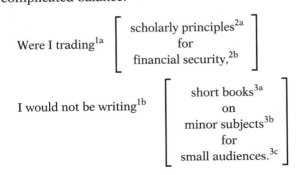

Were I trading[1a]
> scholarly principles[2a]
> for
> financial security,[2b]

I would not be writing[1b]
> short books[3a]
> on
> minor subjects[3b]
> for
> small audiences.[3c]

That sentence balances

- a SUBORDINATE CLAUSE (1a), *Were I trading*, against the MAIN CLAUSE (1b), *I would not be writing;*
- the object of that subordinate clause (2a) *scholarly principles*, against the object in the prepositional phrase (2b) *financial security;*
- the object in the main clause (3a) *short books*, against the objects in two prepositional phrases, (3b) *minor subjects*, and (3c) *small audiences* (and note the balance of *short, minor*, and *small*).

Used to excess, these patterns can seem merely clever, but used prudently, they can emphasize an important point or conclude the line of an argument with a flourish that careful readers notice.

These patterns can also help your own thinking by encouraging you to think of things you might not have otherwise. Suppose you begin a sentence like this:

> In his earliest years, Picasso was a master draftsman of the traditional human form.

Now try this:

> In his earliest years, Picasso was **not only** a master draftsman of the traditional human form, **but also** . . .

Now you have to wonder what else he might have been. Or not have been.

Here's the point: The most striking feature of elegant prose is balanced sentence structures. You can most easily balance one part of a sentence against another by coordinating them with *and, or, nor, but*, and *yet*, but you can also balance noncoordinated phrases and clauses.

CLIMACTIC EMPHASIS

Light and Heavy Words

When we get close to the end of a sentence, we expect words that deserve STRESS (p. 98), so we may feel a sentence is anticlimactic if it ends on words of slight grammatical or semantic weight. At the end of a sentence, prepositions feel light—one reason we sometimes avoid leaving one there. The rhythm of a sentence should carry readers toward strength. Compare:

> Studies into intellectual differences among races is a project that only the most politically naive psychologist is willing to give support to.

> ✓ Studies into intellectual differences among races is a project that only the most politically naive scientist is willing to support.

ADJECTIVES and ADVERBS are heavier than prepositions, but lighter than NOUNS, the heaviest of which are NOMINALIZATIONS. Readers may have problems with nominalizations at the beginning of a sentence, but at the end they provide a satisfyingly climactic thump, particularly when paired. Consider this excerpt from Winston Churchill's "Finest Hour" speech. Churchill ended with a parallelism climaxed by a balanced pair of heavy nominalizations:

> . . . until in God's good time,

$$\text{the New World, with all its} \left\{ \begin{array}{c} \text{power} \\ \text{and} \\ \text{might} \end{array} \right\} \text{steps forth to}$$

$$\left\{ \begin{array}{c} \text{the \textbf{rescue}} \\ \text{and} \\ \text{the \textbf{liberation}} \end{array} \right\} \text{of the old.}$$

He could have written more simply, and more banally:

> . . . until the New World rescues us.

Elegant Stress: Three Devices

Here are three ways to end a sentence with special emphasis.

1. *of* + **Nominalization.** This seems unlikely, but it's true. Look at how Churchill ends his sentence: The light *of* (and an equally light *a* or *the*) quickens the rhythm just before the stress of the climactic monosyllable, *old:*

   > . . . the rescue and the liberation of the **old.**

   We associate this pattern with self-conscious elegance, as in the first few sentences of Edward Gibbon's *History of the Decline and Fall of the Roman Empire:*

✓In the second century of the Christian era, the Empire of Rome comprehended **the fairest part** *of* **the earth,** AND **the most civilized portion** *of* **mankind.** The frontiers of that extensive monarchy were guarded **by ancient renown** AND **disciplined valour.** The gentle but powerful influence of laws and manners had gradually cemented **the union** *of* **the provinces.** Their peaceful inhabitants **enjoyed** AND **abused the advantages** *of* **wealth** AND **luxury.** The image of a free constitution was preserved with decent **reverence:** the Roman senate appeared to possess the sovereign authority, and devolved on the emperors all **the executive powers** *of* **government.**

In comparison, this is flat:

In the second century AD, the Roman Empire comprehended **the earth's fairest, most civilized part.** Ancient renown and disciplined valour guarded **its extensive frontiers.** The gentle but powerful influence of laws and manners had gradually **unified the provinces.** Their peaceful inhabitants enjoyed and abused luxurious wealth while decently preserving what seemed to be **a free constitution.** Appearing to possess the sovereign authority, the Roman senate devolved on the emperors all **executive governmental powers.**

2. **Echoing Salience.** Readers hear special emphasis at the end of a sentence when a word or phrase there echoes or contrasts with the meaning of an earlier one. (These examples are all from Peter Gay's *Style in History.*)

✓I have written these essays to anatomize this familiar yet really strange being, **style the centaur;** the book may be read as an extended critical commentary on Buffon's famous saying that **the style is the man.**

When we hear a stressed word echo the sound of an earlier one, these balances are even more emphatic:

✓Apart from a few mechanical tricks of rhetoric, **manner** is indissolubly linked to **matter; style shapes,** and in turn is **shaped** by, **substance.**

✓It seems frivolous, almost inappropriate, to be **stylish** about **style.**

Gay echoes both the sound and meaning of *manner* in *matter*, *style* in *substance*, *shapes* in *shaped by*, and *stylish* in *style*.

3. **Chiasmus.** This is, admittedly, a device interesting perhaps only to those interested in obscure matters of style. It is called *chiasmus* (pronounced 'kye-AZZ-muss,'), from the Greek word for "crossing."

Chiasmus balances two parts, but the second reverses the order of elements in the first. For example, this would be both coordinate and parallel, but not a chiasmus, because the elements in the two parts are in the same order (AB : AB):

✔ A concise style can improve both
$$\left\{ \begin{array}{c} \textbf{our own}^{1A} \;\; \textit{thinking}^{1B} \\ \text{and} \\ \textbf{our readers'}^{2A} \; \textit{understanding.}^{2B} \end{array} \right\}$$

Were we seeking a special effect, we could reverse the order of elements in the second part to mirror those in the first. Now the pattern is not 1A1B : 2A2B, but rather 1A1B : 2B2A:

✔ A concise style can improve not only
$$\left\{ \begin{array}{c} \textbf{our own}^{1A} \textit{thinking}^{1B} \\ \text{but} \\ \text{the } \textit{understanding}^{2B} \textbf{ of our readers.}^{2A} \end{array} \right\}$$

The next example is more complex. The first two elements are parallel, but the last three mirror one another: AB CDE : AB EDC:

$$\left[\begin{array}{l} \text{You}^{A} \quad \text{reveal}^{B} \quad \textbf{your own}^{C} \; \textit{highest rhetorical}^{D} \; \text{SKILL}^{E} \\ \qquad\qquad\qquad \text{by the way} \\ \text{you}^{A} \quad \text{respect}^{B} \; \text{THE BELIEFS}^{E} \text{ most deeply held}^{D} \; \textbf{by your reader.}^{C} \end{array} \right]$$

Here's the point: An elegant sentence should end strongly. There are four ways to achieve that strength:

1. End your sentence with a strong word, typically a nominalization, or even a pair of them.
2. End your sentence with a prepositional phrase introduced by *of.*
3. End your sentence with echoing salience.
4. End your sentence with a chiasmus.

EXTRAVAGANT ELEGANCE

When writers create balanced RESUMPTIVE and parallel SUMMATIVE MODIFIERS (pp. 144–147), we know they are aiming at something special, as in this next passage by Joyce Carol Oates:

> Far from being locked inside our own skins, inside the "dungeons" of ourselves, we are now able to recognize that our minds belong, quite naturally, to a collective "mind," a mind in which we share everything that is mental, most obviously language itself, and that the old boundary of the skin is not boundary at all but a membrane connecting the inner and outer experience of existence. Our intelligence, our wit, our cleverness, our unique personalities—all are simultaneously "our own" possessions and the world's.

> —Joyce Carol Oates, "New Heaven and New Earth"

Here is the anatomy of that passage:

Far from being locked **inside** our own skins,

            inside the "dungeons" of ourselves,

we are now able to recognize

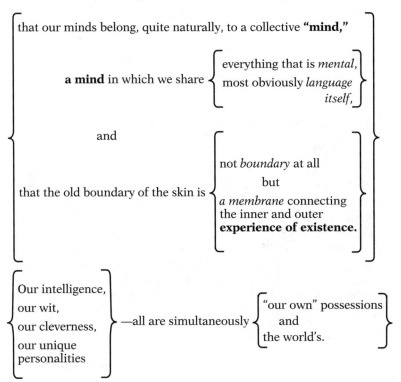

In addition to all the coordination, note the two resumptive modifiers:

> Far from being locked **inside** our own skins,
>   **inside** the "dungeons" of ourselves, . . .
>
> our minds belong . . . to a collective "**mind,**"
>   a **mind** in which we share . . .

Note too the two nominalizations stressed at the end of the first sentence and the coordinate nominalizations at the end of the second:

> . . . the inner and outer experience of existence.
>
> . . . "our own" possessions and the world's.

But such patterns can be more elaborate yet. Here is the climactic sentence from Frederick Jackson Turner's *The Frontier in American History:*

> This then is the heritage of the pioneer experience—a passionate belief that a democracy was possible which should leave the individual a part to play in a free society and not make him a cog in a machine operated from above; which trusted in the common man, in his tolerance, his ability to adjust differences with good humor, and to work out an American type from the contributions of all nations—a type for which he would fight against those who challenged it in arms, and for which in time of war he would make sacrifices, even the temporary sacrifice of individual freedom and his life, lest that freedom be lost forever.

Here is its structure made visible. Note the following:

- The summative modifier in the opening segment: *a passionate belief in . . .*

- The increased length and weight of the second element in each coordination, even the coordinations inside coordinations.

- The two resumptive modifiers beginning with *type* and *sacrifice.*

This then is the heritage of the pioneer experience—
[summative modifier]   a passionate belief that a democracy was possible

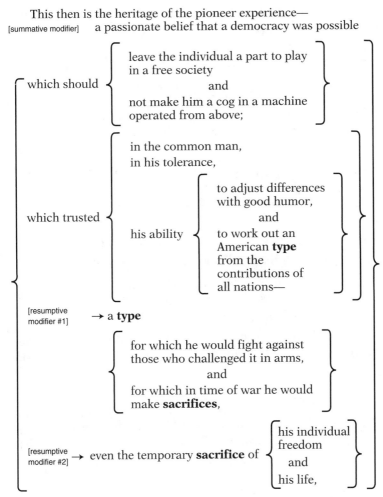

which should {
leave the individual a part to play in a free society
and
not make him a cog in a machine operated from above;
}

which trusted {
in the common man,
in his tolerance,
his ability {
to adjust differences with good humor,
and
to work out an American **type** from the contributions of all nations—
}
}

[resumptive modifier #1] → a **type**

{
for which he would fight against those who challenged it in arms,
and
for which in time of war he would make **sacrifices**,
}

[resumptive modifier #2] → even the temporary **sacrifice** of {
his individual freedom
and
his life,
}

lest that freedom be lost forever.

That may be over the top, especially the quadruple chiasmus in the last 15 words:

the temporary[1] <u>sacrifice</u>[2]   of individual FREEDOM[3] and *his life*[4],

lest[4]   that FREEDOM[3] be   <u>lost</u>[2]   **forever**[1].

The meaning of *temporary* balances *forever; sacrifice* balances *lost; freedom* balances *freedom;* and the sound of *life* balances the sound of *lest* (not to mention the echo of *lest* in *lost*). You just don't see that kind of sentence any more.

Exercise 9.1

You develop a knack for balance by imitating models, not word for word, just their general pattern:

> Survival in the wilderness requires the energy and wit to overcome the brute facts of an uncooperative Nature but rewards the person who acquires that power with the satisfaction of having done it once and with the confidence of being able to do it again.

Think of a subject close to that of the model to make your imitation easy—the academic life, then follow its outline:

> Life as a college student offers a few years of intellectual excitement but imposes a sense of anxiety on those who look ahead and know that its end is in sight.

Use models you find here or in sermons, political speeches, and dictionaries of quotations.

Exercise 9.2

Here are some first halves of sentences to finish with balancing last halves. For example, given this:

> Those who keep silent over the loss of small freedoms . . .

finish with something like this:

> . . . will be silenced when they protest the loss of large ones.

1. Those who keep silent over the loss of small freedoms. . .

2. While the strong are often afraid to admit weakness, the weak . . .

3. We should pay more attention to those politicians who tell us how to make what we have better than to those . . .

4. When parents raise children who do not value the importance of hard work, the adults those children become will . . .

5. Some teachers mistake neat papers that rehash old ideas for . . .

Exercise 9.3

These sentences end weakly. Edit them for clarity and concision, then revise them so that they end on more heavily stressed words, particularly with prepositional phrases beginning with *of.* For example:

> Our interest in paranormal phenomena testifies to the fact that we have **empty spirits and shallow minds.**

> ✓Our interest in paranormal phenomena testifies to **the emptiness of our spirits and the shallowness of our minds.**

In the first three, I boldface words you might nominalize.

1. If we invest our sweat in these projects, we must avoid appearing to work only because we are **interested** in ourselves.

2. The blueprint for the political campaign was concocted by those who were not sensitive to what we **needed** most critically.

3. Throughout history, science has made progress because dedicated scientists have ignored a **hostile** public that is uninformed.

4. Not one tendency in our governmental system has brought about more changes in American daily life than federal governmental agencies that are very powerful.

5. The day is gone when school systems' boards of education have the expectation that local taxpayers will automatically go along with whatever extravagant things that incompetent bureaucrats decide to do.

Nuances of Length and Rhythm

We usually feel the length of a sentence is an issue only when each in a series is only fifteen or so words long, or much longer. In artful prose, length is designed. Some stylists write short sentences to strike a note of urgency:

> Toward noon Petrograd again became the field of military action; rifles and machine guns rang out everywhere. It was not easy to tell who was shooting or where. One thing was clear; the past and the future were exchanging shots. There was much casual firing; young boys were shooting off revolvers unexpectedly acquired. The arsenal was wrecked . . . Shots rang out on both sides. But the board fence stood in the way, dividing the soldiers from the revolution. The attackers decided to break down the fence. They broke down part of it and set fire to the rest. About twenty barracks came into view. The bicyclists were concentrated in two or three of them. The empty barracks were set fire to at once.
>
> —Leon Trotsky, *The Russian Revolution,* trans. Max Eastman

Or terse certainty:

> The teacher or lecturer is a danger. He very seldom recognizes his nature or his position. The lecturer is a man who must talk for an hour. France may possibly have acquired the intellectual leadership of Europe when their academic period was cut down to 40 minutes. I also have lectured. The lecturer's first problem is to have enough words to fill 40 or 60 minutes. The professor is paid for his time, his results are almost impossible to estimate . . . No teacher has ever failed from ignorance. That is empiric professional knowledge. Teachers fail because they cannot "handle the class." Real education must ultimately be limited to men who INSIST on knowing, the rest is mere sheep-herding.
>
> —Ezra Pound, *ABC of Reading*

Or passion. Here, D. H. Lawrence breaks sentences into FRAGMENTS and what could have been a long paragraph into breathless utterances.

> Let us look at this American artist first. How did he ever get to America, to start with? Why isn't he a European still, like his father before him?

Now listen to me, don't listen to him. He'll tell you the lie you expect. Which is partly your fault for expecting it.

He didn't come in search of freedom of worship. England had more freedom of worship in the year 1700 than America had. Won by Englishmen who wanted freedom and so stopped at home and fought for it. And got it. Freedom of worship? Read the history of New England during the first century of its existence.

Freedom anyhow? The land of the free! This the land of the free! Why, if I say anything that displeases them, the free mob will lynch me, and that's my freedom. Free? Why I have never been in any country where the individual has such an abject fear of his fellow countrymen. Because, as I say, they are free to lynch him the moment he shows he is not one of them. . . .

All right then, what did they come for? For lots of reasons. Perhaps least of all in search of freedom of any sort: positive freedom, that is.

—D. H. Lawrence, *Studies in Classic American Literature*

Self-conscious stylists also write extravagantly long sentences. Here is just a piece of one describing a protest march:

In any event, up at the front of this March, in the first line, back of that hollow square of monitors, Mailer and Lowell walked in this barrage of cameras, helicopters, TV cars, monitors, loudspeakers, and wavering buckling twisting line of notables, arms linked (line twisting so much that at times the movement was in file, one arm locked ahead, one behind, then the line would undulate about and the other arm would be ahead) speeding up a few steps, slowing down while a great happiness came back into the day as if finally one stood under some mythical arch in the great vault of history, helicopters buzzing about, chop-chop, and the sense of America divided on this day now liberated some undiscovered patriotism in Mailer so that he felt a sharp searing love for his country in this moment and on this day, crossing some divide in his own mind wider than the Potomac, a love so lacerated he felt as if a marriage were being torn and children lost—never does one love so much as then, obviously, then—and an odor of wood smoke, from where you knew not, was also in the air, a smoke of dignity and some calm heroism, not unlike the sense of freedom which also comes when a marriage is burst—Mailer knew for the first time why men in the front line of battle are almost always ready to die; there is a promise of some swift transit . . . [it goes on]

—Norman Mailer, *The Armies of the Night*

That bit of a sentence does not sprawl:

- Mailer opens with short, staccato phrases to suggest confusion, but he controls them by coordination.
- He continues the sentence by coordinating free modifiers: *arms linked . . . (line twisting . . .) speeding up. . .*
- After several more free modifiers, he continues with a resumptive modifier: *a love so lacerated . . .*
- After another GRAMMATICAL SENTENCE, he adds another resumptive modifier: *a smoke of dignity and some calm heroism . . .*

We almost feel we are overhearing his stream of thought. But of course, such a sentence is the product not of impulse of but of deliberate art.

> ***Here's the point:*** You should be concerned about sentence length only if they are all longer than thirty words or so or shorter than fifteen. Your sentences will vary naturally if you simply edit them in the ways you've seen here.

Exercise 9.4

Combine Lawrence and Pound's sentences into longer ones, like Mailer's. Break up Mailer's sentence into shorter ones in the style of Lawrence and Pound. How do they differ? Imitate the style of Lawrence, Pound, and Mailer. Then transform your Lawrence imitation into a Mailer imitation, and vice versa. Only by expressing the same ideas in different styles can you see how different styles can seem to change ideas (a self-conscious chiasmus there).

METAPHOR

Clarity, vigor, symmetry, rhythm—prose so graced is a great achievement. But it does not excite admiration for the reach of its writer's imagination. This next passage displays all these stylistic devices, but goes beyond craft to reveal a truth about pleasure through a figure of speech embedded in a comparison that is itself metaphorical (I boldface the metaphors):

> The secret of the enjoyment of pleasure is to know when to stop. . . . We do this every time we listen to music. We do not **seize hold** of a particular chord or phrase and shout at the orchestra to go on playing it for the rest of the evening; on the contrary, however much we may like that particular moment of music, we know that its perpetuation would interrupt and **kill** the movement of the melody. We understand that the beauty of a symphony is less in these musical moments than in the whole movement from beginning to end. If the symphony tries to go on too long, if at a certain point the composer **exhausts** his creative ability and tries to carry on just for the sake of **filling** in the required **space** of time, then we begin to fidget in our chairs, feeling that he has denied the natural rhythm, has **broken the smooth curve from birth to death,** and that though a **pretense of life** is being made, it is in fact a **living death**.
>
> —Alan W. Watts, *The Meaning of Happiness*

Watts could have written this:

> . . . however much we like that moment, we know that its perpetuation would interrupt and spoil the movement of the melody. We begin to fidget, feeling he has denied the natural rhythm, has interrupted the regular movement from beginning to end, and that though he makes a pretense of wholeness, it is in fact a repeated end.

The sentences are clear, but lack that startling metaphor of birth and of its smooth curve into death.

Metaphor can vivify all kinds of prose. Social critics use it:

> The schoolmaster is the person who takes the children off the parents' hands for a consideration. That is to say, he establishes a child prison, engages a number of employee schoolmasters as turnkeys, and covers up the essential cruelty and unnaturalness of the situation by torturing the children if they do not learn, and calling this process, which is within the capacity of any fool or blackguard, by the sacred name of Teaching.
>
> —George Bernard Shaw, *Sham Education*

So do historians:

> This is what may be called the common-sense view of history. History consists of a corpus of ascertained facts. The facts are available to the historian in documents, inscriptions, and so on, like fish on

the fishmonger's slab. The historian collects them, takes them home, and cooks and serves them in whatever style appeals to him. Acton, whose culinary tastes were austere, wanted them served plain . . . Sir George Clark, critical as he was of Acton's attitude, himself contrasts the "hard core of facts" in history with the "surrounding pulp of disputable interpretation"—forgetting perhaps that the pulpy part of the fruit is more rewarding than the hard core.

—E. H. Carr, *What Is History?*

So do biologists:

Some of you may have been thinking that, instead of delivering a scientific address, I have been indulging in a flight of fancy. It is a flight, but not of mere fancy, nor is it just an individual indulgence. It is my small personal attempt to share in the flight of the mind into new realms of our cosmic environment. We have evolved wings for such flights, in shape of the disciplined scientific imagination. Support for those wings is provided by the atmosphere of knowledge created by human science and learning: so far as this supporting atmosphere extends, so far can our wings take us in our exploration.

—Julian Huxley, "New Bottles for Old Wine," *Journal of the Royal Anthropological Institute*

And philosophers:

Quine has long professed his skepticism about the possibility of making any sense of the refractory idioms of intentionality, so he needs opacity only to provide a quarantine barrier protecting the healthy, extensional part of a sentence from the infected part.

—Daniel C. Dennett, "Beyond Belief"

And even physicists, when they lack terms for new ideas:

Whereas the lepton pair has a positive rest mass when it is regarded as a single particle moving with a velocity equal to the vector sum of the motions of its two components, a photon always has zero rest mass. This difference can be glossed over, however, by treating the lepton pair as the offspring of the decay of a short-lived photonlike parent called a virtual photon.

—Leon M. Lederman, "The Upsilon Particle," *Scientific American*

These metaphors serve different ends. Shaw and Carr use metaphor to intensify their language. Dennett and Lederman use their comparisons simply to explain, and maybe to play a bit.

Of metaphor, Aristotle wrote,

> By far the greatest thing is to be a master of metaphor. It is the one thing that cannot be learned from others. It is a sign of genius, for a good metaphor implies an intuitive perception of similarity among dissimilars.

But when that perception is not quite right, we can seem foolish— Huxley comes close with his wings of inquiry flapping in an atmosphere of knowledge.

We have to be especially careful that a metaphor does not distort the idea that we want to express, like this:

> Societies give birth to new values through the osmotic flow of daily social interaction. Conflicts evolve when old values collide with new, a process that frequently spawns a new set of values that synthesize the conflict into a reconciliation of opposites.

The birth metaphor suggests a traumatic event, but new values, it is claimed, result from osmotic flow, a process of invisibly small events. Conflicts do not "evolve"; they more often occur in an instant, as implied by the metaphor of collision. The spawning image echoes the metaphor of birth, but by this point the image is a bit silly.

Had the writer thought more carefully, he might have expressed himself more exactly—and gracefully—in literal language:

> ✓ As we interact in small ways, we gradually create new social values. When we behave according to an old value and someone else according to a new one, our values may conflict, but they may also create a third value that reconciles the conflict.

Metaphors can also embarrass us when their literal meanings unexpectedly revive, as in this student example:

> The classic blitzkrieg relies on a tank-heavy offensive force, supported by ground-support aircraft, to destroy the defender's ability to fight by running amuck [sic] in his undefended rear, after penetrating his forward defenses.

Here's the point: The risk in striving for elegance is that you fail spectacularly and never risk it again. I can only encourage you to accept with good humor those first awkward failures that we all survive.

SUMMING UP

The qualities of elegance are so varied and subtle that no summary can capture them. Nevertheless, elegant passages typically have three characteristics that seem incompatible, but are not:

- The simplicity of characters as subjects and actions as verbs.
- The complexity of balanced syntax, meaning, sound, and rhythm.
- The emphasis of a strongly stressed ending.

Walter Lippmann's passage illustrates all three:

> The national unity of a free people depends upon a sufficiently even balance of political power to make it impracticable for the administration to be arbitrary and for the opposition to be revolutionary and irreconcilable. Where that balance no longer exists, democracy perishes. For unless all the citizens of a state are forced by circumstances to compromise, unless they feel that they can affect policy but that no one can wholly dominate it, unless by habit and necessity they have to give and take, freedom cannot be maintained.

He uses only five nominalizations in 88 words: *balance* twice, and *unity, necessity,* and *freedom* once each. Almost all subjects are short, naming his key characters.

The only way to acquire an elegant style is to read enough of it until you get a sense of how it works in your nerves and bones. Only then can you look at your own prose and know when it is elegant, or just inflated. The only reliable rule, I think, is "Less is more." Of the many graces of style, compression is still the first.

S U M M A R Y : P A R T 3

In addition to the principles we laid out in Part 2, we add these four:

1. Prune redundancy.
2. Get to the verb in the main clause quickly.
    a. Keep introductory clauses and phrases short.
    b. Keep subjects short.
    c. Don't interrupt the subject-verb connection.
3. Avoid extending the line of a sentence by attaching more than one subordinate clause to one of the same kind. Instead,
    a. coordinate phrases and clauses, balanced ones if you seek a special effect.
    b. use resumptive, summative, and free modifiers.
4. Try balancing parts of sentences against one another, especially their last few words.

PART FOUR

Ethics

Ethics is in origin the art of recommending to others the sacrifices required for cooperation with oneself.

—BERTRAND RUSSELL

Lesson

10

The Ethics of Prose

There is no artifice as good and desirable as simplicity.
—St. Francis de Sales

Everything should be made as simple as possible, but not simpler.
—Albert Einstein

Affected simplicity is refined imposture.
—La Rochefoucauld

*Many a writer seems to think he is never profound except when he
can't understand his own meaning.*
—George D. Prentice

*Everyone calls "clear" those ideas which have the
same degree of confusion as his own.*
—Marcel Proust

*Essentially style resembles good manners. It comes of endeavouring
to understand others, of thinking for them rather than yourself—
or thinking, that is, with the heart as well as the head.*
—Sir Arthur Quiller-Couch

Beyond Polish

It is easy to think that attention to style is simply a way to polish your sentences, to make them merely more appealing, But more than appeal is at stake in choosing subjects and verbs in these two sentences:

> 1a. **Serbs and Albanians** DISTRUST each other because **they** HAVE ENGAGED in generations of cultural conflict.
>
> 1b. **Generations of cultural conflict** HAVE CREATED distrust between Serbs and Albanians.

Which sentence better reflects what causes distrust between Serbs and Albanians—their deliberate actions, as in (1a), or the circumstances of their history, as in (1b)? In fact, our choices of subjects and verbs even reflect a philosophy of human action: Do we freely choose to act, or do our circumstances choose our actions for us? It is not a stretch to see in our choices a reflection of that age-old debate about free will and determinism. So our choices of what character to tell a story about—people or their circumstances—involve more than ease of reading; indeed, even more than a philosophy of action, because those choices have an ethical dimension, as well.

The Ethical Responsibilities of Writers and Readers

In the last nine lessons, I have relentlessly emphasized the responsibility we owe our readers to be clear, but as socially responsible readers, we also have a responsibility toward writers to read hard enough to understand the necessary complexity in what they write. Genuinely complex ideas can't always be expressed in Dick-and-Jane sentences. It would be impossible, for example, for an engineer to revise this into language clear to everyone:

> The drag force on a particle of diameter d moving with speed u relative to a fluid of density p and viscosity μ is usually modeled by $F = 0.5C_D u^2 A$, where A is the cross-sectional area of the particle at right angles to the motion.

To be sure, some readers invest less time and effort than what they are reading deserves. But most of us work hard to understand—at least until we decide that a writer hasn't worked equally hard to help us, or, worse, has deliberately made our reading more difficult than it has to be. Once we decide that a writer was careless or thoughtless—well, the number of our days is too few to spend them on the writing of those indifferent to our needs.

But that response to gratuitous complexity in what we read only re-emphasizes our own responsibility when we write, for it seems axiomatic that if we don't want others to impose on us writing that is carelessly complex, then we ought not impose that kind of writing on others. If we are socially responsible writers, we work hard to make our ideas no more difficult than they have to be.

Responsible writers follow a rule whose more general model you probably recognize:

> Write to others as you would have others write to you.

Few of us deliberately flout that principle. It's just that we are all inclined to think that our own writing is so clear that if our readers struggle to understand it, then the source of their problem must be not in our incompetent writing but in their incompetent reading.

But that is a serious mistake, because a writer indifferent to his readers' needs risks more than losing merely their attention. He risks losing what writers since Aristotle have called a reliable *ethos*. Your ethos is the character readers infer from your writing: Does it make them think you are thoughtfully diffident or arrogantly certain? Amiably candid or impersonally aloof? Over time, the ethos you project in individual pieces of writing settles into your reputation, and we tend to trust most a writer with a reputation for being thoughtful, reliable, and aware of her readers' needs. So it's not just altruistically generous to go an extra step to help readers understand. It's pragmatically smart.

But there is more at stake here than just reputation.

AN ETHIC OF STYLE

What is at stake is the ethical basis of a literate society. Writing is ethical when as a matter of principle, we would trade places with our intended readers and willingly experience what they do as they read our writing. Since none of us would willingly submit ourselves to the effort of hacking through gratuitously unclear writing, it seems self-evidently unethical to impose that kind of writing on others. Unfortunately, it's not quite that simple. How, for example, do we think about those who write opaquely without knowing they do; or those who knowingly write that way but defend it?

Unintended Obscurity

Those who write in ways that seem dense and convoluted rarely think they do, much less intend to. Their own writing is clear to them, so they think it must be clear to others. Then they are surprised when their readers say it is not. For example, I do not believe that the writers of this next passage *intended* to write it as unclearly as they did:

> A major condition affecting adult reliance on early communicative patterns is the extent to which the communication has been planned prior to its delivery. Adult speech behaviour takes on many of the characteristics of child language, where the communication is spontaneous and relatively unpredictable.
>
> —E. Ochs and B. Schieffelin, *Planned and Unplanned Discourse*

That means (I think),

> When adults speak spontaneously they rely on patterns of child language.

The authors might object that I have oversimplified their meaning, but those eleven words express what I got from their forty-four.

The ethical issue here is not those two writers' willful indifference, but their innocent ignorance. In that case, when writers don't know better, readers who do (as I hope you do now) have the duty to meet another term of the reader-writer contract: not just to read carefully, but when given the opportunity, to respond candidly and helpfully.

I know that many of you think you are in no position to do that. But as presumptuous as it may sound, you can, for example, express a useful opinion to teachers about their selection of books, if you do it responsibly, like rewriting a part that seems unnecessarily difficult to demonstrate the soundness of your views.

Intended Misdirection

The ethics of writing are clearer when a writer hides behind language deliberately. For example, a few years ago, the Sears Company was accused of overcharging for automobile repairs. Sears responded with an ad saying:

With over two million automotive customers serviced last year in California alone, mistakes may have occurred. However, Sears wants you to know that we would never intentionally violate the trust customers have shown in our company for 105 years.

In the first sentence, the writer avoided mentioning Sears as the party responsible for mistakes. He could have used a PASSIVE VERB:

> . . . mistakes **may have been made.**

But that would have encouraged us to wonder "By whom?" Instead, the writer found a verb that moved Sears into the background by saying mistakes just *occurred*, seemingly on their own.

In the second sentence of that ad, though, the writer made *Sears* the specific responsible agent, because he wanted to emphasize Sears' good actions.

> **Sears** . . . would never intentionally violate . . .

If we revise the first sentence to make Sears explicit and the second to hide Sears, we get a very different effect:

> When we serviced over two million automotive customers last year in California, we made mistakes. However, you should know that no intentional violation of 105 years of trust occurred.

The misdirection in that ad seems harmless enough, but now consider this letter from a natural gas utility telling me and hundreds of thousands of other customers that it was raising our rates. (The TOPIC/SUBJECT in every CLAUSE, MAIN or SUBORDINATE, is boldfaced.)

> **The Illinois Commerce Commission** has authorized a restructuring of our rates together with an increase in Service Charge revenues effective with service rendered on and after November 12, 1990. **This** is the first increase in rates for Peoples Gas in over six years. **The restructuring of rates** is consistent with the policy of the Public Utilities Act that **rates for service to various classes of utility customers** be based upon the cost of providing that service. **The new rates** move revenues from every class of customer closer to the cost actually incurred to provide gas service.

That notice is a model of misdirection: After the first sentence, the writer never begins a sentence with a human character, least of all the character whose interests are most at stake—me, the reader. He (or perhaps she) mentions me only twice, in the third person, never as a topic/agent/subject:

> for services to various classes of utility **customers**
>
> move revenues from every class of **customer**

The writer mentions the company only once, in the third person, and not as a responsible topic/agent/subject:

> increase in rates for **Peoples Gas**

Had the company wanted to make clear who the real "doer" was and who was being done to, the notice would have read more like this:

> According to the Illinois Commerce Commission, **we** can now charge you more for your gas service after November 12, 1990. **We** have not made you pay more in over six years, but under the Public Utilities Act, now **we** can.

If the writer *intended* to deflect responsibility, then we can reasonably charge him with breaching the first Rule of Ethical Writing, for surely, he would not want that same kind of writing directed to him, systematically hiding who is doing what.

Here is a passage that raises ethical issues involving life and death. Some time ago, the Government Accounting Office investigated why more than half the automobile owners who got recall letters did not comply with them. It found that they could not understand the letters or were not moved by them. I received the following. It shows how writers can meet a legal obligation while evading an ethical one (I number the sentences):

> [1]A defect which involves the possible failure of a frame support plate may exist on your vehicle. [2]This plate (front suspension pivot bar support plate) connects a portion of the front suspension to the vehicle frame, and [3]its failure could affect vehicle directional control, particularly during heavy brake application. [4]In addition, your vehicle may require adjustment service to the hood secondary catch system. [5]The secondary catch may be misaligned so that the hood may not be adequately restrained to prevent hood fly-up in the event the primary latch is inadvertently left unengaged. [6]Sudden hood fly-up beyond the secondary catch while driving could impair driver visibility. [7]In certain circumstances, occurrence of either of the above conditions could result in vehicle crash without prior warning.

(When asked what make of car the letter refers to, I dodge the question.)

First, look at the subject/topics of the sentences.

[1]a defect	[2]this plate	[3]its failure
[4]your vehicle	[5]the secondary catch	
[6]sudden hood fly-up	[7]occurrence of either condition	

The topic of that story is not me, the driver, but my car and its parts. In fact, the writers ignored me almost entirely (I am in *your vehicle* twice and *driver* once) and omitted all references to themselves. In sum, it says,

> There is a car that might have defective parts. Its plate could fail and its hood fly up. If they do, it could crash and nobody will warn it.

The writers—probably a committee of lawyers—also NOMINALIZED VERBS and made others passive when they referred to actions that might frighten me:

failure	vehicle directional control	heavy brake application
be misaligned	not restrained	hood fly-up
left unengaged	driver visibility	warning

If the writers intended to deflect my fear and maybe my anger, then they violated their ethical duty to write to me as they would have me write to them, for surely they would not swap places with readers deliberately lulled into ignoring a condition that threatened their lives. If they would not, then by their prose style they breached their ethical duty to write to others as they would have others write to them.

Of course, being candid has its costs. I would be naive to claim that we are all free to write as we please, especially when a job depends on protecting an employer's self-interest. Maybe the writers of that letter felt coerced into writing it as they did. But that doesn't mitigate the consequences. When we knowingly write in ways that we would not want others to write to us, we at least abrade the fabric of trust that sustains a civil society.

We should not confuse unethical indirectness with the human impulse to soften bad news. When a supervisor says:

> I'm afraid our new funding didn't come through.

we know it means "You have no job." But that indirectness is motivated not by dishonesty, but by kindness.

It is important to note exactly where these writers focused their attention: They chose the subject/topics of their sentences very carefully, in all three cases choosing subject/topics that deflected attention from themselves and from their reader (me). Subjects are a key element when we want to be clear. But they are also crucial when we want to be honest or misleading.

Exercise 10.1

Revise the gas rate notice, using *you* as a topic/agent/subject. Then revise again, using *we*. For example:

> As the Illinois Commerce Commission has authorized, **you** will have to pay us higher service charges after November 12, 1990/**we** can charge you more after November 12 . . .

Would the company resist sending either revision? Why? Was the original "good" writing? What do you mean by "good"?

Exercise 10.2

Revise the recall letter, making *you* the subject of as many verbs and naming as many actions in verbs as you can. One of the sentences will read,

> If **you** BRAKE hard and the plate FAILS, **you** will . . .

Would the company be reluctant to send out that version? Is the original letter "good" writing? Which of the following, if either, is closer to the "truth"? Is that even the right question?

> If the plate fails, you could crash.
>
> If the plate fails, your car could crash.

Are the ethical issues involved here different from those in the Sears ad or the gas company notice?

Rationalizing Opacity

A more complicated ethical issue is responding to those who know they write in a complex style, but claim they must, because they are breaking new intellectual ground. Are they right, or is that just self-indulgence? This is a vexing question not just because we can settle it only case-by-case, but because we may not be able to settle it at all, at least not to everyone's satisfaction.

Here, for example, is a sentence from a leading figure in contemporary literary theory:

> If, for a while, the ruse of desire is calculable for the uses of discipline soon the repetition of guilt, justification, pseudo-scientific theories, superstition, spurious authorities and classifications can be seen as the desperate effort to "normalize" *formally* the disturbance of a discourse of splitting that violates the rational, enlightened claims of its enunciatory modality.
>
> —Homi K. Babba

Is that the expression of a thought so complex, so nuanced that what it says can be said only as it's said? Or is it babble? How do we decide whether in fact his nuances are, at least for ordinarily competent readers, just not accessible given the time most of us have for finding them?

Most of us think that what we have to say is worth our readers' time. But we usually think we've said it more clearly than our readers think we have, because we know the nuanced complexity we intended. We can never be sure, however, that our readers, even our best readers, will devote the time necessary to find them.

We owe readers an ethical duty to write precise and nuanced prose, but we ought not assume that they owe us an indefinite amount of their time to unpack it. If we choose to write in ways that we think represent the full complexity of our nuanced thinking, knowing that readers will think our writing is too dense and complex—well, it's a free country. In the marketplace of ideas, truth is the most important value, but not the only one. Another is the time it takes to dig it out of extremely complex writing.

At the end of the day, I can suggest only that when writers claim their prose style must be dense because their ideas are new, they are, as a matter of simple fact, more often wrong than right. The philosopher of language Ludwig Wittgenstein said,

> Whatever can be thought can be thought clearly; whatever can be written can be written clearly.

I'd like to add a nuance of my own:

> With a bit more effort, whatever we can think and write can usually be thought and written *more* clearly.

Salutary Complexity/Subversive Clarity

There are two more defenses of complexity: One claims that complexity is good for us, the other that clarity is bad.

As to the first claim, some argue that the harder we have to work to understand what we read, the more deeply we think. Everyone should be happy to know that no evidence supports such a claim, and substantial evidence contradicts it.

As to the second claim, some argue that "clarity" is a device wielded by those in power to mislead us about the real powers that control our lives. By making things deceptively simple, they say, those who feed us information oversimplify it, rendering us unable to understand the full complexity of our political and social circumstances. Here is an example:

> The call to write curriculum in a language that is touted as clear and accessible is evidence of a moral and political vision that increasingly collapses under the weight of its own anti-intellectualism . . . [T]hose who make a call for clear writing synonymous with an attack on critical educators have missed the role that the "language of clarity" plays in a dominant culture that cleverly and powerfully uses "clear" and "simplistic" language to systematically undermine and prevent the conditions from arising for a public culture to engage in rudimentary forms of complex and critical thinking.
>
> —Stanley Aronowitz, *Postmodern Education*

He makes one good point: Language is deeply implicated in politics, ideology, and control. In our earliest history, the educated elite used writing itself to exclude the illiterate, then Latin and French to exclude those who knew only English. In more recent history, those defending authority of a variety of kinds have relied on a vocabulary thick with Latinate nominalizations and on a Standard English that requires those Outs aspiring to join the Ins to submit to a decade-long education, during which time they are expected to acquire not only their language but their values, as well.

In the same way, clarity is not a natural virtue corrupted by fallen academics, bureaucrats, and others jealous to preserve their authority. It is a value that is created by society, and that society must work hard to maintain, for it is not just hard to write clearly; it is almost an unnatural act.

So is "clarity" an ideological value? Of course it is. How could it be otherwise? But those who attack clarity as part of an ideological conspiracy are as wrong as those who attack science on the same grounds: Neither science nor clarity is a threat; the threat is from those who use clarity (or science) deceptively. So it is not clarity that subverts, but the unethical use of it. We must simply insist that, in principle, those who manage our affairs have a duty to tell us the truth as clearly as they can. They probably won't, but that just shifts the burden to us.

With every sentence we write we have to choose, and the ethical quality of those choices depends on the motives that drive them. Only by knowing motives can we know whether a writer of clear prose would willingly be the object of such writing, to be influenced (or manipulated) in the same way, with the same result.

AN EXTENDED ANALYSIS

It's easy to abuse writers who manipulate us. It's more difficult to think about these matters when we are manipulated by writers whom we would never charge with deceit. But it is just such cases that force us to think hard about matters of style and ethics.

The most celebrated texts in our history are the Declaration of Independence, the Constitution, Abraham Lincoln's Gettysburg Address, and his Second Inaugural Address. In previous editions of this book, I discussed how the styles of the Gettysburg Address and the Declaration are not innocently clear. Here I examine the style of Lincoln's Second Inaugural Address.

Lincoln delivered it in March 1865, just before the end of the Civil War. He knew the North would win, but worried that it would punish the South for both slavery and the carnage of the war. As we have seen, he was right to worry. Anticipating that outcome, Lincoln tried to reconcile North and South in words engraved in our national memory:

> With malice toward none; with charity for all; with firmness in the right, as God gives us to see the right, let us strive on to finish the

work we are in; to bind up the nation's wounds; to care for him who shall have borne the battle, and for his widow, and his orphan—to do all which may achieve and cherish a just, and a lasting peace, among ourselves, and with all nations.

We have, however, forgotten his opening sentences, because we are stirred by neither the elegance of their language nor the loftiness of their thought:

Fellow-countrymen: At this second appearing to take the oath of the presidential office, there is less occasion for an extended address than there was at the first. Then a statement, somewhat in detail, of a course to be pursued, seemed fitting and proper. Now, at the expiration of four years, during which public declarations have been constantly called forth on every point and phase of the great contest which still absorbs the attention and engrosses the energies of the nation, little that is new could be presented. The progress of our arms, upon which all else chiefly depends, is as well known to the public as to myself; and it is, I trust, reasonably satisfactory and encouraging to all. With high hope for the future, no prediction in regard to it is ventured.

In fact, were that paragraph anonymous, we might judge it pedestrian, because it is as abstract and impersonal as the worst institutional prose. He could have written this:

Fellow-countrymen: As **I appear** here for the second time to take the oath of the presidential office, **I** have less occasion to **address** you at length than **I** did at the first. Then **I** thought it fitting and proper that **I state** in detail the course to be pursued . . .

In fact, that is close to the style of his First Inaugural Address:

Fellow-citizens of the United States: In compliance with a custom as old as the government itself, **I appear** before you to address you briefly, and to take before you the oath prescribed by the Constitution . . . **I** do not **consider** it necessary at present for me to discuss . . .

Or he could have written this:

Fellow-countrymen: As **we** meet for this second taking of the oath of the presidential office, **we** have less need for an extended address than **we** had at the first. Then **we** felt a statement, describing in detail, the course **we** would pursue, would be fitting and proper . . .

And that is close to the style of the Gettysburg Address:

Now **we** are engaged in a great Civil War, testing whether that nation, or any nation so conceived and so dedicated, can long endure. **We** are met on a great battlefield of that war. **We** have come to dedicate a portion of that field . . .

In fact, Lincoln seems so intent on being impersonal that in his last sentence he dangled a modifier:

With high hope for the future, no prediction in regard to it is ventured.

Either Lincoln dozed, or he had something else in mind.

In that first paragraph, the topics of his sentences deflect our attention from the participants and focus it on the event and his message:

this second appearing to take the oath of presidential office, there is . . .

a statement . . . seemed fitting

public declarations . . . have been constantly called forth

little that is new . . . could be presented

The progress of our arms . . . is well known

it [progress of arms] . . . is encouraging to all.

no prediction is ventured.

Why did he choose that impersonality (assuming he did)? We might understand if we look at the rest of the speech. As you read, notice his subjects (boldfaced):

On the occasion corresponding to this four years ago, **all thoughts** were anxiously directed to an impending civil war. **All** dreaded it—**all** sought to avert it. While **the inaugural address** was being delivered from this place, devoted altogether to saving the Union without war, **insurgent agents** were in the city seeking to destroy it without war—seeking to dissolve the Union, and divide effects, by negotiation. **Both parties** deprecated war, but **one of them** would make war rather than let **the nation** survive; and **the other** would accept war rather than let **it** perish. And **the war** came.

One eighth of the whole population were colored slaves, not distributed generally over the Union, but localized in the southern part of it. **These slaves** constituted a peculiar and powerful interest.

All knew that **this interest** was, somehow, the cause of the war. **To strengthen, perpetuate, and extend this interest** was the object for which **the insurgents** would rend the Union, even by war; while **the government** claimed no right to do more than to restrict the territorial enlargement of it. **Neither party** expected for the war the magnitude or the duration which **it** has already attained. **Neither** anticipated that **the cause of the conflict** might cease with, or even before, **the conflict** itself should cease. **Each** looked for an easier triumph and a result less fundamental and astounding. **Both** read the same Bible, and pray to the same God; and **each** invokes His aid against the other. It may seem strange that **any men** should dare to ask a just God's assistance in wringing their bread from the sweat of other men's faces; but let **us** judge not, that **we** be not judged. **The prayers of both** could not be answered; **that of neither** has been answered fully. **The Almighty** has His own purposes. "Woe unto the world because of offences! for it must needs be that offences come; but woe to that man by whom the offence cometh." If we shall suppose that **American slavery** is one of **those offences which** in the providence of God, must needs come, but which, having continued through His appointed time, **He** now wills to remove, and that **He** gives to both North and South, this terrible war as the woe due to those by whom **the offence** came, shall **we** discern therein any departure from those divine attributes which **the believers in a Living God** always ascribe to Him? Fondly do **we** hope—fervently do **we** pray—that **this mighty scourge of war** may speedily pass away. Yet, if **God** wills that **it** continue until **all the wealth piled by the bondman's two hundred and fifty years of unrequited toil** shall be sunk, and until **every drop of blood drawn with the lash** shall be paid by another drawn with the sword, as was said three thousand years ago, so still **it** must be said, "**the judgments of the Lord**, are true and righteous altogether."

  With malice toward none; with charity for all; with firmness in the right, as **God** gives us to see the right, let **us** strive on to finish the work **we** are in; to bind up the nation's wounds; to care for **him who** shall have borne the battle, and for his widow, and his orphan—to do all which may achieve and cherish a just, and a lasting peace, among ourselves, and with all nations.

In the first sentence of the second paragraph, Lincoln continues the impersonal style of his introduction, both nominalized and passive:

On the occasion corresponding to this four years ago, **all thoughts** were . . . directed to an impending civil war.

He could have written *everyone was thinking.*

Then for two short clauses, he switches to the simplicity we expect:

All dreaded it—**all** sought to avert it.

But in the next sentence, he adopts the impersonal passive again:

While **the inaugural address** was being delivered . . .

Then he returns to the direct, subject/agent–verb/action style for several sentences (note, however, that the subjects are not specific):

insurgent agents were in the city seeking to destroy it

Both parties deprecated war

one of them would make war

the other would accept war

And **the war** came.

(How can war just "come"? How else could he have expressed that idea?)

He then writes an oddly awkward and passive sentence about slavery:

One eighth of the whole population were colored slaves, not distributed generally over the Union, but localized in the southern part of it.

This would have been more direct:

One eighth of the population were slaves, most of them in the South.

In the indirectness of that sentence, Lincoln seems to hold slavery at a distance. He does the same in the next two sentences. They begin clearly, but toward their ends, they slip into impersonality:

These slaves constituted a peculiar and powerful interest.

All knew that **this interest** was, somehow, the cause of the war.

(Why didn't he write, *All knew that slavery caused the war*, or even, *The South caused the war*?)

Most of the subjects and verbs in the rest of the sentences reflect the direct style that we associate with Lincoln (but note how indirectly he keeps referring to slavery; I boldface references to it):

> **To strengthen, perpetuate, and extend this interest** was the object
> **the insurgents** would rend the Union
> **the government** claimed no right to do more than to restrict **the territorial enlargement of it**
> **Neither party** expected for the war the magnitude or the duration **it** has already attained
> **Neither** anticipated
> **the cause of the conflict** might cease
> **the conflict** itself should cease

(How can slavery and the war just "cease"? How else could he have written that?)

At this point, Lincoln's style quickens through a series of short clauses as he introduces God as a character, not yet as an active agent, but as a passive OBJECT of prayers and requests:

> **Each** looked for an easier triumph
> **Both** read the same Bible, and pray to the same **God.**
> **each** invokes **His** aid against the other.
> **any men** should dare to ask a just God's assistance in wringing their bread from the sweat of other men's faces
> let **us** judge not

Then in three short passive clauses, Lincoln implies that God can act, but has not yet acted as either side has prayed:

> that **we** be not judged [by God?]
> **The prayers of both** could not be answered;
> **that of neither** has been answered fully.

Lincoln then returns to his direct active style, naming God in the subject of four of the next eleven clauses as an acting, purposeful agent:

> **The Almighty** has His own purposes.
> If **we** shall suppose that
> **American slavery** . . . must needs come
> **He** now wills to remove
> **He** gives to both North and South this terrible war
> shall **we** discern therein any departure from those attributes

the believers in a living God always ascribe to Him?

Fondly do **we** hope—fervently do **we** pray

this mighty scourge of war may speedily pass away

Yet, if **God** wills that

it continue until

all the wealth piled . . . toil shall be sunk,

every drop of blood . . . shall be paid by another

the judgments of the Lord, are true

Then the majestic climax we all remember:

With malice toward none . . . let **us** strive on to finish the work we are in;

In other words, once Lincoln gets past that first abstract and indirect paragraph and a half, he generally demonstrates what we take to be his classic American style: clear, candid, simple, and direct.

With one exception.

Of all the sentences crafted by American writers, none, I think, is craftier than this one, the longest in the speech, and by far the most complex:

If we shall suppose that American slavery is one of those offences which in the providence of God, must needs come, but which, having continued through His appointed time, He now wills to remove, and that He gives to both North and South this terrible war as the woe due to those by whom the offence came, shall we discern therein any departure from those divine attributes which the believers in a living God always ascribe to Him?

In that seventy-eight-word sentence. Lincoln argues that the North has no right to punish the South for the war, because the war was brought by God:

He gives to both North and South this terrible war . . .

Nor was it the North that ended slavery. God did that, too:

He now wills to remove [this offence of American slavery]

And (as he implies a few sentences later) it will not be a triumphant North that ends the war, but God, at a time of His own choosing:

If **God** wills [to] continue [the war]

In other words, the North has no right to punish the South for the war or to take credit for ending it or slavery: It's God's doing. That's the point of the speech.

But before he made God responsible for the war and its end, he wrote this oddly indirect passage about the origin of slavery:

> **American slavery** is one of those **offences which** in the providence of God, must needs come

(It recalls "the war came," also apparently on its own, and that the conflict and cause of the conflict should just "cease.")

This clause is ambiguous in two ways: First, how are we to understand the phrase "American slavery"? Is "American" the agent of slavery as in "Americans enslave Africans," or its object, as in "Americans are enslaved"? Or both?

Second, how are we to understand the verb *continued?*

> . . . one of those offences . . . which, having continued through His appointed time, He now wills to remove

It could mean *the offence of slavery continued through His appointed time,* or it could mean *God continued the offense of slavery.* Which is it? Or is it both?

But what really distinguishes this passage is its nominalizations. There are only five in these seventy-eight words, a low proportion for a dramatic speech. But three of them occur in just the first sixteen words. We could revise them into verbs and assign them subject/agents:

American **slavery**	→ Americans **ENSLAVE** Africans
is one of those **offences**	→ Americans **OFFENDED** God
which in the **providence** of God	→ God **PROVIDES** [something]

If we reassemble those clauses into a sentence, we get a startling claim:

> God provided that Americans enslave Africans, and that offended God.

Might we reasonably suppose that Lincoln thought such a direct statement would raise a theological issue so thorny that, at least on this occasion, he would just as soon avoid it?

To be sure, Lincoln believed that God had ordained every terrible thing that happened to both North and South. And he had no problem saying clearly that God *gave* the war to both sides, that God *willed* the end of slavery (as opposed to its just "ceasing," as he had written earlier), and though he prays the war will "pass away," he also knows that God might *will* it to continue.

But he seems unwilling to make slavery God's explicit responsibility. He uses direct verbs to express God's agency in bringing the war and ending both it and slavery, but he nominalizes verbs that would make God responsible for slavery, then buries that agency in the middle of the sentence (*in the providence of God*).

That seventy-eight-word sentence is, I think, the stylistic *tour de force* of American literature. But what does that have to do with his impersonal opening paragraph? Perhaps this: Lincoln believed that the enormity of the war was God's doing and that both North and South had earned God's punishment. In fact, the only time he refers to North or South by name, he makes them the object of God's wrath:

> He gives to both North and South this terrible war . . .

He made all the other subject/topic/agents nonspecific, even vague: *agents, parties, one, the other, both, all, each, neither, any man.* In fact, Lincoln seems deliberately to avoid assigning any action to any specific agent, until he introduces God.

And perhaps that explains the impersonality of that opening paragraph. Knowing he would later focus on God as the only specific agent in the story of the Civil War, he wanted to create an indefinite, impersonal blue/gray–gray/blue background to subordinate everyone else's role in American history, including his own, to God's direct agency.

It is a great speech, especially that last sentence whose words are part of our national conscience. But even the parts that feel uninspired now seem at least explicable.

But now recall the question that motivated this discussion: What are we to make of these stylistic sleights-of-hand, of the hyper-complexity of that key sentence? How do we judge the way Lincoln (what word do we use—manipulates? handles? manages?) shapes the responses of his audience? In so doing, was he unethical? The easy answer is no, and I think that's right, at least if we judge by his intentions. But the question forces us to think hard about the ethic of clarity as an unqualified, foundational value. Lincoln was not clear, and, I think, deliberately and rightly so.

Exercise 10.3

There are 702 words in the Second Inaugural. In most prose, the proportion of nominalizations to other words is roughly 1:10, with 1:6 high and 1:20 very low. Count the nominalizations in this speech. What do you make of their proportion to all words? We saw that nine nominalizations appeared in the first 134 words, or about 1:15. What is the proportion in the rest of the speech? Where are the other nominalizations concentrated? Why? Do you think that proportion affects how we respond to this speech?

Exercise 10.4

Pick out every mention of the word *war* or references to it. (There are sixteen.) Look at its function in each sentence: Is it a subject or object? Does Lincoln seem to use the word systematically? Compare it to how he uses the word *slavery* and words for it, such as *interest* and *cause*.

Exercise 10.5

Lincoln distanced God from slavery as deliberately as the writer of the automobile recall letter distanced the manufacturer from its defective product. What kinds of ethical distinctions, if any, would you make between them?

Exercise 10.6

Break up the "If we shall suppose" sentence into shorter sentences. What is the effect? You could begin

Suppose that American slavery . . .

Exercise 10.7

Read the Declaration of Independence. It is divided into three parts:

- A philosophical explanation of when a people may replace one form of government with another. Most of the subjects in this part are abstractions.
- Beginning at "To prove this," a list of charges against King George. Most of the subjects in this section are *he*.
- Beginning at "In every stage of these Oppressions," an account of attempts to avoid separation, followed by the last sentence declaring independence. Most of the subjects in this section are *we*.

Jefferson seemed systematically to shift topics through each section. Why? Here is the first sentence of the first section:

> When in the Course of human events, **it becomes necessary** for one people to dissolve the political bands which have connected them with another . . .

He could have written:

> In the course of human events, **we** decided that **we** had to dissolve . . .

He wrote the first charge against King George like this:

> **He** has refused his Assent to Laws.

He could have written it like either of these two:

> There have been **repeated refusals** of Assent to Laws.
> **We** have been refused his Assent to Laws.

And he wrote the first sentence of the last part like this:

> Nor have **We** been wanting in attention to our British brethren.

He could have written it like either of these two:

> Nor have **our British brethren** been wanting for our attention.
> **Attention** has been directed to our British brethern as well.

Can you explain why Jefferson systematically varied the topics as he did? What effect was he seeking? Revise some sentences in the first part so that they are more like sentences in the last part, some sentences in the last part so that they are more like those in the first part, then some of the sentences in the middle part so that they are more like those in either the first or last parts. What effect do those changes have? In particular, what do you make of these next constructions? (Review p. 196.) Subjects are italicized, verbs capitalized:

> a decent *respect* to the opinions of mankind REQUIRES
>
> *Prudence*, indeed, will DICTATE
>
> all *experience* hath SHEWN
>
> the *necessity* . . . CONSTRAINS them to alter their . . . Government
>
> the *necessity* . . . DENOUNCES [proclaims] our Separation

Exercise 10.8

Revise Lincoln's Gettysburg Address so that the topics are not human characters, but abstractions or the place. The first sentence might be,

> Fourscore and seven years ago, **this continent** witnessed our fathers' bringing forth a new nation. **It** was conceived in Liberty and dedicated to the proposition that **equality** is the birthright of all.

How do the new topics change the impact of the speech?

Exercise 10.9

There are 262 words in the Gettysburg Address. Count the nominalizations (ignore the words *living* and the *dead*, but include *battle* in *battleground*). How does the relative frequency of nominalizations affect the way this speech strikes you? Where are most of the nominalizations? Why there?

SUMMING UP

How, finally, do we decide what counts as "good" writing? Is it clear, graceful, and candid, even if it fails to achieve its end? Or is it writing that gets its job done, regardless of its intention and means? The best writing is both, of course. But we have a problem so long as *good* can mean either ethically sound or pragmatically successful. We can resolve that dilemma by our First Principle of Writing: We write well when we would willingly experience what our readers do when they read what we've written. That puts the burden on us to imagine our readers and their feelings.

If you are even moderately advanced in your academic or professional career, the issues we've examined are familiar. You've experienced the consequences of unclear writing, especially when it is your own. If you are in your early years of college, though, you may wonder whether all this talk about clarity, ethics, and ethos is just a lot of finger wagging. At the moment, you may be happy just to find enough words to fill up three pages, much less worry how clear they are. And you may be reading textbooks that have been written, rewritten, revised, and edited to make them clear to first-year students. So you may not yet have experienced carelessly dense writing. But it's only a matter of time before you will.

If that's so, why struggle toward clarity when obscurity seems to pay off? And on top of that, why not follow your predictable and virtually irresistible desire to sound like someone who belongs in the world you're struggling to join? What experienced readers know, and you eventually will, is that clear and graceful writers are so few that we are deeply grateful when we find them.

I also know that for many writers the pleasure of crafting a good paragraph is often just in the achievement of it. It is an ethical satisfaction some of us find not just in writing, but in everything we do: We take pleasure in doing good work, no matter the job, a view expressed by the philosopher Alfred North Whitehead, with both clarity and grace:

> Finally, there should grow the most austere of all mental qualities; I mean the sense for style. It is an aesthetic sense, based on admiration for the direct attainment of a foreseen end, simply and without waste. Style in art, style in literature, style in science, style in logic, style in

practical execution have fundamentally the same aesthetic qualities, namely, attainment and restraint. The love of a subject in itself and for itself, where it is not the sleepy pleasure of pacing a mental quarter-deck, is the love of style as manifested in that study. Here we are brought back to the position from which we started, the utility of education. Style, in its finest sense, is the last acquirement of the educated mind; it is also the most useful. It pervades the whole being. The administrator with a sense for style hates waste; the engineer with a sense for style economizes his material; the artisan with a sense for style prefers good work. Style is the ultimate morality of mind.

—Alfred North Whitehead, *The Aims of Education and Other Essays*

EPILOGUE

From Clarity to Coherence

We want what we read to be clear, but it has to be coherent, because while we can hack our way through unclear sentences, incoherence just defeats us. In Lessons Five and Six, I looked at three things that contribute to what I'll call "local" coherence, the coherence that unifies an individual passage:

- Individual sentences follow the old-new principle, connecting to the one before and after. See p. 80 for an example.
- Sentences in a passage focus on a just few topics. See p. 85.
- The passage, whether a paragraph or a section, opens with a short segment that (1) announces key concepts in what follows and (2) states its point or claim. See p. 107.

But there is a larger, more important sense of coherence that depends on our unifying locally coherent passages into a globally coherent whole. We do that when we understand the point of what we are reading and why we are reading it. In this Epilogue, I look at four elements that help readers see that larger sense of coherence, particularly how you use the introduction to what you write to motivate readers to read the rest purposefully and attentively. It's the first step in helping them think that you write not just clearly but coherently.

CREATING GLOBAL COHERENCE

Readers judge your writing to be globally coherent when they

- see your main point;
- understand the relevance of its parts to that point;
- recognize the principle behind the order of those parts; and
- read it all purposefully and attentively.

Your challenge is to help them do that.

1. Make Your Main Point Clear

Just as each section and paragraph should have a point or claim of its own, so must your whole piece of writing (another term is *thesis*). If you are writing an argument, your main point will probably be a claim proposing that your readers (or someone) *do* something:

> To manage the problem of binge drinking by college students, colleges must educate first-year students about its risks.

Or it might ask them not to act, but just to *understand* or *believe* something:

> A tendency toward binge drinking by first-year college students appears to correlate with a tendency toward risk-taking.

Or it might describe information that your readers will find in what follows:

> In this report, we describe programs run by several colleges to educate first-year students in the risks of binge drinking.

Some writers hold off stating their main claim until their conclusion, fearing that if readers don't like it, they will stop reading. That's usually a bad strategy. Most of us can see an unwelcome claim coming long before we read it. More important, when we see a point in an introduction, we can judge the relevance of everything that follows (a principle that also applies to sections and paragraphs). If we can't see the relevance of what we read, we may judge it to be incoherent. So it's a good idea to state your main point early, at the end of your introduction. (Apply the same principle to most of your paragraphs and sections, as well.)

2. Make Everything Relevant to Your Point

I'm sorry to say I can't be helpful about relevance, because it is so abstract; I can only list some of its kinds. Readers will judge parts of a piece of writing to be relevant to its main point (or to its sub-points) if they think those parts are any of these:

- Background/contextual information on the topic.
- A reason supporting the main point.
- Evidence, facts, or data supporting a reason.
- An explanation of complex ideas.
- An explanation of your reasoning or methods.
- Consideration of other points of view.
- Personal reflection on any of this.

If your readers can't put most of what they read into one of those categories, they are likely to judge it incoherent.

3. Make Your Organization Clear

Readers want to see not just the relevance of the parts of your writing to your point, but the principle you used in arranging their order. We look for three kinds of order: coordinate, chronological, and logical.

- **Coordinate.** Two or more sections are coordinate with one another when they are like pillars supporting a roof. *There are three reasons why. . .* , and each section discusses a reason supporting your point. You must, however, order those sections so that their sequence makes sense to your reader—by importance, complexity, and so on. Then you must clearly signal that order with *first, second, . . .* or *also, another, more important, in addition,* and so on.
- **Chronological.** Parts are ordered from earlier-to-later (or vice-versa), either as a narrative or as cause-and-effect. Signal time with *first, then, finally;* signal cause-and-effect with *as a result, because of that,* and so on.

- **Logical.** Parts are ordered by example and generalization (or vice-versa), premise and conclusion (or vice-versa), or by assertion and contradiction. Signal logic with *for example, in contrast, therefore, consequently*, and so on.

Once you settle on a way to order the parts, make sure your readers can see where one part stops and another begins. Use signaling words generously and headings, if they are appropriate. (Organize each section and paragraph by one of those principles, as well.)

To make their plan clear, experienced writers often preview it, as I did:

> In this Epilogue, I look at four elements that help readers see that larger sense of coherence, particularly how you use the introduction to what you write to motivate readers to read the rest purposefully and attentively.

4. Motivate Your Readers to Read Purposefully

We depend on all those elements to find the coherence in what we read, but we must be *motivated* to look for it, to read purposefully. And we read most purposefully when we read about a problem and a solution that we care about. That means that even before you begin drafting, you must see your task as writing something that will solve a problem that is *important to your readers*. Try to imagine that problem from *their* point of view; then when you draft, state it in your introduction so clearly that they recognize their interest in seeing how you solve it. Readers are less likely to care about what you write if you offer only a topic, because a mere topic gives them no good reason to read on (unless they have an intrinsic interest in that topic).

Compare these two introductions. The first offers only a topic; it does not motivate us to care about it:

> When college students go out to drink, many "binge," drinking until they are intoxicated or even pass out. This behavior has been growing at colleges and universities everywhere. It once was done mostly by men, but now even women are bingeing. It has drawn the attention of concerned parents, college administrators, and even researchers, and has been widely reported in newspapers around the country.

In contrast, this next introduction both tells us why we should care about bingeing and sketches a solution:

Drinking has been part of American college life for more than three centuries. It has been accepted, even expected, as part of growing up. But a style of college drinking known as "binge" drinking, drinking to get intoxicated quickly, is spreading. Bingeing is far from harmless. In the last six months, it has been cited in three deaths from alcohol poisoning, two from falls, and one in a car crash. It crosses the line from fun to a recklessness that kills and injures not just drinkers but those around them. We cannot end it, but we can control its worst costs by educating students in managing its risks.

In what follows, I explain how that introduction motivates purposeful reading. To do that, I first have to explain how problems work.

TWO KINDS OF PROBLEMS

There are two kinds of problems that motivate us to read purposefully: *pragmatic* and *conceptual*. They motivate our reading in different ways.

Pragmatic Problems

A pragmatic problem is the kind we avoid because it makes us unhappy. If we can't avoid it, we have to *do* something to make it go away. So we pay attention if you describe a problem we care about and offer a solution. You can name a pragmatic problem in a word or two: *AIDS, terrorism, racial profiling*. But its name is only half of the problem—we'll call it its *condition*. The second part of a problem is the effect of that condition—call it the *cost* of the problem: AIDS causes suffering, terrorism causes death, high tuition causes hardship, and costs like those make us unhappy. To define a problem fully, you have to name *both* its condition and its costs.

You may think that the costs of problems like homelessness, drugs, or binge drinking are so obvious that you don't have to name them. But your readers may not know those costs as well as you do, or even know them at all. For example, you might think that the costs of binge drinking in college are obvious—the drinker's injury, or even death. But a callous reader might think, *So what?* If so, you have not named costs that *your reader* has to pay.

But if you cite as a cost injury to *others*, that reader might respond not with, *So what*, but with, *What do we do?* To identify costs, imagine readers who keep asking, *So what?* to the cost of the condition, until you *know* that they would ask, *What do we do?*

At that point you have purposeful readers who will work hard to make sense of what you have written.

Here is that better introduction with its parts labeled (I insert *So what?* where a reader would want to know the costs of not solving the problem):

> Drinking has been part of American college life for more than three centuries. It has been accepted, even expected, as part of growing up. But a style of college drinking known as "binge" drinking, drinking to get intoxicated quickly, is spreading. _{condition} [*So what?*] Bingeing is far from harmless. In the last six months, it has been cited in three deaths from alcohol poisoning, two from falls, and one in a car crash. It crosses the line from fun to a recklessness that kills and injures not just drinkers but those around them. _{cost} We cannot end it, but we can control its worst costs by educating students in managing its risks. _{solution}

The other introduction only implies a problem:

> When college students drink, many "binge," consuming large amounts of alcohol at one sitting until they pass out. This behavior has been growing . . . . It once was mostly a male form of behavior, but now even women are bingeing in increasing numbers. This behavior has drawn the attention of parents, administrators, and even state legislators. [*So what?*]

Sometimes, a writer writes about a pragmatic problem not to solve it, but simply to show us that it exists. We can, for example, turn that first introduction into a problem-*posing* one simply by omitting the solution:

> Drinking has been part of American college life . . . , It has been accepted . . . as part of growing up. But . . . "binge" drinking, drinking to get intoxicated quickly, is spreading, _{condition} [*So what?*] and it is far from harmless. _{cost/main claim}

What follows would be organized around a list of its costs.

Conceptual Problems

Conceptual problems have the same parts as pragmatic ones, a condition and its costs, but beyond that, they are very different.

- Pragmatic problems are everywhere, but conceptual ones are typically posed and solved in academic settings.

- Those whose business is solving them don't avoid them; in fact, they look for them, and the harder they are, the better.

- The condition of a pragmatic problem can be anything, but the condition of a conceptual one is always something we do not know or understand. And, as we shall see, so is its cost.

- Most important, we solve pragmatic problems by getting readers to do something (or to support someone else's doing something), but we solve conceptual problems by getting readers simply to *understand* or *believe* something.

Those new to academic research often find conceptual problems difficult to grasp, so I'll discuss them in some detail.

Defining a Conceptual Problem

We can phrase the condition of conceptual problems as something that is not known or understood:

> We don't know how many stars are in the sky. _{condition}

(Here is where it gets complicated.) We phrase the cost of a conceptual problem as a second, *more important* thing that is also not known, as a direct consequence of not knowing the first thing. That second thing we don't know should answer someone who asks of the first thing that skeptical question, *So what if you never find out?* Imagine this conversation:

> We don't know how many stars are in the sky. _{condition/first thing not known}
>
> *So what if you never find out?*
>
> Until we do, we can't know something more important: Does the universe have enough gravity to hold it together? _{cost/second thing not known}

If that person doesn't again ask, *So what?*, but wants to know how many stars are in the sky *so that* he can know whether there is enough gravity for the universe to hold together, then you've stated a cost that makes him think that the first question is worth not only answering, but asking, and that you have posed a good conceptual problem.

But what if he asks again, *So what?*

> So what if you don't know whether there's enough gravity to hold the universe together?

At that point, you'd have to state something still more important to know:

> If we don't know whether the universe has enough gravity to hold it together, then we can't answer a more important question yet: Will the universe one day cease to exist? _{cost/third thing not known}

If that person asked, *So what?* again, you'd have to think, *Wrong audience.*

All this is very hard to grasp if you are new to doing and reporting academic research. But you must understand it, if you expect your readers to read purposefully and attentively. We are all motivated to read about pragmatic problems, because they are the kind that we all want to eliminate. But those new to academic research don't know what questions make good conceptual problems. To find them, newcomers have to read the books and journals in their field and talk with teachers and colleagues.

Introducing Conceptual Problems

To introduce a conceptual problem, focus on what your readers don't know but should want to. (What follows is abbreviated; each sentence could be expanded to several):

> As health care workers have reported, a style of drinking known as "bingeing" has spread across campuses, causing death and injury to drinkers and those around them. The causes and long-term effects of alcoholism are well understood. But the causes of bingeing by first- and second-year college students are not well understood. _{condition} [*So what?*] Until we understand those causes better, we cannot know whether college bingeing leads to alcohol problems after college. _{cost} Our study of 300 first- and second-year college students who reported bingeing once a week suggests that most students binge because of social situations unique to the first years of college, because when they leave college, they seem to have no more alcohol problems than those who do not binge regularly. _{solution}

If readers start reading a report thinking it will discuss merely the *topic* of college bingeing (and they have no intrinsic interest in it), they are unlikely to be motivated to read attentively. But once they can see that answering a question about college bingeing might answer a more important question about adult alcoholism, then they may be more motivated to read attentively, because now they

see that they don't know something they should. Once you motivate readers to read purposefully, they will work hard to find the
coherence in what you write.

COMMON GROUND

You should know about one more element of an introduction, because experienced writers use it so often to motivate readers to read.
We call it *common ground*. We used it in the introduction above:

> **As health care workers have reported, a style of drinking known
> as "bingeing" has spread across campuses, causing death and in-
> jury to drinkers and those around them. The causes and long-
> term effects of alcoholism are well understood**. _{common ground} But
> the causes of bingeing . . .

I began that introduction with two uncontroversial claims that I
hoped you would accept: Bingeing is spreading and the long-term
effects of alcoholism are understood. Then I qualified it with a *but*
that introduced the problem: *But the causes of bingeing . . .* Experienced writers regularly use that move to motivate readers to
read on to find out why what they thought was so is not. It is the
most common introductory move of experienced writers: Open
with a seeming truth, then contradict or qualify it.

Here's the point: We can get through unclear writing, but
incoherence just defeats us. Readers will judge your writing
coherent when they see this:

- Your sentences follow the old-new principle.
- They have consistent topic strings.
- Paragraphs, sections, and the whole open with a short
  segment that (1) introduces key concepts that you develop and (2) states the point of that paragraph, section,
  or whole.
- Everything is relevant to one of the points, subordinate
  or main.
- The order of the parts is apparent and makes sense.

- Most important, your readers see the problem you are addressing and are motivated enough to care about it and its solution to read on purposefully and attentively.

Purposeful and attentive readers are more likely to find coherence in what you write. You motivate purposeful reading with this plan for introductions:

Common Ground + [Condition + Cost] $_{problem}$ + Solution/Main Point

REVISING FOR COHERENCE: A CHECKLIST

Readers create coherence by using the cues that they find in what they read so that they can organize the knowledge they get out of it. As they do that, they also depend on knowledge they bring to their reading, because the more they know about a subject, the better they can shape whatever new they learn about it.

As writers, we can't control how much readers know, but we can help them work with the knowledge they have. What follows is a way to diagnose how well you do that. It is a mechanical process, but it has to be, because when you read your own writing, you will read into it what you hoped to mean when you wrote it, something beyond your readers' ability. What they see is what they get. Following these steps won't guarantee that your readers will think your writing is coherent, but they will help.

1. **Have you motivated readers with the costs of a problem?**
   Look for a few sentences close to (not *at*) the end of your introduction that answer the question, *So what?*

   - If you cannot find them, think again about your problem.

2. **Do readers see your Solution/Main Point/Claim/Purpose?**
   Underline your Main Point in both your introduction and conclusion.

   - If the Main Point in your conclusion is not more detailed, more complex than the one in your introduction, make it so.

   - If you withheld your Main Point until your conclusion, underline the last few sentences in your introduction.

- If your introduction does not introduce key concepts that you use in the Main Point in your conclusion, work them in.

3. **Can readers see both where each section stops and the next begins and why the sections are ordered as they are?**

   a. Draw a line between each section (and subsection, if they are long).

      - If a section does not open with a short segment, a sentence or two that introduce that section, write one.

   b. Circle the first few words of the first sentence in each segment.

      - If those words do not signal readers they are starting a new section, add some that do.

      - If those words do not signal how each section relates to the previous one, revise them so that they do.

      - If a long section (more than a page) does not end with a sentence that wraps up that section, add it.

4. **Can readers see the point of each section?**

   a. Highlight the sentence that states the point of each section.

      - If you can't find a point, create one.

      - If that point is not at the end of a short introductory segment, you must have good reason for why it is not.

   b. Read those short opening segments as if they were a paragraph.

      - If they do not make sequential sense, revise them so that they do.

5. **Can readers see throughout your writing the key ideas they saw in your introduction and will see in your conclusion?**

   a. Circle four or five key concepts in your Main Point in both your introduction and conclusion; if you withheld your Main Point until your conclusion, circle four or five key concepts in the last two sentences of your introduction.

- If you cannot find four or five key concepts, in your conclusion and introduction, revise them to make them more explicit.

b. In the rest of your piece of writing, circle those same concepts, synonyms for them, and concepts closely related to them.

- If you circle few words, revise each section to include more of them.

c. For each section, find its point, circle its key words; then circle the same and related words in the rest of that section.

- If you find few, revise to include them.

d. Read the body of your piece of writing, watching for frequently repeated concepts that you did *not* use in your introduction.

- If you find any, revise your introduction to include them.

6. **Can readers see how everything is relevant to a point?** Identify the relevance of each section (even each sentence) to its point. (See p. 211 for kinds of relevance.)

- If you cannot identify the relevance of anything, clarify or cut it.

7. **Can readers see how subject/topics in sentences in a section are a related string of familiar characters?**

a. For each sentence in a section, underline its first several words.

- If those words are not subject/topics making a set of related words that name your main characters, revise so they are.

b. Do the underlined words name concepts that readers would expect, given the topic or remember from a sentence that they just read?

- If not, revise.

APPENDIX
Punctuation

---

*I know there are some Persons who affect to despise it, and treat
this whole Subject with the utmost Contempt, as a Trifle far
below their Notice, and a Formality unworthy of their Regard:
They do not hold it difficult, but despicable; and neglect it, as being
above it. Yet many learned Men have been highly sensible to its Use;
and some ingenious and elegant Writers have condescended to point
their Works with Care; and very eminent Scholars have not disdained
to teach the Method of doing it with Propriety.*
—James Burrow

*In music, the punctuation is absolutely strict; the bars and rests
are absolutely defined. But our prose cannot be quite strict,
because we have to relate it to the audience. In other words
we are continually changing the score.*
—Sir Ralph Richardson

*One who uses many periods is a philosopher;
many interrogations, a student; many exclamations, a fanatic.*
—J. L. Basford

*There are some punctuations that are interesting
and there are some that are not.*
—Gertrude Stein

*Anyone who can improve a sentence of mine by the omission or
placing of a comma is looked upon as my dearest friend.*
—George Moore

Most of us think commas and semicolons are about as interesting as sorting socks. Used thoughtfully, however, punctuation can help readers not only understand a complex sentence but help them see its nuances. It takes more than a few commas to turn a monotone into the Hallelujah Chorus, but a little care can produce gratifying results.

SOME BASIC CONCEPTS

I'll address punctuation as a functional problem: How do we punctuate the end of a sentence, its beginning, and its middle? But first, I have to distinguish two kinds of sentences.

Punctuated and Grammatical Sentences

I'll call whatever begins with a capital letter and ends with a period or question/exclamation mark a *punctuated sentence*. We have to distinguish two kinds of punctuated sentences, because readers do; the one you are reading, for example, is one long punctuated sentence, but it does not feel as long as another long sentence you will read in a moment; I have chosen to punctuate as one sentence what I might have punctuated as a series of shorter ones; those semicolons and the comma before *but* could have been periods, for example—and that dash could have been a period too.

Here is the sentence you just read repunctuated with virtually no change in its grammar:

> We have to distinguish two kinds of punctuated sentences because readers do. The one you are reading, for example, is one short punctuated sentence. But this paragraph does not feel as long as another sentence you will read in a moment. I have chosen to punctuate as separate sentences what I earlier punctuated as one long one. The period before *but*, for example, could have been a comma. The last two periods could have been semicolons. And that period could have been a dash.

On the other hand, I can write a different kind of long punctuated sentence, one that I can not break into shorter sentences merely by replacing commas and semicolons with periods, because it is a sentence consisting of several SUBORDINATE CLAUSES, all depending on one MAIN or INDEPENDENT CLAUSE—a complex construction that you have almost finished but that probably feels longer than that first long sentence, even though it is actually shorter.

The difference between those two long punctuated sentences is this: Both let you pause for a breath, but the first one doesn't force you to hold in mind a lot of complex grammatical relations, because it consists of little independent grammatical sentences, clauses that we call independent clauses. At the comma, semicolons, and dash, your mind treats what follows as a new sentence, and so grammatically speaking, you start fresh.

On the other hand, that second long sentence forces you to keep sorting out its grammar, right to the end. Just as that first long sentence does, the second one starts with an independent clause:

> I can write a different kind of sentence . . .

But instead of continuing with a series of independent grammatical sentences that you can process individually, it continues with a series of subordinate clauses that you have to keep integrating into a grammatical whole:

> . . . a sentence
>
> [1][that I can not break into shorter punctuated sentences merely by replacing commas and semicolons with periods],
>
> [2][because it is a sentence consisting of several subordinate clauses, all of them depending on one main or independent clause]
>
> [3]—a complex structure like this one
>
> [4][that you have almost finished] but
>
> [5][that probably feels longer than that sentence in the previous paragraph]
>
> [6][even though it is actually shorter].

In this second sentence, you have to keep figuring out to the end how its parts fit together, and that requires more mental work.

We have to distinguish those two kinds of punctuated sentences, because readers respond to them differently: they may complain about the length of both, but it is easier for them to read a long punctuated sentence consisting of short grammatical sentences than it is for them to read a long punctuated sentence that is one long grammatical sentence.

Exercise A.1

Revise that second long sentence beginning with "I can write a different kind of sentence" making some of the subordinate clauses independent clauses. Then set those independent clauses off first with commas, semicolons, and colons. Then punctuate that revised sentence a second time, this time with periods. How have you changed the style of the sentence? Which revision changes the style of the original sentence more radically: periods, or commas and semicolons?

SIMPLE, COMPOUND, AND COMPLEX SENTENCES

At this point, you may be thinking about sentences called "simple," "compound," and "complex." Most of us learned that if a sentence is a single independent clause, it is *simple*:

> SIMPLE: English dictionaries date back more than 400 years.

If it consists of two or more independent clauses, it is *compound*:

> COMPOUND: [English dictionaries date back more than 400 years][1],
> [but the greatest is the *Oxford English Dictionary*][2].

If it has an independent clause and at least one subordinate clause, it is *complex*.

> COMPLEX: [While there are many good dictionaries] subordinate clause
> [the greatest is the *Oxford English Dictionary*] independent
> clause·

But that terminology is misleading, because it encourages us to think that a grammatically simple sentence should *feel* simpler than one that is grammatically complex. For example, most readers think that of the next two, the grammatically simple sentence *feels* more complex than the grammatically complex one:

GRAMMATICALLY SIMPLE: Our review of the test led to our decision as to its suspension as a result of complaints by teachers.

GRAMMATICALLY COMPLEX: When we reviewed the test, we decided to suspend it because teachers complained about it.

Like the words *active* and *passive,* the terms *simple* and *complex* can refer both to our impressions and to grammatical structure.

In what follows, then, I use terms that are a bit different from those you might recall. I will refer only to grammatical and punctuated sentences.

- The term *grammatical sentence* refers to a single independent clause plus all of its attached subordinate clauses, if any. The term therefore covers both simple and complex sentences:

  I left.

  I left because I was tired.

- What we learned to call a *compound* sentence includes at least two grammatical sentences.

  I left,_{grammatical sentence 1} but I returned_{grammatical sentence 2}.

- A *punctuated* sentence may therefore consist of a single grammatical sentence or several.

Punctuating the Ends of Grammatical Sentences

Beyond all other considerations, you have to let readers know where one grammatical sentence stops and the next begins, unlike this sentence:

In 1957 and again in 1960, Congress passed civil rights laws that remedied problems of registration and voting this had significant political consequences throughout the South.

You can separate a pair of grammatical sentences in ten ways. Three are common:

Three Common Forms of End Punctuation

1. Period (or Question/Exclamation Mark) Alone

   The simplest way to signal the end of a grammatical sentence is with a period:

✓In 1957 and 1960, Congress passed laws that remedied problems of registration and **voting. This** had significant political consequences throughout the South.

But if you create too many short punctuated sentences, your readers may feel your prose is choppy or simplistic. Experienced writers revise a series of short grammatical sentences into subordinate clauses or phrases, turning two or more grammatical sentences into one:

✓**After Congress passed laws in 1957 and 1960 to remedy problems of registration and voting,** those laws had significant political consequences throughout the South.

✓The laws **that Congress passed in 1957 and 1960 remedying problems of registration and voting** had significant political consequences throughout the South.

Be cautious, though: Combine too many short grammatical sentences, and you create a sentence that sprawls.

2. Semicolon Alone

A semicolon is like a soft period; whatever is on either side of it should usually be a grammatical sentence (with an exception we'll discuss later). Use a semicolon only when the second grammatical sentence is closely linked to the first:

✓In 1957 and again in 1960, Congress passed laws that remedied problems of registration and **voting; those** laws had significant political consequences throughout the South.

If readers can't see a link between them, they experience a small twinge of confusion:

In 1957 and again in 1960, Congress passed laws in order to remedy problems of registration and **voting; by 1995** Southern states had thousands of sheriffs, mayors, and other officials from their Afro-American communities.

A few shared concepts would make the connections clearer:

✓In 1957 and again in 1960, Congress passed civil rights laws in order to remedy racial problems of registration and voting, particularly in the South; by 1995 Southern states had elected thousands of sheriffs, mayors, and other officials from their African-American communities.

A SPECIAL PROBLEM WITH *HOWEVER:* There is a common context where even well-educated writers confuse readers by using a comma where they should use a semicolon or period: It is when they end one grammatical sentence and begin another with *however*. The punctuation in this next example is wrong because we don't know whether the *however* goes with the first grammatical sentence or with the second:

> Taxpayers have supported public education, **however,** they now object because taxes have risen so steeply.

That first grammatical sentence must end with a period or a semicolon to signal readers that they have finished one independent clause and are beginning another. So if the *however* goes with the second clause, then a semicolon or period should precede it:

> ✓Taxpayers have supported public education**; however,** they now object because taxes have risen so steeply.

A fairly reliable rule: If you have more than ten or so words before a *however* and as many after, you probably need to change the comma *before* the *however* to a semicolon or period, because that *however* probably begins a new grammatical sentence.

3. Comma + Coordinating Conjunction

   Readers recognize the end of a grammatical sentence when they see a comma followed by

   - a coordinating conjunction: *and, but, yet, for, so, or, nor,*
   - followed by another subject and verb.

   > ✓In the 1950s religion was viewed as a bulwark against communism, **so** it was not long after that that atheism was felt to threaten national security.

   > ✓American intellectuals have often followed Europeans, **but** our culture has proven inhospitable to their brand of socialism.

But choose a period if the two grammatical sentences are long and have their own internal punctuation.

When readers begin a coordinated series of three or more grammatical sentences, they accept just a comma between them, but only if they are short and have no internal punctuation:

> ✓Baseball satisfies our love of **precision, basketball** speaks to our love of speed and **grace, and** football appeals to our lust for violence.

If either of the first two clauses has internal punctuation, separate them with a semicolon:

> ✓Baseball, the oldest indigenous American sport and essentially a rural one, satisfies our admiration for **precision; basketball**, our newest sport and now more urban than rural, speaks to our love of speed and **grace; and** football, a sport both rural and urban, appeals to our lust for violence.

AN EXCEPTION: Omit the comma between a coordinated pair of short grammatical sentences if you introduce them with a modifier that applies to both of them:

> ✓By 1995, the economies of the Soviet Union's former satellites had begun to **rebound but** Russia's had yet to hit bottom.

Four Less Common Forms of End Punctuation

4. Period + Coordinating Conjunction

   Some readers think it's wrong to begin a punctuated sentence with a coordinating conjunction such as *and* or *but*. But they are wrong; this is entirely correct:

> ✓Education cannot guarantee a **democracy. But** without it, democracy cannot survive.

Use this pattern no more than once a page or so, especially with *and*.

5. Semicolon + Coordinating Conjunction

   Writers rarely end one grammatical sentence with a semicolon and begin the next with a coordinating conjunction, so generally avoid this:

> In the 1950s religion was viewed as a bulwark against **communism; so** it was not long after that atheism was felt to threaten national security.

Use a comma. On the other hand, readers are grateful for a semicolon if the two grammatical sentences are long with their own internal commas:

> ✓Problem solving, one of the most active areas of psychology, has made great strides in the last decade, particularly in understanding the problem-solving strategies of experts; **so** it is no surprise that educators have followed that research with interest.

They would probably appreciate a period even more.

6. Comma Alone

Though readers ordinarily do not expect to see just a comma separate two grammatical sentences, they are not confused if they are short and closely linked in meaning, such as cause-effect, first-second, if-then, etc. Be sure, though, that neither has internal commas; this would be confusing:

> Women, who have always been underpaid, no longer accept that discriminatory treatment, they are now doing something about it.

This is clearer:

> ✓Women have always been under**paid, they** are now doing something about it.

But a warning: Although writers of the best prose do this, many teachers consider it an error, so be sure of your readers before you experiment.

7. Conjunction Alone

It is also common to signal a close link between short grammatical sentences with a coordinating conjunction alone, omitting the comma:

> ✓Oscar Wilde violated a fundamental law of British **society and** we know what happened to him.

But the same warning: Though writers of the best prose do this, many teachers consider it an error.

Three Special Cases: Colon, Dash, Parentheses

8. Colon

Discerning readers think you are a more than common writer if you end a sentence with an appropriate colon: They take it as shorthand for *to illustrate, for example, that is, let me expand on, therefore:*

> ✓Only one question **remains: What** if we lose money?

> ✓Dance is not widely **supported: No** company operates at a profit, and there are few outside major cities.

A colon signals more obviously than a comma or semi-colon that you are self-consciously balancing the structure, sound, and meaning of one clause against another:

> ✓Civil disobedience is the public conscience of a democracy: mass enthusiasm is the public consensus of a tyranny.

A rule of thumb: Avoid a colon if it breaks a clause into two pieces, neither of which is a grammatically complete sentence, like this:

> **Genetic counseling requires: a knowledge** of statistical genetics, an awareness of choices open to parents, and the psychological competence to deal with emotional trauma.

Neither chunk before or after that colon could be a grammatical sentence. Instead, put the colon after a whole SUBJECT-VERB-OBJECT structure:

> ✓**Genetic counseling requires the following: a thorough** knowledge of statistical genetics, an awareness of choices open to parents, and the psychological competence to deal with emotional trauma.

In that sentence, the reader completes a chunk of a clause that could stand as a punctuated sentence, even though what follows is part of it. If you follow the colon with a grammatical sentence, you might capitalize the first word or not, depending on how much you want to emphasize what follows.

9. Dash

You can signal the same balance more informally with a dash—it suggests a casual afterthought:

> ✓Stonehenge is a **wonder—only** a genius could have conceived it.

Try that with a colon: It makes a difference.

10. Parentheses

You can attach a short grammatical sentence to another grammatical sentence with parentheses, if what is in the parentheses is like a short afterthought. Put the period outside the last parenthesis:

> Stonehenge is a **wonder (only** a genius could have conceived it**).**

Summary: Ten Ways to End a Grammatical Sentence

1. Parentheses   I win (you lose).
2. Comma alone   I win, you lose.
3. Conjunction alone I win and you lose.
4. Dash   I win—you lose.

5. Comma + coordinating conjunction	I win, and you lose.
6. Semicolon	I win; you lose.
7. Colon	I win: you lose.
8. Semicolon + coordinating conjunction	I win; and you lose.
9. Period + coordinating conjunction	I win. And you lose.
10. Period	I win. You lose.

Readers take these ways of ending grammatical sentences as increasingly emphatic (personal taste varies). If you choose punctuation that separates grammatical sentences only slightly—just a comma or conjunction—be certain your readers recognize that those clauses are closely linked.

PUNCTUATING BEGINNINGS

Punctuation at the beginning of a sentence is no problem when the sentence begins directly with its subject, as this one does. However, as with this one, when it forces a reader to plow through several introductory words, phrases, and clauses, especially when they have their own internal punctuation, and readers might be confused by it all (as you probably are right now), forget trying to punctuate it right: Rewrite it.

There are a few rules that your readers expect you to follow, but more often you have to rely on your judgment.

Five Reliable Rules

1. Always separate an introductory element from the subject that follows it if a reader might misunderstand the structure of the sentence. Do not do this:

   > When a lawyer concludes her argument has to be easily remembered by a jury.

   Do this:

   > ✓When a lawyer **concludes, her** argument has to be easily remembered by a jury.

2. Never put a semicolon at the end of an introductory clause or phrase, no matter how long. Readers take semicolons to

signal the end of a grammatical sentence (but see p. 238).
Not this:

> Although the Administration knew that Iraq's invasion of
> Kuwait threatened American interests in Saudi **Arabia; it** did
> not immediately prepare a military response.

Always use a comma there:

> ✓ The Administration knew that Iraq's invasion of Kuwait
> threatened American interests in Saudi **Arabia, but** it did not
> immediately prepare a military response.

But if that element is long and complicated, consider
breaking it out as a grammatical sentence.

3. Never put a comma right after a subordinating conjunction. Not this:

> **Although, the** art of punctuation is simple, it is rarely mastered.

4. Do not put a comma after the coordinating conjunctions
   and, but, yet, for, so, or, and *nor,* if the next element is the
   subject. Do not do this:

> **But, we** cannot know whether life on other planets exists.

Some writers who punctuate heavily put a comma after a
coordinating conjunction if an introductory word or
phrase follows:

> ✓ **Yet, during this period, prices** continued to rise.

Heavy punctuation retards a reader a bit, but it's your
choice. These are also correct and for the reader, perhaps
a bit swifter:

> ✓ Yet during this **period, prices** continued to rise.

> ✓ Yet during this **period prices** continued to rise.

5. Put a comma after an introductory word or phrase that
   comments on the whole of the following sentence or after
   a conjunction that connects one sentence to another.
      These include elements like *fortunately, possibly, perhaps,* etc., and conjunctions like *however, nevertheless, regardless,* etc. Since readers hear sentences in their mind's
   ear, they expect a pause after such words.

✓**Fortunately, we** proved our point.

Consider revising, however, if you find yourself starting many sentences with an introductory element and a comma. When we read a series of such sentences, we feel the whole passage is hesitant.

THREE COMMON EXCEPTIONS: We typically omit a comma after *now, thus,* and *hence:*

✓**Now it** is clear that many will not support this position.

✓**Thus the** only alternative is to choose some other action.

Three Reliable Principles

1. Readers need no punctuation after a short introductory phrase directly before a subject:

   ✓**Once again we** find similar responses to such stimuli.

   ✓**In 1945 few** realized how the war had transformed us.

   It is not wrong to put a comma there, but it slows readers just as you may want them to be picking up speed.

2. Readers need a comma after a long introductory phrase or clause:

   ✓When a lawyer begins her opening statement with a dry recital of the law and how it must be applied to the case before the **court, the** jury is likely to nod off.

   But there are other considerations: How long is too long and how closely do you want to connect the meanings of the two clauses? Readers don't need a comma when the clause is shorter than, say, ten or so words, its subject is the same as the subject of the main clause, and its meaning closely depends on the meaning of the main clause:

   ✓When **Hitler** realized that he had lost the **war he** ordered his army to raze every city through which it retreated.

   But if the subjects of the clauses differ and the ideas contrast, a comma helps the reader sense the opposition. Compare:

   ✓Since **we** accepted the IRS' **data we** dropped further appeals.

   ✓Although the **IRS** overruled **us, we** still follow our procedures.

3. Readers do not expect a comma to separate a subject from its verb. Do not do this:

> A sentence that consists of many complex subordinate clauses and long phrases that all precede a **verb, may** seem to some students to demand a comma somewhere.

Readers generally dislike long subjects, so keep them short, making a comma unnecessary. Readers need a comma between a subject and a verb only when a phrase or clause clearly interrupts that expected connection. (See the next section on interruptions.)

Occasionally, you cannot avoid a long subject, especially if it consists of a list of items with internal punctuation, like this:

> **The President, the Vice-President, the Secretaries of the Departments, Senators, members of the House of Representatives, and Supreme Court Justices, take** an oath that pledges them to uphold the Constitution.

In these circumstances, help your readers sort out the subject from the rest of the sentence by creating a summative subject, a second one- or two-word subject that sums up the longer one.

> ✓The President, the Vice-President, the Secretaries of the Departments, Senators, members of the House of Representatives, and Supreme Court Justices: **all** take an oath that pledges them to uphold the Constitution.

To create such a subject, do this:

- Insert a colon or a dash at the end of that long subject:

> The President, the Vice-President, the Secretaries of the Departments, Senators, members of the House of Representatives, and Supreme Court Justices:

- Then insert a word that summarizes the preceding list:

> ✓The President, the Vice-President, the Secretaries of the Departments, Senators, members of the House of Representatives, and Supreme Court Justices: **all** take an oath that pledges them to uphold the Constitution.

Choose a dash or a colon depending on how formal you want to seem.

PUNCTUATING MIDDLES

This is where explanations get messy, because to punctuate inside a grammatical sentence—more specifically, inside a clause—you have to consider not only the grammar of that clause, but the nuances of its rhythm, its meaning, and the emphasis that you want your readers to hear in their mind's ear.

Interruptions

When you insert an interrupting phrase or clause between a subject and verb or verb and object, readers have a harder time making the grammatical connections that hold those basic elements of a sentence together. So in general, avoid interruptions (see p. 139), except for reasons of emphasis or nuance. In that case, you have to help your reader recognize the interruption by setting it off with *paired* commas or dashes:

> A sentence, **if it consists of many complex subordinate clauses and long phrases and all precede a verb**, may seem to need commas.

Readers need commas before and after short ADVERBIAL PHRASES, depending on the emphasis you want them to feel. The general principle is that readers feel emphasis falls on what immediately precedes and follows a pause. Compare the different emphases in these:

- ✓Modern poetry has become more relevant to the average reader **in recent years.**

- ✓Modern poetry **has, in recent years, become** more relevant to the average reader.

- ✓Modern poetry has **become, in recent years, more** relevant to the average reader.

- ✓The antagonism between Congress and the president has created utter distrust **among every group of voters.**

- ✓The antagonism between Congress and the president has created, **among every group of voters,** utter distrust.

Loose Commentary

"Loose commentary" differs from an interruption, because you can usually move an interruption elsewhere in a sentence. But loose commentary modifies what it is next to, and so it cannot be moved. It still needs to be set off with commas, parentheses, or dashes. It is difficult to explain exactly what counts as loose commentary because it depends on both grammar and meaning. One familiar distinction is between RESTRICTIVE and NONRESTRICTIVE MODIFIERS (see pp. 118–119) and APPOSITIVES.

We use no commas with restrictive modifiers, modifiers that uniquely identify the noun they modify:

> ✓ The **house that I live in** is 100 years old.

But we always set off nonrestrictive modifiers with *paired* commas (unless the modifier ends the sentence), because they are loose commentary, not necessary to our understanding the meaning of the sentence:

> ✓ We had to reconstruct the **larynx, which is the source of voice,** with cartilage from the shoulder.

An appositive is actually just a truncated nonrestrictive clause:

> ✓ We had to rebuild the **larynx, ~~which is~~ the source of voice,** with cartilage from the shoulder.

> You can achieve a more casual effect with a dash:

> ✓ We had to rebuild the **larynx—which is the source of voice—with** cartilage from the shoulder.

A dash is useful when the loose commentary has internal commas. Readers find this confusing:

> The nations of Central Europe, Poland, Hungary, Romania, Bulgaria, the Czech Republic, Slovakia, Bosnia, Serbia have for centuries been in the middle of an East-West tug-of-war.

They understand this kind of structure more easily if they can see that loose modifier set off with dashes or parentheses:

> ✓ The nations of Central **Europe—Poland, Hungary, Romania, Bulgaria, the Czech Republic, Slovakia, Bosnia, Serbia—have** for centuries been in the middle of an East-West tug-of-war.

Use parentheses when you want your reader to hear your comment as a *sotto voce* aside:

> ✓The brain **(at least that part that controls nonprimitive functions)** may comprise several little brains operating simultaneously.

or use it as an explanatory footnote inside a sentence:

> ✓Lamarck **(1744–1829)** was a pre-Darwinian evolutionist.
> ✓The poetry of the *fin de siécle* **(end of the century)** was characterized by a world-weariness and fashionable despair.

When loose commentary is at the end of a sentence, use a comma to separate it from the first part of the sentence. Be certain, however, that the meaning of the commentary is not crucial to the meaning of the sentence. Contrast these:

> ✓I wandered through **Europe, seeking a place** where I could write undisturbed.
> ✓I spent my **time seeking a place** where I could write undisturbed.

> ✓Offices will be closed July **2–6, as announced in the daily bulletin.**
> ✓When closing offices, secure all safes **as prescribed in the Manual.**

> ✓Historians have studied social changes**, at least in this country.**
> ✓These records must be kept **at least until the IRS reviews them.**

PUNCTUATING COORDINATED ELEMENTS

Punctuating Two Coordinate Elements

Generally speaking, do not insert a comma between just two coordinated elements. Compare these:

> As computers have become **sophisticated, and** powerful they have taken over more **clerical, and** bookkeeping tasks.
> ✓As computers have become **sophisticated and** powerful they have taken over more **clerical and** bookkeeping tasks.

Three Exceptions

1. For a dramatic contrast, put a comma after even a short coordinate element if you want to emphasize a contradiction between the two:

✓ The ocean is nature's most glorious **creation, and** its most destructive.

This use of a comma is especially emphatic before a *but:*

✓ Organ transplants are becoming more **common, but** not less expensive.

2. If you want your readers to feel the cumulative power of a coordinated pair (or more), drop the *and* and leave just a comma. Compare these:

   ✓ Lincoln never had a formal **education and** never owned a large library.

   ✓ Lincoln never had a formal **education, never** owned a large library.

   ✓ The lesson of the pioneers was to ignore conditions that seemed difficult or even **overwhelming and** to get on with the business of subduing a hostile environment.

   ✓ The lesson of the pioneers was to ignore conditions that seemed difficult or even **overwhelming, to** get on with the business of subduing a hostile environment.

3. Put a comma between long coordinate pairs only if you think your readers need a chance to breathe or to sort out the grammar. Compare:

   It is in the graveyard that Hamlet finally realizes that the inevitable end of life is the **grave and clay** and that regardless of one's station in **life the** end of all pretentiousness and all plotting and counter-plotting must be dust.

   A comma after *clay* and *life* signals a natural pause:

   ✓ It is in the graveyard that Hamlet finally realizes that the inevitable end of all life is the **grave and clay, and that** regardless of one's station in **life, the** end of all pretentiousness and all plotting and counter-plotting must be dust.

   More important, the comma after *clay* sorts out the structure of a potentially confusing *grave and clay and that regardless.*

   In this next sentence, the first half of a coordination is long, so a reader might have a problem connecting the second half of the coordination to its origin:

   Conrad's *Heart of Darkness* brilliantly dramatizes those primitive impulses that lie deep in each of us and stir only in our darkest **dreams but asserts** the need for the values that control those impulses.

A comma after *dreams* would clearly mark the end of one coordinate member and the beginning of the next:

✓ Conrad's *Heart of Darkness* brilliantly dramatizes those primitive impulses that lie deep in each of us and stir only in our darkest **dreams, but asserts** the need for the values that control those impulses.

On the other hand, if you find yourself trying to make sense out of a complicated sentence with punctuation alone, you probably need to revise the whole sentence.

Punctuating a Series of Three or More Coordinated Elements

Finally, there is the matter of punctuating a series of three or more coordinated elements. You can put a comma before the last element or not, depending on your taste:

✓ His wit, his **charm and his loyalty** made him our friend.

✓ His wit, his **charm, and his loyalty** made him our friend.

Both are correct, but be consistent. If any of the items in the series has its own internal commas, then readers rely on semicolons to see how they should group the items:

✓ In mystery novels, the principal action ought to be economical, organic, and **logical; fascinating**, yet not **exotic; clear,** but complicated enough to hold the reader's interest.

Here's the point: You can rely on four principles.

1. Inside a clause, always use *paired* marks of punctuation—commas, parentheses, or dashes. Never use semicolons.
2. Set off what prominently interrupts grammatical connections with commas, parentheses, or dashes. Never use semicolons.

3. Set off loose commentary with commas, parentheses, or dashes. Never use semicolons.
4. Use commas to separate items in a series. Use semicolons to set off items in a series only when they have internal commas (see p. 238).

SUMMING UP

Rather than summarize this detailed material, I offer just three bits of advice:

- Always signal the end of a grammatical sentence.
- Always observe the five reliable rules.
- Always set off long interrupting elements with commas.

Beyond that, use your judgment: Punctuate in ways that help your readers see the connections and separations that they have to see to make sense of your sentences. That means you must put yourself in the place of your reader, not easy to do, but something you must learn. On the other hand, write a clearly structured sentence in the first place, and your punctuation will take care of itself.

Exercise A.2

These passages lack their original punctuation. Slash marks indicate grammatical sentences. Punctuate them three times, once using the least punctuation possible, a second time using as much varied punctuation as you can, and then a third time as you think best. You might also analyze these passages for features of elegance, especially how their sentences begin and end. You can even improve some.

1. Scientists and philosophers of science tend to speak as if "scientific language" were intrinsically precise as if those who use it must understand one another's meaning even if they disagree / but in fact scientific language is not as different from ordinary language as is com-

monly believed / it too is subject to imprecision and ambiguity and hence to imperfect understanding / moreover new theories or arguments are rarely if ever constructed by way of clear-cut steps of induction deduction and verification or falsification / neither are they defended rejected or accepted in so straightforward a manner / in practice scientists combine the rules of scientific methodology with a generous admixture of intuition aesthetics and philosophical commitment / the importance of what are sometimes called extra-rational or extra-logical components of thought in the *discovery* of a new principle or law is generally acknowledged / . . . but the role of these extralogical components in persuasion and acceptance in making an argument convincing is less frequently discussed partly because they are less visible / the ways in which the credibility or effectiveness of an argument depends on the realm of common experiences on extensive practice in communicating those experiences in a common language are hard to see precisely because such commonalities are taken for granted / only when we step out of such a "consensual domain" when we can stand out on the periphery of a community with a common language do we begin to become aware of the unarticulated premises mutual understandings and assumed practices of the group even in those subjects that lend themselves most readily to quantification / discourse depends heavily on conventions and interpretation conventions that are acquired over years of practice and participation in a community.

—Evelyn Fox Keller, *A Feeling for the Organism:
The Life and Work of Barbara McClintock*

2. In fact of course the notion of universal knowledge has always been an illusion / but it is an illusion fostered by the monistic view of the world in which a few great central truths determine in all its wonderful and amazing proliferation everything else that is true / we

are not today tempted to search for these keys that un-lock the whole of human knowledge and of man's ex-perience / we know that we are ignorant / we are well taught it / and the more surely and deeply we know our own job the better able we are to appreciate the full measure of our pervasive ignorance / we know that these are inherent limits compounded no doubt and exaggerated by that sloth and that complacency with-out which we would not be men at all / but knowledge rests on knowledge / what is new is meaningful be-cause it departs slightly from what was known before / this is a world of frontiers where even the liveliest of actors or observers will be absent most of the time from most of them / perhaps this sense was not so sharp in the village that village which we have learned a little about but probably do not understand too well the village of slow change and isolation and fixed cul-ture which evokes our nostalgia even if not our full comprehension / perhaps in the villages men were not so lonely / perhaps they found in each other a fixed community a fixed and only slowly growing store of knowledge of a single world / even that we may doubt / for there seem to be always in the culture of such times and places vast domains of mystery if not un-knowable then imperfectly known endless and open.

—J. Robert Oppenheimer, "The Sciences and Man's Community,"
from *Science and the Common Understanding*

GLOSSARY

Grammar is the ground of all.
—WILLIAM LANGLAND

Most of the grounds of the world's troubles are matters of grammar.
—MONTAIGNE

*There is a satisfactory boniness about grammar which the
flesh of sheer vocabulary requires before it can become
vertebrate and walk the earth. But to study it for its own sake,
without relating it to function, is utter madness.*
—ANTHONY BURGESS

*Thou hast most traitorously corrupted the youth of the realm in
erecting a grammar school. . . It will be proved to thy face, that thou
hast men about thee that usually talk of a noun and a verb, and such
abominable words as no Christian ear can endure to hear.*
—WILLIAM SHAKESPEARE, 2 HENRY VI, 4.7

W hat follows is no tight theory of grammar, just definitions useful for the terms in this book. Where the text discusses something at length, I refer you to those pages. If you want to do a quick review to get started, read the entries on SUBJECT, SIMPLE SUBJECT, WHOLE SUBJECT, and VERB.

Action: Prototypically, action is expressed by a verb: *move, hate, think, discover.* But actions also appear in NOMINALIZATIONS: *movement, hatred, thought, discovery.* Actions are also implied in some adjectives: *advisable, resultant, explanatory,* etc.

Active: See p. 61.

Adjective: A word you can put *very* in front of: *very old, very interesting.* There are some exceptions: *major, additional,* etc. Since this is also a test for ADVERBS, you can distinguish adjectives from adverbs by trying them out between *the* and a noun: *The* **occupational** *hazard, the* **major** *reason,* etc. Unfortunately, some nouns occur in the same position—*the* **chemical** *hazard.*

Adjective Phrase: An ADJECTIVE and what attaches to it: *so* **full** *that it burst.*

Adjectival Clause: Adjectival clauses modify nouns. Also called RELATIVE clauses, they usually begin with a relative pronoun: *which, that, whom, whose, who.* There are two kinds: RESTRICTIVE and NONRESTRICTIVE.

Restrictive	The book **that** *I read* was good.
Nonrestrictive	My car, **which** *you saw,* is gone.

Adverb: Adverbs modify all parts of speech except NOUNS:

Adjectives	**extremely** large, **rather** old
Verbs	**frequently** spoke, **often** slept
Adverbs	**very** carefully, **somewhat** rudely often
Articles	**precisely** the man I meant, **just** the thing I need
Sentences	**Fortunately,** we were on time.

Adverb Phrase: An adverb and what attaches to it: *as* **soon** *as I could.*

Adverbial Clause: This is a kind of SUBORDINATE CLAUSE. It modifies a VERB or ADJECTIVE, indicating time, cause, condition, etc. It usually begins with SUBORDINATING CONJUNCTIONS such as *because, when, if, since, while, unless:*

> **If you leave,** I will stop.   **Because he left,** I did too.

Agent: Prototypically, agents are flesh-and-blood, but for our purposes, an agent is the *seeming* source of any ACTION, the entity without which the action could not occur: ***She** criticized the program in this report.* Often, we can make the means by which we do something a seeming agent: ***This report** criticizes the program.* Do not confuse agents with SUBJECTS. Agents prototypically are subjects, but an agent can be in a grammatical OBJECT: *I underwent an interrogation by **the police.***

Appositive: See p. 236.

Article: They are easier to list than to define: *a, an, the, this, these, that, those.*

Character: See pp. 53–59.

Clause: A clause has two defining characteristics:

1. It is a sequence of at least one SUBJECT + VERB.
2. The verb agrees with the subject in number and can be made past or present.

By this definition, these are clauses:

> She left   that they leave   if she left   why he is leaving

These next are not, because the verbal forms cannot be made past tense nor do they agree in number with the putative subject:

> for them to **go**   her **having gone**

Complement: Whatever completes a VERB:

> I am **home.**   You seem **tired.**   She helped **me.**

Compound Noun: See pp. 71–72.

Conjunction: Usually defined as a word that links words, PHRASES, or CLAUSES. They are easier to illustrate than define (the first two are also categorized as SUBORDINATING conjunctions):

ADVERBIAL **conjunctions**	because, although, when, since, etc.
RELATIVE **conjunctions**	who, whom, whose, which, that
SENTENCE **conjunctions**	thus, however, therefore, nevertheless
COORDINATING **conjunctions**	and, but, yet, for, so, or, nor
CORRELATIVE **conjunctions**	both X and Y, not only X but Y, (n)either X (n)or Y, X as well as Y

Coordination: Coordination joins two grammatical units of the same order with *and, or, nor, but, yet*:

Same part of speech	you **and** I, red **and** black, run **or** jump.
PHRASES	in the house **but** not in the basement.
CLAUSES	when I leave **or** when you arrive.

Dangling Modifier: See p. 67.

Dependent Clause: Any CLAUSE that cannot be punctuated as a MAIN CLAUSE, one beginning with a capital letter and ending with a period or question mark. It usually begins with a subordinating conjunction such as *because, if, when, which, that*:

why he left   because he left   which he left

Direct Object: The NOUN that follows a TRANSITIVE VERB and can be made the SUBJECT of a PASSIVE verb:

I found **the money.** → **The money** was found by me.

Finite Verb: A verb that can be made past or present. These are finite verbs because we can change their tense from past to present and vice versa:

She **wants** to leave. ↔ She **wantED** to leave.

These are not finite verbs because we cannot change the INFINITIVE to a past tense:

She wants to **leaves.** ⇜ She wants to **leaveD.**

Fragment: A PHRASE or DEPENDENT CLAUSE that begins with a capital letter and ends with a period, question mark, or exclamation mark:

Because I left.   Though I am here!   What you did?

These are complete sentences:

> He left because I did.   Though I am here, she is not.   I know what we did.

Free Modifier: See p. 146.

Gerund: A NOMINALIZATION created by adding -*ing* to a VERB:

> When she **left** we were happy. → Her **leaving** made us happy.

Goal: That toward which the ACTION of a VERB is directed. In most cases, goals are DIRECT OBJECTS:

> I see **you.**   I broke **the dish.**   I built **a house.**

But in some cases, the literal goal can be the SUBJECT of an ACTIVE VERB:

> **I** underwent an interrogation.   **She** received a warm welcome.

Grammatical Sentence: See pp. 222–224.

Hedge: See p. 125.

Independent Clause: A CLAUSE that does not modify anything else in a sentence.

Infinitive: A VERB that cannot be made past or present. It often is preceded by the word *to: He decided to **stay.*** But sometimes not: *We helped him **repair** the door.*

Intensifier: See p. 127.

Intransitive Verb: A verb that does not take an OBJECT and so cannot be made PASSIVE. These are not TRANSITIVE verbs:

> He **exists.**   They **left** town.   She **became** a doctor.

Linking Verb: A VERB with a COMPLEMENT that refers to its SUBJECT.

> He **is** my brother.   They **became** teachers.   She **seems** reliable.

Main Clause: A main or independent clause can be punctuated as an independent sentence:

> I left.   Why did you leave?   We are leaving.

A SUBORDINATE or DEPENDENT CLAUSE cannot be punctuated as an independent sentence. These would be incorrectly punctuated:

> Because she left.   That they left.   Whom you spoke to.

Main Subject: SUBJECT of the MAIN CLAUSE.

Metadiscourse: See p. 66.

Nominalization: See pp. 41–43.

Nonrestrictive Clause: See pp. 18–19.

Noun: A word that fits this frame: *The* [   ] *is good.* Some are concrete: *dog, rock, car;* others abstract: *ambition, space, speed.* The nouns that most concern us are NOMINALIZATIONS, nouns derived from VERBS or ADJECTIVES: *act → action, wide → width*

Noun Clause: A noun clause functions like a noun, as the subject or object of a verb: **That you are here** *proves **that you love me.***

Object: There are three kinds:

1. DIRECT object: the NOUN following a TRANSITIVE VERB:
   I *read* **the book.**   We *followed* **the car.**
2. PREPOSITIONAL object: the noun following a preposition:
   in **the house**   *by* **the walk**   *across* **the street**   *with* **fervor**
3. INDIRECT object: the noun between a VERB and its direct object:
   I *gave* **him** a tip.

Parallel: Sequences of coordinated words, PHRASES, or CLAUSES are parallel when they are of the same grammatical structure. This is parallel:

   I decided to work hard and do a good job.

This is not:

   I decided to work hard and that I should do a good job.

Passive: See p. 61.

Past Participle: Usually the same form as the past tense *-ed: jumped, worked.* Irregular VERBS have irregular forms: *seen, broken, swum,* etc.

Phrase: A group of words constituting a unit but not including a SUBJECT and a FINITE VERB: *the dog, too old, was leaving, in the house, ready to work*

Possessive: *my, your, his, her, its, their* or a NOUN ending with *-'s* or *-s': the **dog's** tail*

Predicate: Whatever follows the whole SUBJECT, beginning with the VERB PHRASE, including the COMPLEMENT and what attaches to it:

He **[left yesterday to buy a hat]**_{predicate}.

Preposition: Easier to list than to define: *in, on, up, over, of, at, by,* etc.

Prepositional Phrase: The preposition plus OBJECT: *in the house*

Present Participle: The *-ing* form of a VERB: *running, thinking*

Progressive: The PRESENT PARTICIPLE form of the VERB: ***Running*** *streams are beautiful.*

Punctuated Sentence: See pp. 222–224.

Relative Clause: See pp. 18–19.

Relative Pronoun: *who, whom, which, whose, that*

Restrictive Clause: See pp. 18–19.

Resumptive Modifier: See p. 144.

Run-on Sentence: A PUNCTUATED SENTENCE consisting of two or more GRAMMATICAL SENTENCES not separated by either a COORDINATING CONJUNCTION or any mark of punctuation this entry illustrates a run-on sentence.

Simple Subject: The simple subject is the smallest unit inside the WHOLE SUBJECT that determines whether a VERB will be singular or plural:

[The **books** _{simple subject} that are required reading] _{whole subject} **are** listed.

The simple subject should be as close to its verb as you can get it.

If **a book** is required reading, **it** is listed.

Stress: See p. 98.

Subject: The subject is what the VERB agrees with in number:

Two men *are* at the door.   **One man** *is* at the door.

Distinguish the WHOLE SUBJECT from its SIMPLE SUBJECT.

Subjunctive: A form of the VERB used to talk about events that are contrary to fact:

> If he **were** President . . .

Subordinate Clause: A clause that usually begins with a SUBORDINATING CONJUNCTION such as *if, when, unless,* or *which, that, who.* There are three kinds of subordinate clauses: NOUN, ADVERBIAL, and ADJECTIVAL.

Subordinating Conjunction: *Because, if, when, since, unless, which, who, that, whose,* etc.

Summative Modifier: See p. 145.

Summative Subject: See p. 234.

Theme: The key concepts that run through a series of sentences.

Topic: See p. 84.

Topic String: A topic string is the sequence of TOPICS through a passage.

Transitive Verb: A VERB with a DIRECT OBJECT. The direct object prototypically "receives" an ACTION. The prototypical direct object can be made the SUBJECT of a PASSIVE verb:

> We **read** the book. → The book **was read** by us.

By this definition, *resemble, become,* and *stand* (as in *He stands six feet tall*) are not transitive.

Verb: The word that must agree with the SUBJECT in number and that can be inflected for past or present:

> The book **is** ready.   The books **were** returned.

Whole Subject: You can identify a whole subject once you identify its VERB: Put a *who* or a *what* in front of the verb and turn the sentence into a question. The fullest answer to the question is the whole subject:

> The ability of the city to manage education is an accepted fact.
> Question: **What** is an accepted fact?
> Answer (and whole subject): The ability of the city to manage education.

Distinguish the whole subject from the simple subject:

> The **ability** of the city to manage education **is** an accepted fact.

SUGGESTED ANSWERS

You will almost certainly come up with answers different from these, many probably much better. Don't worry whether yours is word-for-word like mine; focus only on the general principle of the lesson and exercise.

EXERCISE 3.4

1a. Verbs: argued, elevate. No nominalizations.

1b. Verbs: been. Nominalizations: speculation, improvement, achievement.

3a. Verbs: identified, failed, develop, immunize. Nominalizations: risk.

3b. Verbs: met. Nominalizations: attempts, defining, employment, failure.

5a. Verbs: caused. Nominalizations: loss, share, disappearance.

5b. Verbs: discover, use, teach, learn. Nominalizations: instruction.

7a. Verbs: fail, realize, are unprepared, protect, adjust. Nominalizations: life.

7b. Verbs: have come, are. Nominalizations: understanding, increases, resistance, costs, education.

EXERCISE 3.5

1b. Some educators have speculated whether a good family environment improves educational achievement (helps students achieve more).

3b. Economists have attempted but failed to formulate principles to define full employment.

5a. When domestic auto makers lost market to the Japanese, hundreds of thousands of jobs disappeared.

7b. Many colleges understand that they can no longer continue to increase tuition because parents are resisting the soaring cost of higher education.

EXERCISE 3.6

1. Lincoln hoped to preserve the Union without war, but when the South attacked Fort Sumter, war became inevitable.
3. Business executives predicted that the economy would quickly revive.
5. Because the health industry cannot control costs, the public may decide that Congress must act.
7. Several candidates attempted to explain why more people voted in this year's elections.
9. The business sector did not independently study why the trade surplus suddenly increased.
11. The CIA is uncertain whether Korea intends to cease missile testing.
13. If the data contradict each other, you must explain why.
15. They performed the play enthusiastically, but did not stage it intelligently.

EXERCISE 3.7

There are many plausible alternatives here, depending on the characters we invent.

1. Although we have used models to teach prose style, students do not always write more clearly or directly.
3. If members depart from established procedures, the Board may terminate their membership.
5. To implement a new curriculum successfully, faculty and students must cooperate to set goals that they can achieve within a reasonable time.

EXERCISE 4.1

1. Historians have re-assessed the place of Columbus in Western history because they have interpreted the discovery of America in new ways.

3. To write more coherently, trace the transitions in a book or well-written article.

5. Networks are aware that they have to revise their programming because viewers are watching cable and videos more.

EXERCISE 4.2

1. Those on welfare become independent when they learn skills valued by the marketplace. [I like the passive here in order to stress "marketplace."]

3. In this article, I argue that the United States fought the Vietnam War to extend its influence in Southeast Asia and did not end it until North Vietnam made it clear that it could be defeated only if the U.S. used atomic weapons.

5. Bierce presents the first section of . . . dispassionately. In the first sentence, he describes . . . but he takes all emotion away from them . . . In paragraph 2, he describes . . . but betrays no feeling because he uses neutral and unemotional language. He presents this entire . . . even though he fills it with details. [Some will object here that the repeated use of "Bierce/he" is monotonous. Two points: first, most of us never notice when subjects are repeated, and second, we can make more changes: "Even though this section is devoid of emotion, it has many details." Again, the question is *not* which is the correct revision, but how we think about it and decide what we like best. That means going beyond simply repeating the rule, "write in the active voice."]

EXERCISE 4.3

1. We believe that students binge because they do not understand the risks of alcohol.

3. We suggest that Russia's economy has improved because it has successfully exported more crude oil for hard currency.

5. In Section IV, I argue that the indigenous culture overcultivated the land at the base of the mesa and thereby exhausted it as a food-producing area.

7. To evaluate how the flow rate changed, the current flow rate was compared to the original rate on the basis of figures collected by Jordan in his study of diversion patterns of slow-growth swamps. [This sentence technically has a dangling modifier, but it is so common that no reader of technical prose would balk. That last clump of nominalizations is acceptable, because it is a technical term.]

Exercise 4.4

1. We analyzed your figures to determine their accuracy. We will announce the results when we think it appropriate.

3. When the author treats the conspiracy theories, he abandons his impassioned narrative style and adopts a cautious one, but when he picks up the narrative line again, he invests his prose with the same vigor and force.

5. For many years, courts have ignored federal regulations concerning the use of wiretaps. Only recently has the Department of Justice imposed tighter restrictions on the circumstances that warrant it.

7. We wrote these directives as simply as possible to communicate effectively with employees who do not read well.

Exercise 4.6

1. The committee on standards for plant safety discussed recent announcements about regulating air quality.

3. The main goal of this article is to describe how readers comprehend text and produce protocols about recall.

5. This paper will investigate how computers [?] process information in games that simulate human cognition.

7. The Social Security program guarantees a potential package of benefits based on what individuals contributed to the program over their lifetime.

Exercise 5.1

1. When Reagan assumed the office of the presidency, he had two aims in mind—the recovery of . . . He succeeded in the first as testified to by the drop in . . . But he had less success with the second, as indicated by our increased involvement . . . Nevertheless, the American voter was pleased by vast increases in the military . . .

Exercise 5.2

1. Except for those areas covered with ice or scorched by continual heat, the earth is covered by vegetation. Plants grow most richly

in fertilized plains and river valleys, but they also grow at the edge of perpetual snow in high mountains. Dense vegetation grows in the ocean and around its edges as well as in and around lakes and swamps. Plants grow in the cracks of busy city sidewalks as well as on seemingly barren cliffs. Vegetation will cover the earth long after we have been swallowed up by evolutionary history.

3. In his paper on children's thinking, Jones stressed the importance of language skills in the ability of children to solve problems. He showed that when children improved their language skills, they improved their ability to solve nonverbal problems. Jones thinks that they performed better because they used previously acquired language habits to articulate the problems and activate knowledge learned through language. We might therefore explore whether children could learn to solve problems better if they practiced how to formulate them.

EXERCISE 5.3

1. Though modern mass communication offers many advantages, it also poses many threats. If it were controlled by a powerful minority, it could manipulate public opinion through biased reporting. And while it provides us with a knowledge of public affairs through its national coverage, it may accentuate divisiveness and factionalism by connecting otherwise isolated, local conflicts into a single larger conflict when it shows us conflicts about the same issues occurring in different places. It will always be true that human nature produces differences of opinion, but the media may reinforce the threat of faction and division when it publishes uninformed opinion in national coverage. According to some, media can suppress faction through education when it communicates the true nature of conflicts, but history has shown that the media give as much coverage to people who encourage conflict as to people who try to remove it.

3. When Truman considered the Oppenheimer committee's recommendation to stop the hydrogen bomb project, he had to consider many issues. Russia and China had just proclaimed a Sino-Soviet bloc, so one issue he had to face was the Cold War. He was also losing support for his foreign policy among Republican leaders in Congress, and when the Russians tested their first atom bomb, the public demanded that he respond strongly. It was inevitable that Truman would conclude he could not let the public think he had

allowed Russia to be first in developing the most powerful weapon yet. In retrospect, according to some historians, Truman should have risked taking the Oppenheimer recommendation, but he had to face political issues that were too powerful to ignore.

EXERCISE 6.1

1. [One can imagine different rationales for different stresses.] In my opinion, at least, the Republic is most threatened by the judiciary's tendency to rewrite the Constitution.

3. In large American universities the opportunities for faculty to work with individual students are limited.

5. College students commonly complain about teachers who assign a long term paper and then give them no comments, but only a grade.

EXERCISE 6.2

1. During the reign of Queen Elizabeth, the story of King Lear and his daughters was so popular that by the time she died, readers could find it in at least a dozen books. Most of these stories, however, did not develop their characters and were simple narratives with an obvious moral. So several versions of this story must have been available to Shakespeare when he began work on *Lear*, perhaps his greatest tragedy. But while he based his characters on these stock figures of legend, he turned them into credible human beings with complex motives.

3. Because the most important event in Thucydides' *History* is Athens' catastrophic Sicilian Invasion, Thucydides devotes three quarters of his book to setting it up. We can see this anticipation especially in how he describes the step-by-step decline in Athenian society so that he could create the inevitability that we associate with the tragic drama.

5. Revenues changed as follows during July 1–August 31: Ohio and Kentucky, up 73% from $32,934 to $56,792; Indiana and Illinois, up 10% from $153,281 to $168,651; Wisconsin and Minnesota, down 5% from $200,102 to $190,580. [The important thing here is to get the sequence of items in a regular order. I could imagine an argument insisting that the percentage be at the end of sentence.]

EXERCISE 6.3

The second sentence best introduces the themes of turmoil and disputed succession to the throne, because it is that sentence that announces those themes in its stress.

EXERCISE 7.1

1. Critics must use complex and abstract terms to analyze literary texts meaningfully.
3. Graduate students face an uncertain future at best in finding good teaching jobs.
5. Most patients who go to a public clinic do not expect special treatment, because their health problems are minor and can be easily treated.

EXERCISE 7.2

1. We can reduce the federal deficit only if we reduce federal spending.
3. A person may be rejected from a cost-sharing educational program only if that person receives a full hearing into why she was rejected. Or: An agency may reject a person from . . . only when that agency provides a full hearing into why it rejected her.
5. If we pay taxes, the government can pay its debts.
7. Catholics and Protestants will reconcile only when they agree on the Pope's authority.

EXERCISE 7.4

1. Recent research has applied schemata theory to the pedagogy of solving mathematical problems. [Sounds dull to me, but who knows?]
3. American and British historians have interpreted what caused the War of 1812 in radically different ways because of their methodological differences. [Sounds significant.]
5. Egyptian and Greek thought influenced scientific thinking. [Sounds banal to me.]
7. I will explore how birth order relates to academic success.

Exercise 7.5

1. On the other hand, some TV programming will always appeal to our most prurient interests.

3. One principle governs how to preserve the wilderness from exploitation.

5. Families and other social units transmit more social values than do schools.

Exercise 8.1

1. Proponents of workfare have not yet shown it is a successful alternative to welfare because they have not shown evidence that it can provide meaningful and regular employment for welfare recipients. Therefore, it is premature to recommend that all the states should fully commit themselves to workfare.

3. One way to prevent foreign piracy of videos and CDs is for the justice systems of foreign countries to move cases faster through their courts and to impose stiffer penalties. But we do not expect any immediate improvement in the level of expertise of judges who hear these cases.

5. The music industry has ignored the problem of how to apply a rating system to offensive lyrics broadcast over FM and AM radio. Until it does, it is unlikely that stations will improve their public image, even if they were willing to discuss such a system.

7. Young people will not be discouraged from smoking just because the film and TV industries agree not to show characters smoking.

9. When Congress voted funds to construct the Interstate Highway System, it did not anticipate inflation, and so the system has run into financial problems.

11. "Reality" shows are the most popular shows on TV because they appeal to our voyeuristic impulses.

13. If carbon monoxide continues to be emitted, world climate will change.

Exercise 8.2

1. Many school systems are returning to the basics, a change that is long overdue.

3. For millennia, we have asked why we age, a mystery that we can answer either biologically or spiritually.

5. Both scientists and lay-people have been troubled by the ethical issues of test-tube fertilization, an event that has changed the way we think about what it means to be human.

7. In the Renaissance, greater affluence and political stability allowed streams of thought to merge, an historical development that both undermined the dominance of religious authority over knowledge and laid the groundwork for everything that we know about the world.

EXERCISE 9.2

1. Those who keep silent over the loss of small freedoms risk being kept silent when they lose big ones.

3. We should pay more attention to those politicians who tell us how to make what we have better than to those who tell us how get what we don't have.

5. Some teachers mistake neat papers that rehash old ideas for great thoughts wrapped in impressive packaging.

EXERCISE 9.3

1. If we invest our sweat in these projects, we must avoid appearing to be working only for our own self-interest.

3. Throughout history, science has progressed because dedicated scientists have ignored the hostility of an uninformed public.

5. Boards of education can no longer expect that taxpayers will support the extravagancies of incompetent bureaucrats.

EXERCISE 10.1

As the Illinois Commerce Commission has authorized, **we** are charging you . . . **We** have not raised rates . . . but **we** are restructuring the rates now . . . so that **we** can we charge you for what **we** pay to provide you with service.

As the Illinois Commerce Commission has authorized, **you** will have to pay . . . **You** have not had to pay . . . , but **you** will now pay rates that have been restructured consistent with the policy of The Public Utilities Act that lets us base what **you** pay on what it costs to provide you with service.

EXERCISE 10.2

Your car may have a defective part that connects the suspension to the frame. If you brake hard and the plate fails, you won't be able to steer. We may also have to adjust the secondary latch on your hood because we may have misaligned it. If you don't latch the primary latch, the secondary latch might not hold the hood down. If the hood flies up while you are driving, you won't be able to see. If either of these things occurs, you could crash.

EXERCISE 10.3

There are forty nominalizations in the speech: Para 1: *appearing, address, statement, expiration, declarations, contest, attention, progress, hope, prediction* (1:13); Para 2: *thoughts, address, saving, effects, negotiation* (1:20); Para 3: *interest, interest, cause, interest, enlargement, cause, conflict, conflict, triumph, result, aid, assistance, wringing, prayers, offenses, offenses, offense, slavery, offenses, providence, offense, departure, toil, judgments, firmness* (1:18). The opening paragraph is highly nominalized. Then it tapers off quite a bit until the passage beginning with *offenses for it must needs be* through *providence*, in which he concentrates six nominalizations in thirty-five words, the highest in the speech. This is clearly the most philosophical section of the speech.

EXERCISE 10.4

Nine mentions of *war* occur in paragraph two, with all of them except the last one an object of some kind. In the last sentence of paragraph two it becomes an acting subject. It becomes an object again, but mostly as an instrument of God.

EXERCISE 10.5

This is a hard question to answer. The difference is that Lincoln had good intentions; the others did not. But do good intentions justify such stylistic sleights-of-hand?

EXERCISE 10.7

The last part of the Declaration topicalizes *we*; the middle part *he*; and the first part abstractions. It is so regular that Jefferson had to have something in mind. I suspect it was this: In the first part, he systemically subordinated the colonist/revolutionaries to abstractions such as duty, prudence, and so on, making them the constrained objects of higher principles: They have no choice in the matter: Necessity requires that they revolt. But once he is past the philosophical foundations of his argument, he can introduce the evidence ("Let facts be submitted . . .") focusing on King George, and then at the end, he can focus on "we" as the dispositive agents who are now entitled to act on their own.

EXERCISE 10.8

Four score and seven years ago, **this continent** witnessed the birth of a new nation . . . Now **a great Civil War** engages us . . . **That war** has given us this great battlefield for a meeting place. **A portion of that field** is ready to receive its dedication . . . **This** is an altogether fitting . . . But in a larger sense, **this ground** will not let us dedicate, . . . **It** has already received that consecration . . . **The world will little note** . . . but **it can never forget** . . . , **This consecrated ground** calls on us the living to . . . , **that this honored place** increases our devotion . . . , **that this place was not died for in vain** . . . **this nation** . . . , **this earth shall not** be deprived of government of . . .

EXERCISE 10.9

The nominalizations: *proposition, battle(field), work, devotion, cause, devotion, birth, freedom, government.* Nine words in 262 is an extraordinarily small number (and *battle* hardly counts), especially since three come in the space of six words "**birth** of **freedom**, and that **government**." The Gettysburg Address has often been praised for its simplicity, but for the wrong reasons. It has nothing to do with the proportion of Anglo-Saxon to borrowed words. It has entirely to do with the lack of abstraction and simple syntax.

EXERCISE A.1

I can write a different kind of punctuated sentence: It would be a sentence that I could not break into shorter sentences merely by replacing commas and semicolons with periods; it would be a sentence consisting of several subordinate clauses: They would all depend on one main or independent clause—it would be a sentence like this one that you have almost finished, but it would probably feel longer than that sentence in the previous paragraph, yet it is shorter.

EXERCISE A.2

Here are the two passages, one with the least punctuation I can imagine and one with much more.

1. Scientists and philosophers . . . precise, as if those . . . disagree. But in fact scientific language . . . believed. It too is subject to . . . understanding. Moreover, new theories . . . falsification. Neither are they defended, rejected or accepted in so straightforward a manner. In practice scientists combine . . . commitment. The importance . . . generally acknowledged. But the role of . . . less visible. The ways in . . . common experiences, on extensive practice . . . taken for granted. Only when we step out of such a "consensual domain," when we can stand out . . . the unarticulated premises, mutual understandings and assumed practices of the group. Even in those subjects . . . to quantification, discourse depends heavily on conventions and interpretation, conventions that are acquired over years of practice and participation in a community.

    Scientists and philosophers of science . . . were intrinsically precise, as if those who use it . . . meaning, even if they disagree. But, in fact, scientific language . . . commonly believed: it, too, is subject to imprecision and ambiguity, and hence to imperfect understanding. Moreover, new theories, or arguments, are rarely, if ever, constructed by way of clear-cut steps of induction, deduction, and verification or falsification; neither are they defended, rejected, or accepted in so straightforward a manner. In practice, scientists combine the rules of scientific methodology with a generous admixture of intuition, aesthetics, and philosophical commitment. The importance of what are, sometimes, called extra-rational, or extralogical components of . . . law is generally acknowledged . . . But the role of these extralogical . . . frequently discussed, partly because they are less visible. The ways in which the credibility, or effectiveness, of an argument depends on the realm of common experiences, on extensive practice . . . a common language, are hard to see precisely, because such commonalities are taken for granted. Only when we step out of such a "consensual domain," when we can stand . . . language, do we begin to become aware of the unarticulated premises, mutual understandings, and assumed practices of the group. Even in those subjects . . . quantification, discourse depends heavily on conventions and interpretation, conventions that . . . participation in a community.

2. In fact of course, the notion of . . . been an illusion. But it is an illusion fostered . . . else that is true. We are not today . . . man's experience. We know that we are ignorant. We are well taught it. And the more surely and deeply we know our own job, the better able . . . pervasive ignorance. We . . . men at all. But knowledge rests on knowledge. What is new is . . . known before. This is a world . . . from most of them. Perhaps this sense was not so sharp in the village, that village which . . . not understand too well, the village of slow change . . . full comprehension. Perhaps in the villages men were not so lonely. Perhaps they found in each other a fixed community, a fixed and . . . single world. Even that we may doubt. For there seem . . . endless and open.

In fact, of course, the notion of universal knowledge . . . illusion, but it is an illusion . . . view of the world, in which a few great, central truths determine, in all its wonderful and amazing proliferation, everything else that is true. We are not, today, tempted to search . . . and of man's experience: we know that we are ignorant; we are well taught it; and the more surely and deeply we know our own job, the better able . . . pervasive ignorance. We know that these are inherent limits, compounded, no doubt, and exaggerated by . . . men at all. But knowledge rests on knowledge: what is new is meaningful, because it departs, slightly, from what was known before. This is a world of frontiers, where even the liveliest . . . of the time, from most of them. Perhaps, this sense was not so sharp in the village, that village which we have learned a little about, but probably do not understand too well—the village of slow change, and isolation, and fixed culture, which evokes our nostalgia, even if not our full comprehension. Perhaps in the villages men were not so lonely; perhaps they found in each other a fixed community, a fixed and . . . single world. Even that we may doubt, for there seem . . . and places, vast domains of mystery, if not unknowable, then imperfectly known—endless and open.

ACKNOWLEDGMENTS

INDEX

Absolute words, 26
Abstraction, 40–46; as characters, 58–59; diagnosing, 41–43; revising, 41–43
Academese, 4
Academic prose, first person in, 65–68
Accept, vs. *except*, 24
Actions, 34–39; in verbs, 34–39; in adjectives, 39; in nouns, 34–39
Active voice, 61–68; impression, 61–62; vs. passive voice, choosing between, 62–63; scientific writing, 65–68; cohesion, 79–80
Adjectives, as actions, 39
Affect, vs. *effect*, 24
Aggravate, vs. *annoy*, 23
And, beginning sentence with, 12, 17, 227
Annan, Noel Gilroy, 19
Annoy, vs. *aggravate*, 23
Anticipate, vs. *expect*, 23
Anxious, vs. *eager*, 23
Any, singular verb with, 22
Aphasia, temporary, 8
Appositive, 236
Aristotle, 179
Arnold, Matthew, 1
Aronowitz, Stanley, 194
As, vs. *because*, 20; vs. *like*, 24; vs. *since*, 20; vs. *while*, 20

Balance, coordinated, 160–62; uncoordinated, 163–64

Baldwin, James, 92
Barzun, Jacques, 18
Basford, J. L., 221
Because, vs. *as*, 20; beginning sentence with, 17
Bhabha, Homi K., 193
Blackmail, vs. *coerce*, 23
Blair, Hugh, 11
Blake, William, 135
Brand, Myles, 59
Bureaucratese, 4
Burgess, Anthony, 243
Burns, Robert, 13
Burrow, James, 221
But, beginning sentence with, 12, 17, 227

Capote, Truman, 115
Carr, E. H., 177–78
Carroll, Lewis, 77
Chadwick, Douglas, 7
Characters, passive verbs, 61–63; as abstractions, 58–59; as subjects, 34–38, 54; diagnosing, 55–56; importance, 54; revising, 55–58
Chiasmus, 167
Churchill, Winston, 165
Clarity, vs. coherence, 78–85; vs. simplemindedness, 50–51; complexity, 136; emphasis, 96–98; subversive, 194–95
Coerce, vs. *blackmail*, 23
Coherence, 46, 83–86; vs. clarity, 78–85; vs. cohesion, 83–86; emphasis, 96; logic, 212; main

point, 107–08, 210–11; organization, 211–12; problems, 213–17; relevance, 211; themes, 105–09; topics, 84–85; diagnosing and revising, 218–20; false, 89–90; global and local, 209–20
Cohesion, 79–82; vs. coherence, 84–85; as old-new, 79–82
Cohort, vs. *consort*, 23
Coleridge, Samuel Taylor, 33
Colon, use, 229–30, 234
Comma, use, 227–28, 229, 232–240
Common ground, 217
Complete, 26
Complex sentences, 224–25
Complexity, clarity, 136; kinds, 96–98; salutary, 194–195
Compound nouns, 71–72
Compound sentence, 224–25
Comprise, vs. *constitute*, 23
Concision, 116–25, 46; excessive, 135; principles, 116–21
Concreteness, 46
Connections, unclear, 154
Consort, vs. *cohort*, 23
Constitute, vs. *comprise*, 23
Continual, vs. *continuous*, 23
Cooper, James Fenimore, 5–6
Coordinated elements, punctuating, 237–39